www.wadsworth.com

www.wadsworth.com is the World Wide Web site for Thomson Wadsworth and is your direct source to dozens of online resources.

At *www.wadsworth.com* you can find out about supplements, demonstration software, and student resources. You can also send email to many of our authors and preview new publications and exciting new technologies.

www.wadsworth.com
Changing the way the world learns®

From the Wadsworth Series in Mass Communication and Journalism

General Mass Communication

Anokwa, Lin, and Salwen, *International Communication: Issues and Controversies*

Biagi, *Media/Impact: An Introduction to Mass Media,* Seventh Edition

Bucy, *Living in the Information Age: A New Media Reader,* Second Edition

Craft, Leigh, and Godfrey, *Electronic Media*

Day, *Ethics in Media Communications: Cases and Controversies,* Fifth Edition

Dennis and Merrill, *Media Debates: Great Issues for the Digital Age,* Fourth Edition

Fellow, *American Media History*

Gillmor, Barron, and Simon, *Mass Communication Law: Cases and Comment,* Sixth Edition

Gillmor, Barron, Simon, and Terry, *Fundamentals of Mass Communication Law*

Hilmes, *Connections: A Broadcast History Reader*

Hilmes, *Only Connect: A Cultural History of Broadcasting in the United States*

Jamieson and Campbell, *The Interplay of Influence: News, Advertising, Politics, and the Mass Media,* Sixth Edition

Kamalipour, *Global Communication*

Lester, *Visual Communication: Images with Messages,* Fourth Edition

Overbeck, *Major Principles of Media Law,* 2006 Edition

Straubhaar and LaRose, *Media Now: Understanding Media, Culture, and Technology,* Fifth Edition

Zelezny, *Communications Law: Liberties, Restraints, and the Modern Media,* Fourth Edition

Zelezny, *Cases in Communications Law,* Fourth Edition

Journalism

Bowles and Borden, *Creative Editing,* Fourth Edition

Chance and McKeen, *Literary Journalism: A Reader*

Craig, *Online Journalism*

Hilliard, *Writing for Television, Radio, and New Media,* Eighth Edition

Kessler and McDonald, *When Words Collide: A Media Writer's Guide to Grammar and Style,* Sixth Edition

Poulter and Tidwell, *News Scene: Interactive Writing Exercises*

Rich, *Writing and Reporting News: A Coaching Method,* Media-Enhanced Fourth Edition

Rich, *Writing and Reporting News: A Coaching Method, Student Exercise Workbook,* Media-Enhanced Fourth Edition

Stephens, *Broadcast News,* Fourth Edition

Wilber and Miller, *Modern Media Writing*

Photojournalism and Photography

Parrish, *Photojournalism: An Introduction*

Public Relations and Advertising

Diggs-Brown and Glou, *The PR Styleguide: Formats for Public Relations Practice*

Hendrix, *Public Relations Cases,* Sixth Edition

Jewler and Drewniany, *Creative Strategy in Advertising,* Eighth Edition

Newsom and Haynes, *Public Relations Writing: Form and Style,* Seventh Edition

Newsom, Turk, and Kruckeberg, *This Is PR: The Realities of Public Relations,* Eighth Edition

Research and Theory

Baxter and Babbie, *The Basics of Communication Research*

Baran and Davis, *Mass Communication Theory: Foundations, Ferment, and Future,* Fourth Edition

Littlejohn, *Theories of Human Communication,* Seventh Edition

Merrigan and Huston, *Communication Research Methods*

Rubin, Rubin, and Piele, *Communication Research: Strategies and Sources,* Sixth Edition

Sparks, *Media Effects Research: A Basic Overview,* Second Edition

Wimmer and Dominick, *Mass Media Research: An Introduction,* Eighth Edition

Media Effects Research

A Basic Overview

Second Edition

GLENN G. SPARKS
Purdue University

THOMSON

TM

WADSWORTH

Australia • Canada • Mexico • Singapore • Spain
United Kingdom • United States

THOMSON
✦ TM
WADSWORTH

Publisher: *Holly J. Allen*
Assistant Editor: *Darlene Amidon-Brent*
Editorial Assistant: *Sarah Allen*
Senior Technology Project Manager: *Jeanette Wiseman*
Marketing Manager: *Mark Orr*
Marketing Assistant: *Andrew Keay*
Marketing Communications Manager: *Shemika Britt*
Project Manager, Editorial Production: *Christine Sosa*

Art Director: *Maria Epes*
Print Buyer: *Doreen Suruki*
Permissions Editor: *Kiely Sisk*
Production Service: *Stratford Publishing Services, Inc.*
Copy Editor: *Judy Ashkenaz*
Cover Designer: *Liz Harasymczuk*
Cover Printer: *Webcom*
Compositor: *Stratford Publishing Services, Inc.*
Printer: *Webcom*

For more information about our products,
contact us at:
Thomson Learning Academic Resource Center
1-800-423-0563

For permission to use material from this text
or product, submit a request online at
http://www.thomsonrights.com.
Any additional questions about permissions
can be submitted by email to
thomsonrights@thomson.com.

Library of Congress Control Number:
2005920412

ISBN 0-534-62917-2

Thomson Higher Education
10 Davis Drive
Belmont, CA 94002-3098
USA

Asia (including India)
Thomson Learning
5 Shenton Way
#01-01 UIC Building
Singapore 068808

Australia/New Zealand
Thomson Learning Australia
102 Dodds Street
Southbank, Victoria 3006
Australia

Canada
Thomson Nelson
1120 Birchmount Road
Toronto, Ontario M1K 5G4
Canada

UK/Europe/Middle East/Africa
Thomson Learning
High Holborn House
50–51 Bedford Row
London WC1R 4LR
United Kingdom

Latin America
Thomson Learning
Seneca, 53
Colonia Polanco
11560 Mexico
D.F. Mexico

Spain (including Portugal)
Thomson Paraninfo
Calle Magallanes, 25
28015 Madrid, Spain

■

Dedicated to Cheri Wilcox Sparks
The love of my life

■

Contents

■

Preface

As I put the finishing touches on the second edition of this text, I find that much of what I wrote in the preface to the first edition is still true. I never intended to write a textbook. I have always identified myself as a researcher and teacher of mass-communication effects—not a textbook writer. My intentions changed after teaching university undergraduates for over two decades. In my course at Purdue University on mass-communication theory, I watch semester after semester as my students gradually sink into the dry-sand prose of most texts that attempt to present theories of mass media. Once the sinking starts, I am almost never able to rescue them. I finally grew tired of this routine.

Since my approach to teaching media theory involves teaching the theoretical concepts in the context of research findings, I decided to try my hand at writing a text that reflected this perspective. Theory is fully realized when it meets the soil of observation. I have found that students can digest incredible doses of theory in the context of discovering what research says about media impact. So, this book attempts to introduce plenty of theoretical ideas—but in the context of asking about the effects of media. If you teach a more conventional media theories course, I am betting that you will find plenty of theory to keep your students occupied. One new feature in this edition is the list of theories and theoretical concepts that are covered in the text (see page 243). If you check out the list, you'll see that the book provides a good deal of contact with the major theoretical ideas in media effects research.

I became convinced to write a book for undergraduate students when I realized that it *was* possible to write a text that was not dry and boring. My two primary exemplars are Robert Cialdini's classic text on persuasion, *Influence,* and Em Griffin's best-selling introduction to communication theory, *A First Look at Communication Theory.* Since Em asked me to advise him about what to include in the mass-communication section of his book, I began thinking more seriously of trying to write a text of my own. Reactions to the first edition indicate that I succeeded beyond my fondest hopes. Those who use the book seem to be genuinely excited about how it connects with undergraduate students. Before you dive in, let me outline just a bit about the guiding philosophy of the book and how I think the text can be used.

Above all else, I have tried to write plainly and in a style that will engage the typical undergraduate student. This means that I often share personal anecdotes and refer to myself in the first person. I am committed to this style. I think students respond better if they can sense that there is a living, breathing human being behind the words. The reactions of my own students have helped to convince me that this is truly the case.

As you evaluate the text, keep in mind that I have attempted only to *introduce* the topic of media effects—not to write everything known by the research community. I believe that textbook writers make a tragic mistake when they try to cover the whole terrain of their topic. This might satisfy textbook reviewers and serve as a valuable reference for scholars, but I don't think it does much good at generating genuine interest among the students who ultimately have to pay for and read the text. Because of my commitment to limiting this textbook to an introduction to media effects, I am certain that some professors will examine this text and spot crucial omissions that simply *must* be included. I am well aware that the book fails to cover everything. I planned it that way. One of my goals is to keep the material manageable so that students will actually read the chapters. I also want students to finish the book and still be interested in finding out more about media effects. I have decided to sacrifice a little breadth on the altar of student interest. I think it is a sacrifice well worth making.

How can this book be used? I think the text can fit into two different kinds of courses. First, it can obviously be used in a mass-communication theory course or a mass media research course. Second, the book can be used as a secondary text in a basic introduction to mass communication. Most of the texts for the basic course have little or no coverage of media effects research. For professors who want their students to develop a deeper understanding of the effects literature, this book should not be too overwhelming as an accompanying volume in the basic introductory course. I have deliberately held the presentation of material to 12 chapters in order for the book to fit comfortably into different course formats. In the 15-week semester, I have found that students would rather ease in and ease out. For years, I attempted to fight that attitude; now I find myself subscribing to it. Once again, my philosophy here is to meet the needs of the audience. If I don't assign a chapter of reading in either the first or last week, I can still assign a chapter per week for the rest of the semester and have one week for some additional reading that I might select. If there is a topic that a professor believes must be in the course that I don't cover, the flexible week fills the need. The chapters are also short enough and easy enough to read that more than one chapter *could* be assigned in a single week for schools that are on a shorter semester. In the end, my primary goal is to have students understand more about media research and still be interested in the topic when they finish reading. The initial evidence suggests that I have succeeded. I am eager to discover if you agree.

If you used the first edition, I hope you'll discover that this edition looks familiar. I haven't made changes just for the sake of making changes. Instead, I've tried to take the main comments from the reviewers on each chapter and attempt to respond in a reasonable way to their suggestions. Essentially, I've tried to update examples and, wherever appropriate, include some of the latest research in a given area. Here are some of the changes that you'll notice:

Chapter 1

- A new study box on media ratings

Chapter 2

- Updated examples of content analysis and experiments
- Expanded discussion of experimental design
- New discussion on epidemiological methods

Chapter 3

- New discussion of World War II experiments on propaganda films

Chapter 4

- New material on TV addiction
- Updated statistics on media use
- Updated discussion on TV viewing and obesity

Chapter 5

- Updated material on violent video games (formerly in chapter 11)
- New study box on enjoyment of media violence

Chapter 6

- Expanded discussion of the theory of excitation transfer
- New study box on the safety-valve hypothesis and catharsis

Chapter 7

- New discussion of empathy in media effects
- New discussion of mood management
- New study box on empathy

Chapter 8

- Updated examples of persuasion in the media
- New study box on media health campaigns

Chapter 9

- Updated examples of research findings

Chapter 10

- Updated examples
- Expanded discussion of latest research on body-image dissatisfaction
- New study box on body-image dissatisfaction

Chapter 11

- New research on the effects of the Internet on social relationships
- New section on thinking about new technology
- New study box on research topics in new technology

Chapter 12

- New discussion on applying Marshall McLuhan's ideas to the 2004 presidential campaign

New Website

There is now a website for instructors and students that contains web links relevant to each chapter, current items in the news pertaining to the chapter topics, and potential exam questions for instructors.

ACKNOWLEDGMENTS

Writing a book of this type is not easy. Very simply, I could never have done it without help from lots of people. My students over the years helped to shape my thinking about a book of this type. To the extent that the book is successful at communicating well about media effects, I am indebted to my students' willingness to share their reactions and insights. Before I ever started my work at Purdue, I was fortunate enough to be mentored in graduate school by Joanne Cantor. Her integrity and dedication to my training as a scholar were unparalleled. I could never have written this text without the kind of education that Joanne provided.

The book would never have been completed if I hadn't been blessed with a working environment that was conducive to productive labor. I have been in the Department of Communication at Purdue University for 19 years. It is a fabulous place to teach, conduct research, write, and generally enjoy life. For these things, I am thankful.

The people at Wadsworth have been fantastic to work with from the beginning. My editor for the first edition, Karen Austin, was particularly helpful. I also appreciate the work of Holly Allen as well as the copy editing by Carolyn Russ and Judy Ashkenaz on the first and second editions, respectively. I also owe a debt of gratitude to the many reviewers on the first version of the manuscript: Andy O. Alali, California State University, Bakersfield; Lisa R. Barry, Albion College; Robert M. Brady, University of Arkansas; Travis Dixon, University of Michigan; Anita Fleming-Rife, Pennsylvania State University; Linda C. Godbold, East Carolina University; Bradley S. Greenberg, Michigan State University; Gerald Kosicki, The Ohio State University; Annie Lang, Indiana University; Miriam J. Metzger, University of California, Santa Barbara; John Sumser, California State University, Stanislaus; and Wayne Wanta, University of Oregon as well as the reviewers who provided comments for the second edition: William P. Eveland Jr., The Ohio State University; Olan Farnall, California State University, Fullerton; Kate Madden, State University of New York, Brockport; Keith R. Stamm, University of Washington; and Nicholas A. Valentino, University of Michigan.

I also owe thanks to my colleague, George Stevens, who has always provided a sounding board for my writing ideas and has been willing to read anything that I write—especially since his retirement from a long and distinguished career as an expert in the law of mass communication.

If you're like me, you find it difficult to sustain work on a project over many months unless you have close friends who bear your burdens, share your joys, and offer words of encouragement. I have a few choice friends who do all of these things. I could write several pages about each of them, but that would undoubtedly embarrass them. So, I will just extend a heartfelt thanks to Em Griffin, Will Miller, Bob Ogles, Stuart Robertson, and John Greene. These are the friends who nourish my soul. I also am incalculably indebted to my parents, Calvin and Betty Sparks, and to my in-laws, Conrad and Laurel Wilcox. Their constant love and devotion to me and my family are nothing short of inspirational.

Finally, I owe everything to my wife, Cheri Sparks. A Ph.D. in her own right, she has contributed to this project in ways too numerous to count. Most importantly, she offered her daily encouragement and support. It was Cheri who convinced me that I ought to try my hand at this project. She is also the mother of my three incredible children, David, Erin, and Jordan. To my family, both immediate and extended, I offer my deepest thanks for helping me in all of the little ways (and big ones too) to achieve whatever I manage to achieve.

1

■

A Scientific Approach
to the Study
of Media Effects

On April 20, 1999, two students at Columbine High School in Littleton, Colorado, stunned their classmates and the nation when they unleashed a horrible assault of gunfire and bombs, leaving many students and one teacher dead. In the national discussion that followed this tragic event, a persistent theme was sounded over and over again: The mass media must share a significant part of the blame for this incident and others like it. President Clinton called upon the producers of mass media messages to reduce gratuitous violence. The clear implication of Clinton's rhetoric was that exposure to violent entertainment images increased the probability of this type of violent behavior. But others disagreed. They charged that media messages were simply a convenient scapegoat distracting us from the real problem of poor parental oversight. In a Gallup poll published 3 weeks after the shootings in Littleton, only 4% of the respondents said that controlling media violence was the most important thing that society could do to prevent other events like the shootings at Columbine. About 12% identified the root cause of the problem as the unrestricted proliferation of guns.[1]

If you listened carefully to any of this national discussion, you may have heard viewpoints that seemed consistent with your own values or political positions. It may have seemed tempting to embrace one or more of the ideas that you heard about how to prevent similar events in the future. In the end, *opinions* about the events in Littleton were easy to come by. But if you were thinking carefully about the variety of opinions that were expressed about the causes of school shootings, you probably realized that opinions were limited in bringing you to an understanding of the truth. Despite the fact that President Clinton was in a position of national leadership, his opinion about the role of the mass media in the Littleton shootings was still only an opinion. To see whether President Clinton's opinion has any scientific merit, you can read more about the actual effects of media violence in chapter 5. In this chapter, you will learn something about how science is different from casual opinion.

WAYS OF KNOWING

Experience

There are many ways that we try to know things about the world around us. One way is through direct **experience.** This approach is sometimes called **empiricism.** Experience is often a very reliable path to knowledge. One morning, after leaving home from the Chicago area without a map, I found myself in Milwaukee, Wisconsin. The only problem was that I was trying to get to Muskegon, Michigan. If you consult a map, you will discover that I had gone up the wrong side of a rather large lake (Lake Michigan). I have now learned from my experience to consult a map before I travel long distances. This knowledge has often saved me from additional navigating disasters. But learning by experience can also be filled with many trials and errors. Progress can be painfully slow and can lead down blind alleys. For nearly 300 years, the people of Europe were afraid to eat tomatoes, which had been introduced from Central America in the 1500s. Personal experience told them that any fruit from the nightshade family was unsafe.[2] Legend has it that someone may have eaten a tomato and died shortly thereafter. In this case, experience proved to be very misleading.

When it comes to our knowledge of media effects, many of us tend to rely on our own personal experience to reach a conclusion. In class discussions about the media violence controversy, it is not uncommon for me to hear students expressing the following viewpoint:

> Well, I don't really think that media violence makes us more violent. After all, look at me. On Saturday mornings, I watched every violent cartoon that the networks put on. Today, I love movies like *The Terminator*. The more blood and guts, the better. My parents love violent movies, too. I grew up on them. But am I a violent person? Of course not! I have never even gotten into a fight. I don't own a gun. I've never been arrested for anything. I'm a peaceful and law-abiding citizen. In fact, my whole life is a personal testimony to the fact that media violence has no negative effect at all. Kids can tell the difference between real violence and fantasy violence. So, I'm sorry, I just don't buy it. Media violence is just fun entertainment. I don't see the harmful effects.

It shouldn't be difficult to recognize that this viewpoint is a great example of knowledge gained through personal experience. It should also be relatively easy to see that a person's individual experience may be a poor guide to the best general knowledge on a given topic. Just as people thought that tomatoes were poisonous for everyone, people might also think that media violence is benign for everyone. In both cases, personal experience might seem to point to a solid conclusion. But a more careful look might show such a conclusion to be solidly wrong. One possibility is that the conclusion from personal experience is valid for oneself but not for others. The fact that violent media might not trigger aggressive behavior for one individual does not necessarily imply that media violence functions the same way for everyone. Another possibility is that one's impression about being invulnerable to media impact is simply incorrect. Perhaps the effects of media violence are difficult for people to detect in themselves—even though the effects are definitely present.

Authority

Another way of knowing is to rely on **authority.** Obviously, we can't know everything there is to know. When we get sick, we usually consult a doctor and follow whatever advice he or she gives. We recognize that long years of study and practice tend to have qualified the doctor as an authority on medical diagnosis. Often the trust we place in medical authorities is rewarded with a cure. But, as some have learned, medical authorities are only human. They make mistakes. Some doctors are better than others. Medical horror stories of incompetent physicians who ruin the lives of their patients are not difficult to find. Blind allegiance to authority can often have debilitating effects on our search for reliable knowledge. Our awareness that doctors generally know more than we do about medical cures can lead to a shortcut in our thinking that results in the conclusion that *any* doctor can be trusted as an authority. That kind of mental shortcut can be dangerous. Another dangerous mental shortcut that often occurs with authority figures is to transfer their authority to an area that is unrelated to the area of expertise. My doctor might be an authority in prescribing medication, but there may be little reason to trust the doctor's advice when it comes to finding a good auto mechanic or trying to figure out the best way to motivate my children to do well in school.

Hundreds of years ago, religious authority figures were adamant that the earth was the center of the universe and that every celestial body revolved around it. However, astronomical discoveries by Copernicus indicated that the earth actually revolved around the sun. Copernicus feared the actions of the church leaders so much that he kept his discoveries secret for over a decade before publishing them. Nearly 100 years later, Galileo was still confronting resistance from the Roman Catholic Church with regard to the Copernican model of the solar system.[3] Many people continued to reject the truth about the movement of the celestial bodies because they relied on religious authorities for all knowledge. In this case, reliance on authority resulted in incorrect beliefs.

Over the years, television network executives have made various statements about the effects of media violence that tend to minimize the possibility of negative impact. Shouldn't these network executives be regarded as authorities on the topic? After all, they are in the day-to-day programming business. They sell advertising time on the basis of their understanding of the effects of commercials. If network executives say that media violence isn't a problem, shouldn't we listen? As we shall see later, one of the problems with arriving at knowledge by appeal to authority is that the supposed authority figures often have various interests to protect. Just as religious authorities rejected new views of the solar system to protect what they believed to be their religious interests, so the TV networks can probably be blamed for issuing statements downplaying the importance of media violence out of their concern for maintaining economic profits.[4]

Science

In the chapters that follow, I have attempted to summarize the scientific evidence on the question of media effects. **Science** is a particular way of knowing. One of the hallmarks of the scientific method is **systematic observation,** as opposed to casual observation. Science combines empiricism with logical thought and is always pressing onward toward greater precision of observation.[5] One of the best arguments in favor of the power of the scientific way of knowing is the observation that *science works.* A commitment to science has brought us powerful antibiotics to cure our diseases. It has also put human beings on the moon. Although science is a human activity that suffers from the multitude of human shortcomings, it is still the most powerful way of knowing that humans have at their disposal. One of the best ways to understand the scientific method of arriving at new knowledge is to understand the **goals of science.**[6] Whether one is doing natural science or social science, the goals are the same. Natural scientists attempt to achieve the goals of science in their study of biology, chemistry, physics, astronomy, and the like. Social scientists attempt to achieve the goals of science in their study of social and psychological phenomena that involve human beings.

GOALS OF SCIENCE

Prediction

Accurate prediction is one of the coveted goals of science. If you turn on the weather forecast tonight on your local TV news, you will discover that the meteorologist has employed a wide array of instruments, maps, and satellite photos in an attempt to provide an accurate prediction of tomorrow's weather. **Prediction** can be defined simply as foretelling the future. Over the years, the science of meteorology has produced increasingly accurate forecasts. Forecasts for a day in advance are usually reliable enough that people can trust them in planning their picnics. When the citizens of Oklahoma City experienced an onslaught of killer tornadoes on May 3, 1999, they had a full 30 minutes of advance warning. In this case, accurate prediction undoubtedly saved lives. But the state of the art is not advanced enough to predict the weather accurately over the long term. Science is in continual pursuit of better prediction.

In the area of media effects, accurate prediction is also one of the chief goals. For example, if researchers can predict ahead of time which children are most likely to imitate violent behavior seen in films, parents might be able to intervene to prevent film exposure. Likewise, if scholars can predict that certain types of characters will facilitate learning on programs like *Sesame Street,* then young children might have a better start upon entering elementary school.

Explanation

Science certainly has no monopoly on prediction. Insurance companies are also in the prediction business. When my daughter, Erin, recently celebrated her 21st birthday, I received notice that my auto insurance rates would be going down. Data collected by the insurance industry led to the prediction that unmarried female drivers who have reached their 21st birthday will be much less likely to have accidents than those who are younger. The next price break won't come until she turns 25. The data also indicate that if she had married at any time after her 17th birthday, she would enjoy the same reduced risk as an unmarried 25-year-old. These statistics are so dramatic that the insurance companies can pass on premium savings to the customer. The insurance companies don't really care much about *why* accidents drop off after female drivers turn 21 (the rate charts for males are more complicated). You can probably identify several possible reasons without thinking too long (more years of driving experience, increased social maturity, and so on). The insurance companies care mainly about the fact that they can predict that the decrease will happen. It is on this point that the scientist and the insurance company may begin to part ways. They are both interested in prediction. But the scientist is also interested in **explanation**—knowing *why* something occurs the way it does.

If prediction means foretelling the future, then what does it mean to say that something has been explained? Think about something simple, like flicking a light switch. If someone asked you to explain why the lights go on and off each time you move the switch, what would you say? You would probably say something about the electric circuitry behind the switch, including wires, lightbulb filaments, and the flow of electricity. All of these ingredients provide a broader framework or pattern that you invoke to help uncover the "why" behind the phenomenon of the light switch. And this is usually what it means to explain something. **Explanations place the phenomenon to be explained into a broader framework or pattern that doesn't really require much additional elaboration.**

Scientists are always searching for the best explanation of why something happens the way it does. You can probably appreciate the fact that arguments will often erupt about the adequacy of specific explanations. A parent might answer a 3-year-old child's question about why the leaves turn colors in autumn by saying something like "That's the way God made trees." In this case, "God" becomes the broader framework or pattern that requires no additional elaboration. Such an answer might satisfy the 3-year-old but seem increasingly inadequate as the child gets older. The child who discovers that asking "why" is appropriate regardless of what explanation parents may provide has actually discovered something very important about explanations. Explanations can continually be scrutinized and pressed until more detail emerges that seems more satisfying. It isn't necessarily the case that an explanation with less detail is wrong. It just might not provide the desired level of intellectual satisfaction. One of the characteristics of science is that it always encourages additional scrutiny.

In media effects research, as in other sciences, scholars argue about how adequate certain explanations are for given research findings. For example, some researchers have located the primary explanation for people's increased tendency toward aggression after seeing media violence in the aggressive images shown in programs or films.[7] Other researchers have argued that these images are not the most important thing. Instead, they have identified the increased physiological arousal caused by exposure to violent images as the critical explanatory ingredient in the increase in aggressive behavior.[8] You will read more about these explanations in chapter 5 on media violence.

Understanding

Good explanations provide a sense of **understanding.** What does it mean to say that we understand how something works? Usually, **understanding has to do with knowing the particular sequence of causal events** that unfold in a given phenomenon of interest. An explanation that yields a high level of understanding of how the light switch turns the light on would be one that ordered the causal chain of events beginning with the flick of the switch and ending with the illumination of the bulb. Because good explanations provide understanding, these two goals of science are closely related and tend to go hand in hand.

In the case of explanations of how watching media violence might increase aggressive behavior, our understanding would not be very deep if the explanation simply amounted to the statement that children watch the shows and then copy what they see. If this were the extent of the explanation, we might ask what really happens between the viewing and the copying. In other words, what is the exact causal sequence of events? Another hallmark of science is the constant quest for deeper levels of understanding.

Control

When scientists can accurately predict, explain, and understand a phenomenon, they are afforded greater **control** over that phenomenon. In the wake of the Oklahoma City tornadoes, a number of news features appeared on TV that explained how the science of meteorology has advanced over the last few decades. With the help of such developments as Doppler radar, satellite cloud images, and computer analyses of storm data, meteorologists are now much better able than in the past to forecast the occurrence of a tornado. Though still far from perfect, the level of explanatory insight that scientists can claim for the tornado phenomenon is greater than it once was. Today's scientists, in contrast to those of the past, understand some of the causal forces that produce these extraordinary storms. Advances in prediction, explanation, and understanding provide a greater sense of control over the tornado event. People who live in areas that the data show are particularly susceptible can now be warned to take safety precautions. Broadcast practices can be modified to get the word out when meteorologists detect the early signs of a tornado.

Much like the scientific investigation of tornadoes, the investigation of media effects also holds ramifications for controlling events. A good example of the control implications of media effects research is easily seen in a recent study conducted by researchers Brad Bushman (Iowa State University) and Joanne Cantor (University of Wisconsin–Madison). Bushman and Cantor discovered that over the years, there had been a total of 18 research reports on how different media ratings systems affected attraction to media content. For example, if a movie is rated R, will people be more attracted to it than if it carried a rating of PG-13? The total number of people involved in these 18 studies exceeded 5,000, so there was a reasonable basis for drawing some firm conclusions. What did Bushman and Cantor discover? In fact, just as they suspected, they found that "media ratings do more to attract than to repel viewers." The research in this area makes a distinction between "descriptive" ratings, which simply provide information about the nature of the content, and "evaluative" ratings, which make recommendations about who should be restricted from media exposure. The rating system used by the Motion Picture Association of America (MPAA) is an evaluative rating system (G, PG, PG-13, R, and NC-17). Both descriptive and evaluative ratings made programming more attractive—particularly for male viewers. The authors believe that the ratings are used by viewers as a general clue as to how much violence, sexual content, or other themes of a mature nature might be present in a movie. Being curious about these themes, children and adolescents are more attracted to films that carry ratings suggesting the presence of this sort of content. One implication of this research is that the ratings system used by the MPAA may actually tend to attract older children to the very film material that is, theoretically, not intended for their consumption. As a result of their study, Bushman and Cantor have several different recommendations about how the entertainment industry ought to use rating systems (see Study Box 1-1).[9] Just as in tornado prediction, an increase in the ability to predict and understand a given media effect results in increased control.

Sometimes the implications for control that may arise out of scientific research are controversial. The MPAA has resisted the policy suggestions that spring from Bushman and Cantor's research. This is not the first time that research has ultimately led to controversy about media policy. Back in 1974, researchers discovered that a short commercial message ("The Swing") that was designed to promote sharing and turn-taking behavior in young children was effective in modifying children's behavior. But the commercial caused great controversy among some people who were concerned about its potential to "brainwash" children. According to these critics, the message about sharing a swing on the playground might promote passive compliance among children who need to learn to stand up for their rights.[10]

STUDY BOX 1-1   Policy Recommendations from Research on the Effects of Media Rating Systems

1. Rating systems need to provide guidance by using a system that people can easily understand without having to memorize definitions or decode letters and icons. Current ratings systems tend to be vague and confusing, and they provide insufficient guidance for parents.
2. Rating systems need to provide information about the *content* of the media. Parents are less interested in what the MPAA recommends for their children and more interested in what specific material is present in movies.
3. The criteria used for assigning ratings need to be explicated clearly. In general, there is a need for the ratings committees to include psychologists, who can explain exactly why certain movies should be rated in a particular way.
4. Many ratings of media material are self-assigned by the distributor or producer of the material. Consumers need to have a procedure for appealing a rating or putting the rating through some sort of public review.
5. The media industries need to devote significant efforts toward educating parents about their rating systems and attempting to make it easier for parents to find ratings information and apply it without confusion.
6. In the American media environment, censorship is not a practical solution. Parents assume the burden for controlling their children's viewing. But if this system is to work effectively, parents must have clear, reliable information about media content.

SOURCE: Summarized and paraphrased from Bushman, B. J., & Cantor, J. (2003). Media ratings for violence and sex: Implications for policymakers and parents. *American Psychologist, 58*(2), 130–141.

Although lawmakers, organizations, and other policymakers might debate the pros and cons of particular strategies for controlling a phenomenon, scientists usually hesitate to become identified too closely with a particular policy. Instead, they are more comfortable pointing out the range of control strategies that are available as a result of the increased ability to predict, explain, and understand a given phenomenon. Although the goal of science is not necessarily to push any particular remedy for controlling an event, scientific progress is generally oriented toward providing greater measures of control over the things that are studied.

HOW ARE THE GOALS OF SCIENCE ACHIEVED?

Theory

When I teach the fundamentals of science to students and I ask them how they think the goals of science are usually achieved, I typically get a variety of answers. Students often identify experiments, testing, observation, data analysis, surveys, and so on. While these are all tools of the scientist, the most powerful way to achieve the goals of prediction, explanation, understanding, and control does not appear on that list. The thing that generates experiments, testing, data analysis, and the like is **theory.**

Scientific theory is a bit different from the kind of theory that we might refer to in everyday conversation. When my wife and I were driving home from campus one evening, we noticed that there was much more traffic than usual and we wondered about the reason for the increase. I announced that I had a theory about the change, and I proceeded to speculate that road construction in another part of town had caused traffic to divert to our usual route home. Thus, we were now in a traffic jam—even though the road construction was nowhere near our location. In this case, my casual use of the term *theory* was really just as a synonym for the word *idea*. I could just as easily have said that I had an *idea* about the traffic change. The meaning would have been the same. But in science, the word *theory* cannot easily be replaced with the word *idea*.

There are several parts to the notion of scientific theory. First, a scientific theory **consists of more than one statement.** My notion of why traffic had increased on our route home was easily stated in a single sentence. But scientific theories take much more than a sentence to state completely. Often, they involve an entire manuscript that might even be as long as a book. Darwin explicated his theory of evolution in a book called *The Origin of Species.*[11] Albert Bandura took an entire book chapter to present his "social cognitive theory of mass communication."[12] You will read more about that theory in chapter 5. The point here is that scientific theories consist of a *set* of statements—not just a single statement.

One of the things that this set of statements does is to **identify the key concepts of the theory and specify how they are related.** In meteorology, a theory about tornado formation might include the concepts of warm air, cold air, and updrafts. The theory might describe how these concepts relate to one another to produce conditions that are favorable for tornadoes. A theory about how media violence affects viewers might describe how the concepts of attention, role models, identification, rewards, and punishments relate to one another to lead to the anticipation of viewers' aggressive behavior.

Perhaps the most important characteristic of scientific theories is that **they yield hypotheses that are testable by observation. A hypothesis is a specific prediction about what will happen under a certain set of well-specified conditions.** Hypotheses are not theories. They are produced by theories. Copernicus presented his heliocentric theory of celestial motion in the 1500s. The theory yielded a hypothesis that the earth rotates around the sun. One way to test this hypothesis was to look at the stars. As one scientist put it, "If Copernicus's theory were true . . . then stars nearer the Earth should seem to change their position relative to more distant stars as the Earth moved around the sun."[13] This change in position is called *parallax*. Once powerful telescopes were invented, parallax was actually observed, thus lending credence to Copernicus's theory. If parallax had never been observed, the heliocentric theory would have eventually been discredited and replaced by a theory that gave a better account of the data.

In the research about media ratings, before they actually looked at the data, Bushman and Cantor thought that there might be evidence for the hypothesis known as the **forbidden fruit effect.** This hypothesis actually comes from a theory in psychology that was formulated years ago by the psychologist Jack Brehm in a theory that he called **psychological reactance theory.**[14] According to this theory, whenever a person's behavioral freedom is threatened or restricted, the person will feel psychological reactance, which is a very unpleasant feeling. In an effort to get rid of this feeling, the person will attempt to restore his or her freedom. One way to accomplish this is to engage in the behavior that is threatened or restricted. Bushman and Cantor thought that perhaps evaluative movie ratings, which suggest restriction of exposure to people of particular ages, might induce psychological reactance. If this was the case, people might be more attracted to movies that carry a restrictive rating. However, the data from their study didn't offer strong evidence for the forbidden fruit effect. As it turned out, although evaluative ratings *did* tend to attract viewers, so did the descriptive ratings, which, theoretically, should not have created any psychological reactance. Descriptive ratings, after all, simply provide a description of the content. They don't make any recommendations about who should be restricted from exposure. Bushman and Cantor concluded, then, that the forbidden fruit effect was not the best way to explain their data. Instead, they thought that both types of ratings were being used as a guide to content that people were curious about.

This example from the research on media ratings illustrates an important point about how the goals of science are actually achieved. Even though theory is a crucial element in the process, there is a constant interplay between theory and data. New theories are often inspired by certain observations. Existing theories are often modified, qualified, or discarded on the basis of data. Ultimately, theory without data is not very useful in contributing to the goals of science. In media effects research, just as in research on physical theory, hypotheses are often proposed from theories and then tested by observing the data.

Falsifiability

What does it mean to say that a theoretical hypothesis must be testable by observing the data? A key aspect of the meaning of testability is that the hypothesis must be **falsifiable.** This does not mean that the hypothesis has to turn out to be false. Instead, it means that **it should be possible to specify ahead of time what sort of data, if observed, would make the hypothesis false.** If one is able to clearly specify in advance the data that would falsify the hypothesis, and those data are never observed in systematic tests, the hypothesis has to be taken seriously. But if one is unable to specify in advance the data that would falsify the hypothesis, then one will not be able to determine whether the hypothesis has any merit. Em Griffin uses an analogy involving a trick basketball shot to illustrate this concept in his book about communication theory.[15] His description reminded me of an experience from my own childhood that makes essentially the same point.

During the summer, I used to play a series of Wiffle-ball games with one of my friends. During that series, my friend boasted that he had found a way to throw a secret pitch that was impossible to hit. The first time he threw me the pitch, I swung and missed. "See," boasted my friend, "the pitch just can't be hit." When I swung and missed a second time, I started to wonder if he might be right. But the third time he gave me the secret pitch, I hit it down the left-field line. Before I could say a word, my friend announced, "That wasn't my secret pitch. I didn't have my fingers lined up right." For several more innings, my friend tried to protect his thesis that the secret pitch could not be hit. Each time I swung and missed, he declared that he had thrown the secret pitch. But when I managed to hit a double or a home run, I would inevitably discover afterwards that it hadn't been the secret pitch after all.

What was wrong with my friend's claim? As he eventually discovered, I couldn't take his thesis about the secret pitch very seriously. If he had really wanted to convince me that the thesis was true, he needed to announce *ahead of time* what would have to happen to disconfirm his claim. He needed to say something like, "This is the secret pitch—and if you hit it, then I can no longer say that my secret pitch is impossible to hit." The fact that he couldn't make his claim a falsifiable one undermined his ability to determine if the claim was valid.

This is exactly the case with scientific theory. If a theory yields a hypothesis that can never be falsified, the theory will not ultimately enjoy acceptance in the scientific community because there is no way to determine if the theory's claims are valid. Sometimes theories, including theories of mass communication that may sound very provocative, are not able to contribute very much to the goals of prediction, explanation, understanding, and control.

THE NATURE OF SCIENCE

Theories that are falsifiable certainly form an important foundation for the achievement of the goals of science. Without research generated by such theories, there would be little progress toward those goals. A great deal of scientific activity is devoted to the actual details of the research process: What methods can be used to actually test a hypothesis? Chapter 2 will introduce you to some of the methods used to investigate mass media effects from a scientific perspective. But before we move along to a consideration of these methods, it is important to understand some of the underlying commitments of the scientific enterprise. Although we live in a culture that enjoys the numerous benefits of these commitments, the commitments themselves are not often articulated clearly—even by scientists.

At this moment, I am witnessing an event that people who lived 100 years ago would find unbelievable. My fingers are tapping on lettered keys, and words are instantly appearing on an illuminated screen. If, during this process, I get a headache, I know that I can take two aspirin tablets and my headache likely will disappear in less than an hour. The application of science is responsible for these benefits—for my opportunity to use the computer and for the relief of my

---

STUDY BOX 1-2   Characteristics of Social Science

Social science is:

Logical: Scientists use inductive and deductive logic to achieve their goals. Theories must not contain logical inconsistencies.

Deterministic: Scientists assume that events happen for reasons. Things do not "just happen."

General: The aim is to understand overall patterns of events. The larger the scope that is explained, the more useful the explanation is.

Parsimonious: The aim is to gain the greatest amount of understanding from the smallest number of variables.

Specific: Scientists must be specific about the methods of measurement used to investigate a given phenomenon.

Empirically verifiable: Propositions and theories must be testable in the real world.

Intersubjective: Descriptions of observations must be sufficiently detailed that other scientists will be able to replicate the observations.

Open to modification: As time passes, new evidence may be expected to revise existing ways of thinking about a phenomenon.

SOURCE: Babbie, Earl R. (1973). *Survey research methods.* Belmont, CA: Wadsworth.

---

headache. It is easy to take the benefits of science for granted while simultaneously remaining ignorant of how these benefits were derived. To the extent that we can understand the underlying nature of science, we will be in a better position to actually implement the scientific method, understand the outcomes of science, and make additional advances. In Study Box 1-2, you will find a brief list of qualities that a sociologist, Earl Babbie, identified as describing the nature of social science.[16] Following this list, I expand on one of the dimensions noted by Babbie, and I also add a few other aspects of science that are important to grasp.

Science Is General

One of the important aspects of science that is often misunderstood is the quest for generality. Think back to the opening discussion about the shootings at Columbine High School. Most of the public discussion that followed this incident focused on uncovering the particular reasons why two young boys would turn guns on their classmates. Social commentators cited a wide range of possible explanations, including parental neglect, social isolation from peers, the influence of violent video games, the impact of a particular scene from the movie *Basketball Diaries,* and the impact of mood-altering drugs. You may have noticed that on the various news and talk shows that proliferated in the aftermath of the shootings, few scientists went before the cameras claiming that the cause of the shootings was easy to identify. Their reluctance to identify the specific causes may not have been very satisfying to the news media, but it made sense from the standpoint of what constitutes good science.

The predominant quest of the news commentators following the Columbine event was to find the particular reason or reasons that it had happened. In research, this would be analogous to a "case study" approach to knowledge. In such an approach, the investigator seeks to describe a given case with as much detail as possible—invoking as many variables as possible—so that a full and complete understanding of the event can be achieved. Once this understanding is reached, it *could* be helpful in generalizing to other cases—but the details of a given case are typically so idiosyncratic that generalizing is likely to be impossible. For example, one of the boys who did the shooting at Columbine was an avid participant in a fantasy baseball league. In the case study approach, this fact could turn out to be highly significant. Perhaps the boy had become disenchanted with his team's progress and his mood had sunk, thus contributing to his outrage.

Unlike the case study approach to knowledge, science searches for general patterns or principles. These patterns are usually stated in terms of probability and attempt to employ as *few* variables as possible. For example, researchers might know that the probability of antisocial behavior among youth increases with parental neglect. Or media researchers might know that boys who play violent video games are more likely to exhibit aggressive behaviors. Notice that it might be difficult or nearly impossible for a scientist to connect these general findings with a specific case. In a given incident, violent video games or parental neglect may have little to do with a specific crime. Even though scientific research on fantasy baseball leagues might reveal that such a hobby is generally healthy (this is purely speculative and hypothetical), it might turn out to be a significant culprit in a crime in any given case.

In the end, case studies do much more to inform us about idiosyncratic cases than they do to help us understand broader patterns. Scientific research does more to inform us about broad, general patterns across large groups of individuals than it does to help us understand the particulars of a given case. Scientists who did participate in the public discussions after the Columbine shootings tended to take the opportunity to discuss the general patterns found in research pertaining to playing violent video games or taking mood-altering drugs. The fact that they stopped short of claiming that these variables had anything to do with the actual shootings at Columbine may have frustrated some viewers. But the commitment of science to uncovering general patterns is viewed among scientists as more valuable to society than an emphasis on specific cases. You would probably appreciate the value of this emphasis if your doctor informed you that the drug you were about to take was effective in 99% of cases. The information about this general pattern of effectiveness would undoubtedly be much more pertinent to your decision to take the drug than would the details of any single case study.

Science Acknowledges the Existence of Objective Truth

It is fashionable today to proclaim that there is no objective **truth** to be uncovered. My students can often be overheard saying that there is no such thing as truth—truth is relative. Something may be true for you but not true for me. When classroom discussions turn to the effects of the media,

I can almost always count on at least one person saying something like the following:

> It is certainly OK for you to believe that media have bad effects on children. I mean, if that's true for you, then no one can really argue with you about that. And I'm certainly not going to argue with you. But for me, the media don't have bad effects on children. I grew up with TV and I don't think it hurt me at all. I kind of liked cartoons and then I got into science fiction for a while. So no one will convince me that it has bad effects. But if it does for you, that's OK. You know—what is true for you is true for you and what is true for me is true for me. There is no such thing as something that's true for everybody.

If all of my students take this sort of perspective, it certainly produces great harmony in the classroom. It sounds very tolerant. But tolerance notwithstanding, there are certain features of the statement that make little sense when subjected to critical scrutiny. Let's start with the last statement: "There is no such thing as something that's true for everybody." The problem can be uncovered quite simply by asking this question about the statement itself: Is this statement true for everybody? If, on the one hand, the statement is true for everybody, then the existence of this fact stands as a complete disconfirmation of the statement itself. If, on the other hand, the statement is *not* true for everybody, then it might not be true for you or me. If it isn't true for you or me, then we can reject the statement as false. In either case, the statement runs into significant problems as a claim to be taken seriously. Two scientists, Theodore Schick Jr. and Lewis Vaughn, have summarized the situation this way:

> Each time we assert that something is the case or we think that something is a certain way, we assume that there is objective reality. Each time a relativist denies it, he entangles himself in self-refutation and contradictions. In the very argument over the existence of objective truth, both those who accept it and those who deny it must assume it or the argument would never get off the ground. (p. 80)[17]

With respect to arguments about media effects, the assertion that the media affect children is incompatible with the assertion that they don't affect children. The two assertions cannot both be true. There is, in fact, an objective reality "out there" to be discovered by the media effects researcher. The fact that the truth is out there to be discovered is no guarantee that scientists will actually discover it. But when one takes a scientific approach, one is definitely committing oneself to the notion that objective truth exists.

Let's go back to the student's statement about media effects, just to make sure that we don't get things confused. It may well be that the media might affect two people differently. If that is the point the student is trying to make, then we surely have to grant it. But when this position gets articulated in a general way that results in the denial of the existence of an objective truth, the scientist would issue a correction. Look again at the student's statement. The actual effects of the media may, in fact, be relative. That is, the media may affect different people differently. But the *fact* that the media affect people differently is an objective truth for everyone. As Schick and Vaughn note, "Certain states-of-affairs . . . may be relative to individuals. *But the truth about those states-of-affairs isn't relative*" [emphasis in original].[18] The point, then, is to recognize that **scientific activity is concerned with uncovering the truth about things.** In the area of media effects, scientists want to uncover the truth about media impact.

Science Assumes a Skeptical Attitude

If you scan through the ads in some popular magazines and newspapers, it probably won't be long before you come to an ad that advertises psychic advice. Such ads were especially prevalent on cable TV until a 2002 decision by the Federal Trade Commission charged that ads placed by "Miss Cleo" were fraudulent because they promised "free" advice but then charged customers large telephone fees. Nevertheless, if you want advice about your future, you can still find a psychic to satisfy your desire. Many self-professed psychics will talk to you over the telephone and tell you things about your life that the psychic supposedly knows only by some psychic process. After you become convinced (if you do) that the psychic knows the details of your life, he or she will proceed to give you advice about how to conduct your future affairs. Of course, this advice usually doesn't come for free. In past years, the telephone industry has done literally billions of dollars of business.[19] Obviously, many people believe the psychics and take their advice. But should they?

A person with a **scientific attitude** would approach the phenomenon of psychic advice with great skepticism. If such a psychic process did actually exist, it would violate the current understanding of natural law. That is, scientists currently would have no way to explain how such a process took place. This feature alone would not cause the scientist to rule out psychic phenomena. For years, scientists could not explain how the firefly lit up, but there was no disagreement that it did. Now, of course, scientists understand the chemistry of the firefly's light so well that they have been able to harness it. Children now carry luminescent sticks on Halloween and wear luminescent necklaces that became possible after the chemistry of the firefly was discovered and explained. However, upon examining the claims of the psychic's ability to see into the future, a scientist still has many unanswered questions. Unlike the firefly phenomenon, about which there was no disagreement, scientists are quite skeptical about the claim that psychics can know the future any better than the average person. If psychics can really see future events, why can't they purchase winning lottery tickets before a drawing for a huge jackpot? Psychics inevitably dodge such questions with a variety of explanations of how the psychic process doesn't permit them to see lottery numbers. But it is harder for the psychic to deal with the fact that certain people who have studied their craft can seem to duplicate their amazing powers—without claiming any psychic ability.

Finally, remember the acid test of science—falsifiability. If the psychic's power is real, then why not offer a specific prediction about a future event that would clearly demonstrate that power? Actually, there is a large monetary award ($1 million) waiting for the first psychic who can meet this challenge success-fully. It is offered by the professional magician and illusionist James Randi.[20] In the final analysis, scientists are skeptical about psychic claims because no scien-tific evidence exists for their validity. Social scientists should likewise be skepti-cal about claims of media impact until clear evidence is offered in favor of those claims. As you will read in some of the later chapters, plenty of ideas have been offered about media effects that turn out not to be supported.

Science Can't Answer Certain Kinds of Questions

Some people think that a scientist is a person who believes that all things are knowable and that scientists know nearly all things. Some people think of sci-entists as "know-it-alls" who look down on others as "know-nothings." Some scientists, unfortunately, don't do a lot to combat this image. One of the things that a good scientist will readily admit is that certain kinds of questions fall outside the purview of scientific investigation. Scientists may have invented the atom bomb, but science can never give a definitive answer to the question of how the bomb should be used. In the area of media effects research, science can tell us *how* viewing violent images is likely to affect children, but it can't tell us *what* the federal government should do about media violence—or whether it should do anything at all.

There are other kinds of mass communication theory and research that won't be presented in this book because they are not really concerned with documenting the effects of the media. These other theories (e.g., critical and normative theories) address questions that scientists can't answer by applying scientific methods. At the same time, these theories can't answer questions about media impact by applying the methods of criticism or interpretation. In their book *Mass Communication Theory,* two media scholars, Stanley Baran and Dennis Davis, present a number of questions that scientific theory is ill equipped to answer, including these: [21]

- Should media do something more than merely distribute whatever content will earn them the greatest profits in the shortest time?
- Should media become involved in identifying and solving social problems?

Likewise, questions such as the following are most appropriately addressed within a scientific framework:

- Does viewing media violence cause people to become desensitized to vio-lence in real life?
- Are the outcomes of political elections affected by the news media's pro-jections of winners prior to the closing of the polls?

Scholars who take different perspectives in their search for knowledge may be trying to answer different questions. Sometimes the tension that exists between scholars who identify with different traditions of inquiry can be alle-viated a bit by recognizing the differences in the kinds of questions that are capable of being addressed from each perspective. Scientists do themselves no favor when they give the impression that their perspective can be used to answer every kind of question. It can't. But the general power of science as a mode of inquiry can hardly be denied. Without the knowledge that has been generated about media effects from a scientific perspective, we would be left with little else but opinion and speculation. Science is not after opinion and speculation. It is after truth. As Ralph Estling, a writer from the United Kingdom, has recently argued in an essay,

> In science, pluralism and tolerance will imperceptibly fade into relativism where there is no such thing as external truth, objective facts, intrinsic, self-sustaining reality, where there is only "my truth" and "your truth." There is never any need to compare, contrast, question, doubt, argue, seek to learn from what the data say and what the Universe tells us. When this happens, truth—for there is such a thing—is in dire peril. And science ceases to function. (p. 55)[22]

Some of the most interesting questions to consider regarding mass media are questions that can't be answered by any sort of scientific study. For example, should journalists be permitted to ride on tanks with the soldiers on the front line? Should individual states design powerful shield laws to protect journalists from having to reveal their confidential sources? Should the Federal Communications Commission (FCC) reinstitute the "fairness doctrine" requiring broadcasters to give coverage of differing viewpoints on controversial issues? Questions such as these are addressed best by normative and critical theory—not scientific theory. On the other hand, questions about how media content affect people's thoughts, feelings, and actions are best addressed by scientific theory. The focus of this book is on theory and research that is properly situated within the scientific tradition of the field.

SUMMARY

This chapter began with a discussion of the tragic events at Columbine High School. Many opinions about the causes of those events were expressed in the popular press, but it is often difficult to determine the truth from sifting through a host of opinions. Personal experience and appeal to authority are different ways of knowing—but they don't apply the systematic observation and logic that is included in a scientific approach. The goals of science are prediction, explanation, understanding, and control. Scientists achieve these goals by advancing theories and testing theoretical hypotheses that are falsifiable. There are a number of important ingredients that characterize a scientific approach. Science is concerned with uncovering truth. But it maintains a **skeptical attitude** and acknowledges that it can't answer every question. Ultimately, the scientific method seeks to make general statements about the way variables are related. Consequently, while scientists may have much to contribute to a general discussion about an event such as the shootings at Columbine High School, they will probably refrain from making statements about the particular causes involved in an isolated incident.

KEY TERMS AND CONCEPTS

Experience 2

Empiricism 2

Authority 3

Science 4

Systematic observation 4

Goals of science 4

Prediction 4

Explanation 5

Understanding 6

Control 6

Theory 9

Hypothesis 9

Forbidden fruit effect 10

Psychological reactance theory 10

Falsifiability 10

Truth 13

Scientific attitude 15

Skeptical attitude 17

To learn more about the topics in this chapter, enter the Key Terms and Concepts found in this chapter as subject and keyword searches on your InfoTrac® College Edition.

NOTES

1. Navarro, J., & Riddle, K. (2004). *Violent media effects* [Online]. Available: http://www.uweb.ucsb.edu/~ker/public_opinion.htm

2. Rhodes, D. (1999). *Tomatoes: General introduction* [Online]. Available: http://www.hort.purdue.edu/rhodcv/hort410/tomat/to00001.htm

3. Schick, T., & Vaughn, L. (1995). *How to think about weird things: Critical thinking for a new age*. Mountain View, CA: Mayfield.

4. Liebert, R. M., & Sprafkin, J. (1988). *The early window: Effects of television on children and youth*. New York: Pergamon Press.

5. Graziano, A. M., & Raulin, M. L. (1989). *Research methods: A process of inquiry*. New York: Harper & Row.

6. Although I have not consulted my notes from graduate school in writing about the goals of science, I am certainly aware that my thinking on this and other topics I discuss in this chapter was crystallized in a course that I took from Professor Joseph Cappella at the University of Wisconsin–Madison in 1981.

7. Jo, E., & Berkowitz, L. (1994). A priming effect analysis of media influences: An update. In J. Bryant & D. Zillmann (Eds.), *Media effects: Advances in theory and research* (pp. 43–60). Hillsdale, NJ: Erlbaum.

8. Zillmann, D. (1991). Television viewing and physiological arousal. In J. Bryant & D. Zillmann (Eds.), *Responding to the screen: Reception and reaction processes* (pp. 103–133). Hillsdale, NJ: Erlbaum.

9. Bushman, B. J., & Cantor, J. (2003). Media ratings for violence and sex: Implications for policymakers and parents. *American Psychologist, 58*(2), 130–141.

10. Liebert, R. M., & Sprafkin, J. (1988). *The early window: Effects of television on children and youth*. New York: Pergamon Press.

11. Darwin, C. (1900). *The origin of species*. New York: Burt.

12. Bandura, A. (1994). Social cognitive theory of mass communication. In J. Bryant & D. Zillmann (Eds.), *Media effects: Advances in theory and research* (pp. 61–90). Hillsdale, NJ: Erlbaum.

13. Schick & Vaughn, *How to think about weird things.*

14. Brehm, J. W. (1966). *A theory of psychological reactance.* New York: Academic Press.

15. Griffin, E. (2000). *A first look at communication theory.* Boston: McGraw-Hill.

16. Babbie, E. R. (1973). *Survey research methods.* Belmont, CA: Wadsworth.

17. Schick, T., & Vaughn, L. (1995). *How to think about weird things: Critical thinking for a new age.* Mountain View, CA: Mayfield.

18. Ibid., p. 81.

19. Nisbet, M. (1998). Psychic telephone networks profit on yearning, gullibility. *Skeptical Inquirer, 22,* 5–6.

20. Special announcement [Online]. Available: http://www.randi.org

21. Baran, J., & Davis, D. K., (1995). *Mass communication theory: Foundations, ferment and future.* Belmont, CA: Wadsworth.

22. Estling, R. (1998, July/August). Is science concerned with truth? *Skeptical Inquirer.*

2

■

Scientific Methods in Media Effects Research

W hen I was about 14 years old, my grandmother came to visit for the summer. She loved to watch soap operas in the middle of the afternoon. My father didn't think much of soap opera content, and he didn't hesitate to voice his opinion that soap operas affect viewers in a negative way. The gist of his complaint was that he thought soap operas encouraged viewers to see their own lives as a constant melodrama. I was never sure that I agreed with my dad about the impact of soap operas on viewers, but his strong opinions on the subject made me wonder. **How would one ever go about discovering the effects of media content?**

Having read chapter 1, you may suspect that a good general answer to this question is to use a scientific approach. But what would such an approach entail? One of the main goals of this chapter is to introduce three specific methods that social scientists use to answer questions related to media impact. Taken together, these methods constitute the main arsenal of the media effects researcher. The three methods are: **content analysis,** the **survey,** and the **experiment.**

ANALYZING MEDIA CONTENT

In general, the first step in scientific investigation is to *describe* the phenomenon of interest with precision. **Content analysis** allows a researcher to describe the nature of the content of communication in a systematic and rigorous fashion. Content analysis can be applied to almost any type of communication, but it is particularly appropriate for mass media messages because it permits us to describe precisely a vast diversity of message content that might otherwise prove elusive. Content analysis is a logical beginning point for the investigation of media effects because it helps us to discover what content is present that might be bringing about various effects. The controversy about the impact of media violence on children would hardly capture our attention if none of the programs or movies that were made contained any violent scenes. On the other hand, it is important to understand that **the results of a content analysis do not permit one to make inferences about the effects of that content.**

I carry a card in my wallet that was distributed by a group called TV Tune-In, located in Cleveland, Ohio. One of the "TV Awareness Facts" that appears on the card is particularly striking: "More guns are fired on TV in one evening than are fired in the course of an entire year by a metropolitan police force of 504 officers!" This fact is based on content analyses of prime-time TV. Researchers arrived at this figure after counting the number of guns fired during an average evening of prime-time offerings. It may seem like an easy jump to move from this fact to the inference that TV influences people to shoot guns. But such an inference would be unjustified. It could be the case that people become disgusted with all the guns fired on TV and consequently use guns less frequently than they would otherwise. The facts themselves that come from a content analysis don't ever permit us to answer the question about the *effects* of the content. To answer that question, other research methods must be used. Before we examine some of those other methods, let's take a closer look at the method of content analysis and examine the role that it can play in mass-communication research.

What Is Content Analysis?

One researcher, Bernard Berelson, defined content analysis in the following way: "Content analysis is a research technique for the *objective, systematic,* and *quantitative* description of the *manifest* content of communication."[1] Essentially, content analysis is a method that allows the researcher to describe messages in quantitative terms even though those messages are essentially verbal or non-quantitative in nature.

Content analysis is *objective* in the sense that the method permits multiple researchers to examine the same content and come to identical conclusions. This is possible because the method is *systematic.* That is, it specifies an unambiguous set of rules or procedures for coding the message content. Theoretically, any **coder** (a person who examines the content and classifies it into categories) who understands the rules or procedures will arrive at the same coding of the message content as any other coder. The data that result from content analysis are *quantitative.* That is, certain aspects of the content are coded and tallied in some quantitative way. This aspect of content analysis is important because it permits the researcher to conduct various statistical tests on the results of the coding.

Finally, content analysis is concerned with the coding of manifest content rather than latent content. **Manifest content** refers to the material that actually appears, uninterpreted, in the message. **Latent content** is content that might become apparent after a coder has interpreted or "read between the lines" of the message before coding. For example, a coder might classify the following statement in a TV sitcom as a compliment: "Gee, Jerry, that's a real attractive outfit you're wearing." The actual statement is the manifest content. The surface meaning of the statement suggests that it should be coded as a compliment. However, it might be apparent from other cues in the program that the statement was uttered with sarcasm and was not actually intended as a compliment. If the coder classified the statement as an insult instead of as a compliment, that would be an example of coding the latent content. As you can probably begin to appreciate, the issue of manifest versus latent content is controversial among content analysts. Some researchers are content to code only the manifest content and discuss alternative interpretations after the data have been analyzed. Other researchers may be interested in coding the latent content directly, as long as agreement among different coders can be established.

Although this overview may provide a general conceptual introduction to content analysis, chances are good that your understanding of this method is still a little vague. An example is in order.

Suppose you believe that the actions of characters in top-grossing movies can potentially influence the culture by setting certain expectations, norms, or standards for a wide variety of behaviors. In particular, suppose you think you have noticed that more characters in recent movies seem to be lighting up cigarettes and smoking than you remember seeing in past years. You want to study the top-grossing films in some systematic fashion to determine whether your casual observation has any merit, but you aren't sure how to proceed. Content analysis is the method that can answer your question.

An Example: The Content of Top-Grossing Movies

If you were actually wondering about this particular question, you wouldn't be alone. In 2004, three researchers wondered about this same question and decided to attempt to get an answer. In order to do so, Stanton Glantz, Karen Kacirk, and Charles McCulloch decided to design a content analysis.[2] A closer look at their study will reveal the essential steps that one goes through in designing this sort of research.

The Sample Every content analysis has to be done on a particular sample of messages. In this case, the researchers wanted to compare movies from 2001 and 2002 with movies from the 1950s. They decided to use the WorldwideBoxOffice Internet site to get a list of movies with their box office revenues. As I write these words, the website lists 54 films for the years 1950 through 1959 and 482 films for 2001 and 2002. The authors don't report in their article the total number of films that were listed when they did their study, so it's possible that more are listed now than when the study was conducted. In any event, on the basis of these numbers, it appears that the authors would have had to set aside a great deal of time to watch more than 500 movies before coming to their conclusion. In fact, they didn't do that. They randomly selected 20 movies from the 1950s and 5 movies from the 20 top-grossing films for the years 2001 and 2002. Their final sample contained just 30 films, so they had to watch movies for only about 60 hours.

Sometimes, the population that a researcher wants to draw from is so large that a smaller **random sample** is chosen. A random sample is one that permits every member of the population to have an equal chance of being selected in the sample. It is a crucial technique if the researcher wants to be able to generalize the results of the sample back to the larger population. In many content analysis problems, the population of interest is so large that it simply wouldn't be worth the time and expense to use all members. That was certainly the case with the study on smoking behavior in movies. The researchers understood that it wasn't necessary to code the smoking behavior in *every* film on the list. Still, some researchers might argue that even though Glantz, Kacirk, and McCulloch sampled a full 20% of the 20 top-grossing films between 2001 and 2002, a sample of only 5 movies is probably too small to allow for any compelling statements about the actual frequency of smoking in the top-grossing films from those years.

Units of Analysis After the sample is selected, the researchers must decide what units of the content will be coded. For example, in a newspaper article, the researcher might code each paragraph for certain attributes. Thus, the paragraph would be the **unit of analysis.** If each sentence were coded, then the sentence would be the unit of analysis. Sometimes TV shows are broken into scenes and each scene is coded. In this case, the scene is the unit of analysis. In the study of movies by Glantz, Kacirk, and McCulloch, they chose each hour of film time as their unit of analysis; that is, each hour of film was coded for smoking behavior.

Categories In every content analysis, the content of the message is coded according to a **category scheme.** Glantz, Kacirk, and McCulloch wanted to code each hour of the movie in several ways. For example, they wanted to count the number of individual incidents of smoking. They also wanted to count the number of tobacco advertisements that appeared in each hour of film. Further, they counted how many ashtrays appeared. Although it isn't clear from their article if these were the only things they counted, they were primarily interested in what they called "tobacco incidents" per hour of the movie.

Sometimes, it is difficult to tell from a research report exactly how the category scheme was actually applied. For example, suppose that during the first 5 minutes of the first hour of a movie, a character is seen smoking a cigarette. Now suppose that the scene switches for the next 10 minutes and then returns to the first scene, where the same character is seen smoking what appears to be the same cigarette. Should this count as a second tobacco incident, or should it simply be considered a continuation of the first one? Whatever the answer to this question might be, it is important that the rules be explained well and then applied consistently by the coders. In this case, the research report was too brief to provide answers to the various questions that might occur to a reader. The only way to discover the answers to questions such as these if they are not contained in the report is to try to contact the authors directly and ask them for details about the coding rules. In this study, a useful measure that apparently was not used by the authors might be the actual length of time during the movie that smoking was depicted on the screen. You might be able to think of other interesting measures that could have been incorporated into the study.

Coding Agreement After the data have been coded by more than one coder, some statistical index of agreement among the coders is computed. Sometimes this statistic is simply calculated by dividing the number of times the coders agree by the total number of coding decisions they make. For example, consider the case of a researcher who wanted to code the smoking incidents in a movie and wanted to know, for each incident, whether a male or female was doing the smoking. Suppose that there were 10 incidents of smoking and that two independent coders watched these incidents and agreed on the sex of the smoker in 9 out of 10 incidents. Their percentage of agreement would be 90% or .90. Although this may seem like a pretty good percentage of agreement, consider the fact that there are only two possible categories in this case: male and female. The possibility of agreeing just by chance is 50%. Because of the possibility of chance agreements, many researchers compute coding agreement (often referred to as **coding reliability**) with a special formula that makes an adjustment for the chance hits. A rule of thumb in content analysis is that coding reliability must be at least .70 (lower levels are accepted if a formula that adjusts for chance agreements is employed). In the study of smoking in movies, the authors asserted that they had coding agreement between multiple coders, but they failed to report the extent to which the coders either agreed or disagreed in the various judgments that they made. In the field of communication and most other social sciences, it normally is not possible to publish a content analysis without providing this type of information.

Statistical Analysis Once the researchers have established coding reliability, the data from the study can be described in statistical terms. In Glantz, Kacirk, and McCulloch's study, it turned out that there were 10.9 smoking incidents per hour in the most recent films from 2001 and 2002. This was nearly identical to the number of incidents per hour (10.7) in the films from the 1950s. The authors also reported that they had published a similar study on movies from 1980 through 1982, where they found only 4.9 incidents per hour.

Interpretation of Findings After the results have been summarized, the authors of a content analysis usually discuss the implications of the study. The authors of the smoking study discussed the fact that although the number of tobacco incidents in movies decreased from the 1950s to the early 1980s, the number in the most recent years seems to have climbed back to the levels of the 1950s. The authors also noted that this change in the frequency of smoking depictions is not consistent with reality. That is, the authors pointed out that whereas 44% of the population smoked in the 1950s, only 22.8% smoked in the year 2000.

If the percentage of smokers in the population was substantially lower in 2000 than in 1950, why don't the films from 2001 and 2002 reflect this reality? There are many possible answers to this question. The authors speculate that Hollywood movie moguls may be taking payment from the tobacco industry to inject more smoking into today's movies. Alternatively, Hollywood may be doing this for free. One gets the impression that Glantz, Kacirk, and McCulloch are not very happy with Hollywood. They state that if the first explanation is correct, then Hollywood is corrupt, and if the second explanation is correct, Hollywood is stupid. In either case, Hollywood doesn't look very good. Ultimately, the authors are concerned about the possibility that when film characters smoke, they might influence film viewers to start smoking or to smoke more. But they stopped short of making any specific claim for the effects of the increase in smoking behavior that they observed in their study. To their credit, they understood that their study did not establish any *effects* of media content. Instead, their study helped us to understand the nature of the content of the media.

Although the results of a content analysis cannot be used to document the effects of the media, these types of studies often have implications for claims about media effects. Suppose that a researcher wanted to investigate the possibility that the decrease in smoking behavior in current films had caused viewers to smoke less. The presumed media effect in this case would be based on an assumption about the prevalence of smoking in movies that Glantz, Kacirk, and McCulloch's study suggests might be false. Smoking behavior in current films may not have decreased at all. This example illustrates an important relationship between content analyses of media content and research on media effects. Ideas about media effects are usually based on some assumptions about the presence or absence of certain kinds of media content. Content analyses are often an excellent way to begin research on media effects because they can confirm or disconfirm these assumptions.

THE SAMPLE SURVEY

Content analysis in mass-communication research focuses on message content. But there are a host of interesting research questions that can't be answered with this method. Many of the most important questions require researchers to investigate *people* instead of message content. One of the best ways of investigating people is to ask them questions directly. The method that is designed particularly for this purpose is the survey. It is often referred to as the **sample survey** because, in most cases, it is based on a random sample of some larger population of interest.

The survey method is probably the one that is most familiar to the average citizen. If you haven't actually participated in a survey as a respondent in the last month, you have almost certainly heard the results of at least one survey reported by the mass media. The quest by politicians and government officials for an accurate gauge of public opinion has served to refine the methods of survey research over the years. Today, sample surveys play a vital part in the governmental process. John Kerry and George Bush used sample surveys throughout the 2004 election season in order to determine where they needed to concentrate their presidential campaigning. The U.S. Census Bureau relies heavily on sample surveys to reveal information about the changing demographics in the population.

In mass-communication research, surveys are invaluable in helping us to understand people's media habits. Through survey research, scholars now have a good sense of how much TV the average person watches, what types of content are most popular, and what people report about their own reactions to that content. The survey, as it turns out, is an excellent method for getting descriptive insight into a given phenomenon.

Beyond simple descriptive data, the survey is an excellent way of exploring relationships between different variables. Suppose, for example, a researcher thought that children who tend to watch lots of television during a typical week also tend to be more obese. This relationship could be uncovered in a sample survey. Phone numbers in a given area might be selected randomly, and parents who answered the phone might be asked a number of questions about their child's weekly TV viewing. After getting estimates of the child's daily viewing, the researcher might also solicit estimates of each child's weight. After the researcher had collected these data, a statistical analysis could be applied to the data to see if the children who watch more TV during the week also tend to be the children who weigh more.

Studies similar to the one described have actually been conducted. For example, a group of researchers writing in the *Journal of the American Medical Association* recently reported a survey of well over 50,000 women. They found that TV viewing was especially related to a significantly higher level of obesity and type 2 diabetes.[3] These research findings are consistent with the results of the survey reported by Larry Tucker and Marilyn Bagwell. These authors surveyed nearly 5,000 adult females and found that obesity was twice as likely to occur among those who viewed 4 or more hours of TV per day as compared to those who viewed less than 1 hour of TV per day.[4] Statistical analyses that reveal this type of finding are an important tool of the mass-communication researcher. This chapter will introduce you to a few of the most important basic concepts. First, let's take a closer look at an example of an actual survey that was conducted to study media effects.

An Example: The Effects
of Talk Show Viewing on Adolescents

At some point in your TV viewing experience, the chances are good that you have watched at least a brief clip from *The Jerry Springer Show.* This program regularly features physical attacks by one guest on another. In some markets, the show airs during the afternoon, when young adolescents have arrived home from school and may be interested in watching TV before beginning their homework. Programs like Jerry Springer's have prompted considerable controversy among parents, educators, and political leaders. Senator Joseph Lieberman complained that some TV talk shows "make the abnormal normal."[5] Politicians in the city of Chicago, where the program is taped, have considered taking various measures against the show. One possibility would include having police officers arrest anyone who engages in physical assault in the studio. Assault, after all, is against the law.

Jerry Springer's show is only one of many talk shows that air daily on TV. There are a total of approximately 20 shows with an estimated 10 million viewers.[6] Two researchers, Stacy Davis and Marie-Louise Mares, decided to move beyond the popular rhetoric about the impact of talk shows. They decided to conduct a survey of adolescents to explore the possibility that watching TV talk shows has negative effects.[7]

The Sample Davis and Mares chose 292 students from two public high schools and one private high school in North Carolina. Because their sample was not randomly selected, the reader must be careful about extending the results to a larger population of high school students. It is always possible that the particular group of students surveyed was different in some way from the larger population of high schoolers. To their credit, the researchers recognized this limitation and cautioned the reader about extrapolating the results to all adolescents.

The Questionnaire The questionnaire itself took about 30 minutes to complete and included a number of questions about attitudes toward social issues that are featured on TV talk shows (such as teen runaways, teen pregnancy, and guns in schools). The second part of the questionnaire included questions about the talk shows that the students watched. These questions were placed later in the survey so that the students would not be thinking about talk shows when they answered the questions about their attitudes.

Descriptive Findings One of the chief advantages of a sample survey is that the researcher can often generate a brief statistical summary that provides a descriptive glimpse of the phenomenon under investigation. This descriptive glimpse may reveal things that no amount of speculation could ever produce. For example, in this case the results revealed that during the school year 46% of the students reported watching a talk show either sometimes or every day. This percentage increased to 68% during the summer. *Ricki Lake* (watched by 41% either sometimes or every day) was the most frequently watched program, followed by *Oprah Winfrey* (36%) and *Montel Williams* (31%).

Statistical Relationships When Davis and Mares examined the relationships between social attitudes expressed by the adolescents and their reported viewing of TV talk shows, they made a number of interesting findings. First, as they expected, there was a tendency for heavy viewers of the talk shows to overestimate the real-world frequency of phenomena like teen sex, teen pregnancy, and teens running away from home. Although most of the adolescents who completed a survey tended to overestimate the frequency of these happenings, the respondents who were heavy talk show viewers overestimated them to a greater extent than did the adolescents who were light viewers.

A second question that Davis and Mares wanted to answer concerned the relationship between talk show viewing and perceptions of the importance of social problems. Do heavy viewers tend to trivialize these problems? The data on this point seem to suggest that trivializing does not take place. In fact, the opposite tendency was uncovered. Especially among older adolescents, heavy talk show viewers were *more* likely to perceive the various problems depicted as significant.

Interpretation of the Findings Davis and Mares stated their conclusions succinctly: "Overall, we conclude that the sweeping condemnation of talk show viewing is rather extreme. Although talk shows may offend some people, these data do not suggest that the youth of the U.S. is corrupted by watching them." Of course, being the careful researchers that they are, Davis and Mares reminded the reader that no direct tests of adolescent *behaviors* were measured in this survey. As they stated, "For example, we do not know whether talk show viewers were more likely to have had sex or become pregnant than non-viewers." But their data did show that the heavy viewers were just as intolerant as the light viewers of the sorts of behaviors that were regularly featured on the shows. "They were equally as likely as light viewers to believe that the victims in the vignettes had been harmed and to think that the antisocial behavior described was wrong."

Types of Surveys The survey conducted by Davis and Mares is one of the most common types of surveys reported in social science research. It was a survey of a single sample of some population. This kind of survey is commonly referred to as a **cross-sectional** survey. The distinguishing characteristic of a cross-sectional survey is that it occurs at a single point in time and involves a single sample. Often, researchers are not satisfied with a single sample. They have research questions that cannot be answered unless a separate questionnaire is administered at more than one point in time. When a researcher designs a survey project that includes more than one sample taken at different points in time, the survey design is referred to as **longitudinal.** There are three kinds of longitudinal survey designs.

The first type of longitudinal design is a **trend study.** Suppose that 5 years after Davis and Mares finished their survey on talk show viewing among high school students, they wondered whether there had been some change in viewing habits among the students at the three respective high schools used in their study. To answer this question, they might return to the same high schools years later and re-administer their questionnaire to another sample of students. By comparing the results of this second questionnaire with the initial results, they would be able to detect changes in the viewing trends among high school students. Notice that in a trend study, the individuals who are surveyed the first time are not the same individuals as those who are surveyed the second time. The only similarities between the two groups would be their enrollment in the same high school, and their same station in life at the time of the survey.

A second type of longitudinal survey is a **cohort study.** Again, suppose that Davis and Mares were interested in any change in the viewing habits among the students in the first study. Instead of surveying different students from the same high schools, the researchers might choose another sample of individuals who were the same age as the individuals in the first sample. For example, they might choose to visit a college campus 4 years after the first survey and administer the questionnaire to college students. These college students would be members of the same age cohort as the high school students in the first survey. But they wouldn't be the same students. Perhaps you have seen news reports on how the attitudes of the post–World War II "baby boomers" have changed as they grew older. These changes are typically detected with a cohort design. If people between the ages of 40 and 50 were surveyed in 1990, then people between the ages of 50 and 60 would be surveyed in 2000. The cohort survey allows the researcher to assess changes in a general cohort group—but not in the same individuals.

The final type of longitudinal survey design is a **panel study.** If the researchers actually wanted to measure the changes in viewing habits in exactly the same individuals, then they would use a panel design. Long-term panel designs are relatively rare because of the time and effort involved in keeping track of the same individuals over time. In chapter 5 on media violence, you will learn about a long-term panel study that followed young children into their adult years. Although such studies are rare in mass-communication research, the results are usually very important in revealing trends that no other method is capable of detecting. Short-term panel designs are used more frequently. Researchers often design short-term panels during political campaigns to track attitudinal changes that might take place in response to media messages and other political events.

THE SEARCH FOR CAUSAL RELATIONSHIPS

Before considering the third general research method used by researchers in mass communication, it is important to understand that one of the principal goals of doing research on media effects is to explore the possibility that media messages bring about some change in people's thoughts, attitudes, emotions, behaviors, and so on. That is, the researcher is interested in documenting **causal relationships** between media and people. Documenting causal relationships is not nearly as easy as one might suspect. There are three general criteria that need to be met before a researcher can make the claim that one thing (the media message) is causing another (a change in attitude or behavior, for example).

Criteria for Causal Relationships

The first thing a researcher needs to establish before making a claim that one thing causes another is that the two things in question are **empirically related to each other.** Recall the studies mentioned earlier that investigated the relationship between TV viewing and obesity. In order to document that watching TV *caused* people to become more obese, researchers first needed to establish that these two variables (TV viewing time and level of obesity) were actually related to each other. As it has turned out in several studies, the two variables are empirically related. That is, there was a tendency for the people who spent more time watching TV to also be the people with higher body weights. Researchers need a specific tool to detect an empirical relationship like this one. They can't simply eyeball the data and make a casual declaration that two variables seem to be either related or unrelated. The methods of science are more precise than that. The most common statistical tool used to determine relationships between two variables is the technique of **correlation.**

Correlation Coefficients When researchers want to know whether two variables are related to each other, they often apply a statistical formula to the data and compute a **correlation coefficient.** The particular formula for the correlation coefficient is commonly available in introductory statistics texts, and you don't need to be concerned with formulas here. But because of their importance in documenting empirical relationships between variables, it is helpful to know how to interpret correlation coefficients.

Correlation coefficients are computed between two variables. The data in the obesity studies conform nicely to the sort of situation where correlation can be useful. The researchers who published these studies had a measure of two different variables for each person in the sample. If increases in one of the variables tended to go along with increases in the other variable, then the two variables would have a **positive correlation.** This was actually the case in the two obesity studies mentioned earlier. People who had higher TV viewing times tended to weigh more. Sometimes, increases in one of the variables tend to go along with *decreases* in the other variable. When this situation arises, the two variables have a **negative correlation.** Some studies have documented a negative correlation between income level and TV viewing. People who make more money tend to watch less TV. Of course, it is not always the case that the two variables being correlated are related to each other in either a positive or negative way. In some cases, the two variables might be unrelated. In order to get a picture of relationships between variables, check out Figure 2-1. This figure displays graphs of five different correlation coefficients.

Interpreting Correlation Coefficients When researchers compute correlation coefficients between two variables, the result is a specific number that provides an index of how strongly the variables are related. The formula for the correlation coefficient is designed so that variables that are perfectly related have an index of +1.0 (if the relationship is positive) or −1.0 (if the relationship is

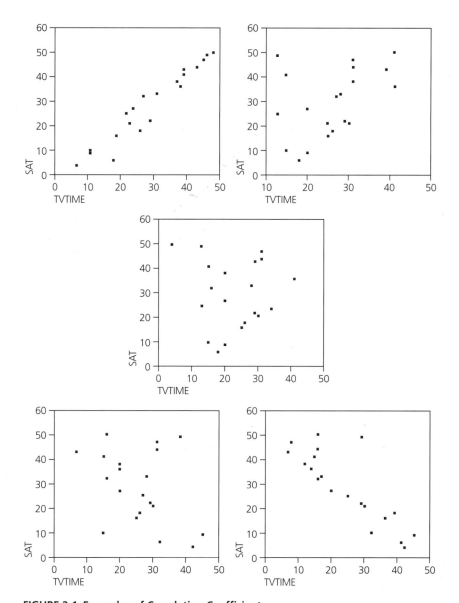

FIGURE 2-1 Examples of Correlation Coefficients
The figure consists of five different scatterplots that illustrate hypothetical
relationships between the number of hours that 20 high school students spent
watching TV during the week before their Scholastic Achievement Test (SAT) and
their SAT scores. Moving from left to right, the two plots on the top show
correlation coefficients of .97 and .48, respectively. As TV time increases, SAT
scores tend to increase, as well. The graph in the middle shows a correlation
coefficient of .03 or nearly zero. The variables appear to be unrelated. The
bottom two graphs show correlation coefficients of −.38 and −.85, respectively.
As TV time increases, SAT scores tend to decrease.

negative). No correlation coefficient can exceed $+1.0$ or -1.0. The smallest correlation that could exist between two variables is no relationship at all—indicated by a coefficient of zero (0.0). Most relationships between two variables fall somewhere between 0.0 and 1.0. The statistical symbol for the coefficient is r. Typically, then, when correlation coefficients are reported, you might read something like $r = .34$ (if the relationship between the variables is positive) or $r = -.21$ (if the relationship between the variables is negative).

Once a correlation coefficient has been computed (usually by a computer), its meaning must be interpreted. Suppose the correlation between two variables is indicated by $r = .45$. What do we know? Although we know that the two variables have some association, we still don't know how likely it is that this result occurred by chance alone. If the correlation between two variables is very likely to occur by chance, then we wouldn't want to attach too much importance to the particular coefficient that was computed. Fortunately, statisticians have determined how likely it is that correlation coefficients of given magnitudes occur by chance, given samples of various sizes. These probabilities appear in statistical tables and are built right into the computer programs that compute correlation coefficients. Scientists have agreed by consensus to adopt a particular standard for determining a chance occurrence. If a statistical result could happen by chance more than 5 times in 100, it is generally considered to be a chance finding. If, on the other hand, a statistical result could happen by chance 5 times in 100 or less, the result is considered unlikely to be due to chance. A statistical result that is unlikely to be due to chance is referred to as a **statistically significant** result. When correlation coefficients are reported in the scientific literature, they usually look something like this: $r = .32, p < .04$. The first part of this expression reports the magnitude of the correlation coefficient. The second part of the expression reports how likely it is that a correlation this large would occur by chance alone. In this case, it would be expected by chance less than 4 times in 100 and thus would be considered statistically significant.

Once a researcher determines that a correlation is statistically significant (that is, unlikely to be due to chance), the first criterion for documenting a causal relationship has been met (see Study Box 2-1 for more detail on interpreting correlation coefficients). The researchers who documented that there was a significant positive correlation between TV viewing and obesity met this first criterion. But recall that there are three criteria for establishing causal relationships. Unless all three are met, the researcher is on faulty ground in declaring a causal relationship between the two variables. Determining that TV viewing and obesity are positively correlated is only the first step.

The second criterion that must be met in order to establish a causal relationship is the **time-order** of the two variables. One thing can't cause another thing unless it precedes it in time. A bullet leaving the chamber of a gun cannot be the cause of the trigger-pull that fired it. In order to clearly establish causality, researchers must document the fact that **the variable doing the causing precedes the variable that is caused.**

This second criterion often is more challenging than it first appears. Think about the surveys that documented an empirical relationship between TV

**STUDY BOX 2-1   Interpreting Magnitudes
                    of Correlation Coefficients**

Correlation coefficients can range in value from -1.0 to $+1.0$. Coefficients are treated as if they were zero (indicating no relationship between the variables), unless the statistical test for significance reveals that the magnitude of the correlation is not likely due to chance. It is important to keep in mind that even in the case of no correlation, the variables still could be related in a *nonlinear* fashion. That is, correlation coefficients test only for linear relationships—not nonlinear ones. Imagine a situation where people who watch no TV at all are very high on knowledge of current events, perhaps from reading a lot. In the same scenario, people who watch large amounts of TV are also well informed, in this case because they watch many news programs. A third group, with the lowest knowledge of current events, consists of moderate watchers of TV. Although this example is completely hypothetical, it does illustrate a nonlinear relationship between TV viewing and knowledge of current events. In such a case, the correlation coefficient would be a poor test of a relationship between the two variables. Fortunately, researchers are able to apply special statistics to cases where variables are related in nonlinear ways.

When a statistical test does indicate that a correlation is not likely to be the result of chance ($p < .05$), then it is important to examine the magnitude of the relationship. One statistician, J. P. Guilford,* suggested that

correlation coefficients between 0.0 and .20 were very slight and should be viewed as indicating nearly no relationship at all. Coefficients between .20 and .40 should be considered as indicating small but definite relationships. Moderate relationships are indicated by coefficients between .40 and .70. Coefficients above .70 (rare in the social sciences) are considered to be substantial and large.

Another way of judging the size of the relationship between two variables is to simply square (r^2) the value of the correlation coefficient. This value, the **coefficient of determination,** provides a statistical indication of how much information or variance in the dependent variable is explained or accounted for by knowing the values of the independent variable. For example, if the correlation between TV viewing and obesity was $r = .30$, $p < .05$, you would know that the relationship was not likely due to chance. In addition, you would know that TV viewing was able to account for 9% ($.30^2 = .09$) of the variance in the measure of obesity. In this example, 91% of the variance in obesity would be unexplained by TV viewing. This is a valuable tool to apply because it tells us something about the relative **statistical importance** of the relationship between the two variables.

*Guilford, J. P. (1956). *Fundamental statistics in psychology and education* (3rd ed.). New York: McGraw-Hill.

---

viewing and obesity. We learned that people who watch a lot of TV tend to have higher body weights. But do we know from the survey data that TV viewing *preceded* body weight in the sequence of time? The answer to this question is clearly no. Because all the data in these surveys were collected at the same point in time using a cross-sectional survey design, the researchers have no way of sorting out which variable came first. Could body weight cause

TV viewing instead of the reverse? If you think about it, that possibility is perfectly plausible. Perhaps, for whatever reasons, some people weigh more than others. Perhaps these heavier people prefer to lead a more passive lifestyle because exercise is an extra effort that strains the body. In their passivity, they might naturally turn to TV as a form of entertainment more frequently than to physical exercise. In this case, a cross-sectional survey is simply an inadequate tool for establishing the time-order between the two variables.

One of the advantages of longitudinal surveys is that they can establish the time-order between variables. In chapter 5 on media violence, you will read about a panel study that found that early viewing of TV violence was significantly correlated with aggressive behavior much later in life. Longitudinal surveys of this type are capable of establishing empirical relationships between two variables as well as establishing the time-order between the variables.

For the sake of our example, let's suppose that the researchers studying TV viewing and obesity had conducted a longitudinal survey and had established that reports of TV viewing in the first survey were significantly correlated with weight gains reported in the second survey. In such a case, both of the first two criteria for establishing causal relationships would have been met. But this is still not enough evidence to establish the causal claim. There is a final criterion that also needs to be met.

After empirical relationships and time-order have been established, a researcher must also establish that the observed relationship is not due to some unmeasured variable causally related to both of the others. All possible **third-variable explanations** must be eliminated. In the studies on TV viewing and obesity, one plausible third-variable explanation for the relationship might be socioeconomic status. People with low incomes may only be able to afford housing in poor, urban areas. Such areas may not provide many opportunities for recreation and physical exercise. People living in these neighborhoods may perceive that they are in danger when they go outside, so they prefer to stay indoors for their recreation, thus burning fewer calories and gaining more weight. TV viewing is the predominant type of entertainment available indoors, so these folks also watch more TV. In this scenario, low income would be causing both TV viewing and obesity. If a researcher examined TV viewing and obesity without including a measure of income, the empirical relationship might emerge and lead the researcher to think that watching TV causes obesity—but this would be a mistaken conclusion. The true cause of the relationship in this case (low income) would remain hidden.

From the preceding discussion, it might seem impossible to design a study that simultaneously meets all three criteria for establishing a causal relationship. If an unmeasured variable might be responsible for the relationship between two measured variables, then clearly a sample survey (whether cross-sectional or longitudinal) can never provide the definitive evidence needed for a causal relationship. Because no survey can measure every possible variable, there is always a chance that a variable that went unmeasured is precisely the one that explains why two measured variables are related to each other. A good survey design can anticipate some of the obvious variables that might play the role of explanatory third variable. Once these variables are measured, they can be tested to see if they might be responsible for an observed relationship between two other variables of interest (this was done in Tucker and Bagwell's study on TV and obesity). But no matter how clever the survey design, no survey can measure everything. Consequently, the survey is, in principle, not capable of satisfying all three of the criteria needed to say that one thing causes another.

Where does this leave us? If the sample survey is capable of establishing only two of the three criteria for causal relationships (empirical relationship and time-order), is there an alternative method that might allow us to meet all three criteria simultaneously? The answer to this question leads to the last of the three fundamental methods used to study media effects: the experiment.

THE EXPERIMENTAL METHOD

Like the survey method, experiments in mass communication gather data directly from people. But unlike the survey, the **experiment** seeks to gather these data under controlled conditions. If an experiment is carefully executed, a researcher is often able to make a case that all three of the criteria for documenting causal relationships have been met. What are the key ingredients that make this possible?

Manipulation of a Key Variable

Once an experimenter has identified a variable (usually called the **independent variable**) that is thought to be a potential cause of another variable (usually called the **dependent variable**), the strategy is to manipulate the independent variable in order to create more than one experimental condition. The purpose of this manipulation is to be able to observe the impact of various levels of the independent variable on some dependent variable. My daughter has always been concerned about drinking too much diet soda. Her concern stems from reports she has heard from her friends that too much of the sugar substitute in diet soda might cause cancer. We did a little investigating and discovered that researchers have completed many experiments on this topic. In this case, the sugar substitute is the potential causal variable. Consequently, researchers manipulated this variable and created a number of experimental conditions. In one condition of a typical experiment, laboratory animals might be injected with very large doses of the substance over a period of weeks. In a second condition, moderate doses might be administered. A third group of animals might get very light doses. The animals in each of these conditions can then be compared for their incidence of cancer.

Random Assignment to Experimental Conditions

One crucial feature in experiments is **random assignment** of people (or animals) to experimental conditions. In experiments on the impact of sugar substitutes, laboratory animals are randomly assigned to one of the doses. Why is random assignment so important? The answer to this question should be clear upon thinking about the population of the laboratory animals. Suppose that one of the cages where a group of the animals is housed resides in a corner of the building that contains cancer-causing asbestos. If all the animals in that cage were placed in the same experimental condition, the researchers might erroneously conclude that the experimental treatment was responsible for a higher incidence of cancer in this condition. Or suppose that some of the animals are already developing the early stages of cancer. If those animals are spread evenly across the experimental groups, then researchers can still detect the impact of the sugar substitute. Random assignment to experimental conditions theoretically makes the experimental groups equivalent just prior to their exposure to the experimental manipulation. Consequently, any difference that emerges after the manipulation can be confidently attributed to the manipulation itself.

Identical Treatment Except for the Manipulation

Random assignment to experimental conditions makes the experimental groups equivalent at the beginning of the experiment. Random assignment must be followed by identical treatment in all ways except for the **manipulation of the variable.** In the sugar substitute experiment, the animals in all three conditions should have identical diets except for the difference in the dose of sugar substitute. They should be housed in identical cages with equal amounts of light and dark, equal numbers of other animals in their cages, and so on. In short, *anything* that introduces a difference in the experimental conditions, except the manipulated variable, must be avoided. Otherwise, once the experiment is over, the researchers can't be confident that differences in the manipulated variable among the experimental groups caused the dependent variable of interest (in this case, incidence of cancer).

Recall the discussion of the three criteria for establishing causal relationships. Survey designs are capable of meeting two of the three: revealing the presence of a relationship and establishing the time-order of the variables. As we saw, however, the survey design could not eliminate all third variables that might present themselves as possible alternative causes to consider in a given relationship. The experimental method, however, is able to meet all three criteria at once. Consider the experiment on sugar substitutes. If one of the conditions shows a higher incidence of cancer, then a relationship between consumption of the substitute and cancer has been found. That's the first criterion. If the experimental groups were equivalent at the beginning of the experiment, then time-order has also been established. The increased incidence of cancer in one of the groups occurred *after* consumption was manipulated. That's the second criterion. Finally, if the experimental groups were equivalent at the beginning of the experiment and were treated equally throughout the experiment except for the manipulation, then there are no third variables that can offer a rival explanation for how differences in cancer emerged in one of the groups. The experiment theoretically controls all possible third variables that might compete with the manipulation to explain the outcome of the experiment. It is this feature of the experiment that makes it such a valuable tool for investigating questions of media effects.

Control Groups

In order to properly assess the impact of a manipulated variable in an experiment, some sort of **control group** is typically used. Suppose that, in the experiment on sugar substitutes, animals in the large-dose group were more likely to develop cancer than animals in the small-dose group. Such a finding might be interpreted to mean that the sugar substitute is dangerous and consumption should be avoided. Notice, however, that the experiment described earlier did not contain a control group that received *no* sugar substitutes. The inclusion of a control group in the experiment might completely change the interpretation of the results. What if, in an experiment that included a no-substitute control group, animals in the control group had the *highest* incidence of cancer? In this case, the interpretation of the results is completely changed. With the inclusion of the control group, it now appears that consumption of any level of the sugar substitute *reduces* the incidence of cancer. Heavy consumption reduces it less than light consumption, but both doses reduce it. These results are completely hypothetical, but they help to illustrate how the inclusion of a control group in an experimental design can often aid the researcher in interpreting the results of an experiment clearly. In order to get a more concrete sense of how the experimental method is applied in mass-communication research, let's look briefly at a real example of a published experiment.

Different Experimental Designs

Not every experiment is designed in exactly the same way. Researchers have various choices to make about how they want to set up a study and what they want to measure at which point in the experimental process. The study of experimental designs can get quite complicated; graduate students frequently take semester-long courses in experimental design. Although that sort of in-depth treatment is far beyond the scope of this text, it might be useful to get at least some passing insight into the types of choices that experimenters have to make.

Consider the case of a researcher who wants to know whether playing certain types of video games causes a person's heart rate to increase. There are at least two possible ways to set up the experiment. In the first approach, the researcher could have people sit quietly before playing one of several different video games in order to get a baseline heart rate reading. Then, immediately after playing a particular game, heart rate could be measured again. By comparing the first reading with the second across groups of people who were randomly assigned to play different games, the researcher could determine which game caused the greatest increase in heart rate. In this case, because the researcher measures heart rate both *before* and *after* playing the game (the game is the experimental stimulus), the experimental design would be called a **pre-test, post-test** design. If the research added a control group condition in which people played no video game between the two heart rate measurements, it would be a **pre-test, post-test, control group** design. In studies where heart rate is measured, the pre-test, post-test design would be a common approach.

A second approach to this experiment is called the **post–test–only** design. You can probably guess what the difference in this design is just by thinking about its name. In the post-test-only design, the researcher would examine heart rate only once, after the game playing is over. What is the logic of taking this approach? Wouldn't the researcher be losing some valuable information by eliminating the first heart rate readings? Perhaps not. If you think about a carefully designed experiment, once the participants have been randomly assigned to the experimental conditions, the groups of people assigned to play different video games should have, on average, heart rates that are statistically equivalent to those of the other group. Recall that random assignment to conditions should theoretically result in groups that are equivalent on any variable of interest. If the heart rates of the different groups are theoretically equivalent at the start of the experiment, a researcher might not care very much about taking a pre-test measurement. It is true, however, that some information is lost with this type of design. In this case, the researcher wouldn't be able to describe how many average beats per minute a group either increased or decreased as a result of playing the game. But the researcher would still be able to make the crucial comparison that the experiment was intended to make. That is, the researcher would still be able to describe the differences in heart rate between the various groups right after the game playing was over.

Is there any reason that a researcher would deliberately want to pass up the pre-test measure? The answer to this question is yes. Consider the situation where the pre-test measure might be a questionnaire about your attitude toward particular video games. Now imagine that after playing a game, you are asked to complete the same attitude measure that you filled out just before the beginning of the experiment. Instead of reporting your true attitude afterwards, you might think about your responses on the first attitude measure and strive to be consistent with your earlier answers. In this case, the pre-test would have sensitized you to the post-test. If that sort of sensitization happens, the whole purpose of the experiment is defeated. Instead of being able to see how the experimental manipulation affected your attitude, the researcher would really be observing how the pre-test measure of attitude affected your response on the post-test. Researchers are often willing to lose a little pre-test information in order to avoid the risk of ruining the whole experiment.

You can probably see from this discussion that designing good experiments requires plenty of careful thought and analysis. It usually takes several years of training before a researcher is able to consistently make good choices about experimental designs.

An Example: The Effects of
Mood on Music Listening Choice

One topic that some media researchers have shown interest in over the years is how our media use affects our emotional moods. In fact, a researcher named Dolf Zillmann has proposed an entire theory on this topic known as **mood–management theory**.[8] The theory states that people deliberately use media messages to alter their moods. For example, suppose you were in a bad mood and you had the chance to listen to different types of music on the radio. What type of music would you choose? Would you prefer joyous, upbeat music or something more somber? Recently, Silvia Knobloch and Dolf Zillmann attempted to answer this question by conducting an experiment to see whether or not a person's mood was causally related to the type of music the person chose to listen to.[9] A closer look at one of these experiments should help you to see how this method works to document media effects.

Participants For this study, the authors recruited 116 college students to participate. About two-thirds of the students were female. All of the recruits were awarded with extra course credit for their participation. They were randomly assigned to one of the three experimental conditions.

Independent Variable The independent variable was mood. In order to test how mood influences choices of music, the researchers first had to know that their participants were in different mood states. All of the participants were asked to look at a series of photos of people and were instructed to identify how the people were feeling. In fact, the researchers made sure that this was a difficult task. None of the people pictured had a clearly identifiable emotional expression. On a random basis, some of the participants were given feedback that their performance on this exercise was excellent—that they had correctly identified the emotions for 85% of the pictures. Other participants were given feedback that their performance was terrible—that they had correctly identified only 15% of the pictures. Depending on the group to which participants were assigned, they ended up in either a good mood or a bad mood. The researchers also had a third group of participants who were told that their performance was just average—that they had correctly identified about 55% of the pictures. This group served as a neutral-mood control group.

Dependent Variable After the picture-rating task, the participants were moved to another situation that they believed was completely unrelated. They were asked to put on headphones and were presented with 8 different songs that they could play over the next 10 minutes. Because there was a total of nearly 30 minutes of music to listen to, the participants had to be selective and presumably listened to the music they liked best.

Experimental Results As the researchers suspected might be the case, the participants who had been put in a bad mood on the picture-rating task were much more likely than the good-mood group to select energetic or joyful music during their 10-minute listening session. The difference between the two groups was statistically significant (that is, the probability that the difference occurred by chance was less than 5 in 100).

Interpretation of Results Research results must always be interpreted. In this case, the authors of the study concluded that the main finding supported the theory of mood management. People who were in bad moods selected media that would make them feel better.

CONTROVERSY ABOUT
RESEARCH METHODS

This chapter has introduced you to the research methods used in media effects studies. As you read about each of the methods, you may have wondered about the extent to which we should rely on them for our understanding of the effects of the media. For example, perhaps it occurred to you that when people are asked questions on a survey, they might not respond with truthful answers. Or maybe you wondered about whether a carefully controlled laboratory experiment can really tell us very much about behavior that happens in more natural environments—are laboratory experiments too artificial? Questions like these are important ones that researchers have debated for years. A full consideration of each potential problem of a particular research method is beyond the scope of this book. If you are interested in these problems, your instructor should be able to point you to additional reading on research methods or even recommend a good course on the topic.

In spite of the difficulties with individual research methods, media effects researchers gain confidence in the results of research studies by examining the same research problem in a number of different ways. If a particular finding seems to show up again and again in studies of different types, scientists would refer to this as replicating a research result with convergent evidence. **Replication** refers to the fact that the same result can be observed over and over again. **Convergence** refers to the fact that the use of different methods still leads to the same general conclusion. In the end, researchers are reluctant to declare that they know anything about media effects until they have results from more than one or two studies. Although no single research method is perfect or beyond criticism, careful application of the three methods discussed in this chapter provides a powerful arsenal of tools for learning about the ways that media messages affect people.

ANOTHER METHODOLOGICAL APPROACH

Although content analyses, surveys, and experiments are the major tools of media effects research, there is another useful tool that is worth mentioning: the **epidemiological approach.** This approach is useful for studying the potential impact of media in the natural world. Epidemiological research is often conducted in the medical arena because it is not ethical to do experiments that might cause severe harm. The best example of this might be research on the effects of smoking on the incidence of cancer. Although researchers would never want to set up a study in which some people were randomly assigned to smoke large numbers of cigarettes, they can still study the potential causal link between smoking and cancer by simply observing what happens to people who smoke compared to those who don't. Essentially, then, the epidemiological approach is an observational science. Unlike the experiment, it doesn't seek to manipulate variables. Instead, it seeks to find connections between variables by simply observing what is happening in the world outside the laboratory.

As you might suspect, because epidemiological researchers can't control variables the way experiments do in the laboratory, the interpretation of results must be done very carefully. There are potentially a whole host of "third variables" that might account for a relationship found in an epidemiological study. For example, maybe smokers also tend to have different diets than non-smokers. Of course, researchers who take the epidemiological approach seek to make simultaneous observations on other variables so that they can rule out these types of explanations for a relationship. When some medical researchers who conduct experiments on laboratory animals discover that tobacco products cause cancer, and others who take the epidemiological approach discover that smokers are more likely to die of cancer than people who don't smoke, the combination of this converging evidence is more convincing than either type of evidence alone.

Similarly, as you will discover in chapter 5, epidemiological studies have revealed that violence in different societies tends to increase with the introduction of television. When this evidence is combined with evidence from carefully controlled laboratory experiments on the effects of media violence on aggression, we get a much more complete and compelling picture of how media violence might actually cause aggression.

SUMMARY

In this chapter, you have been introduced to three major research methods used by media effects scholars: content analysis, the sample survey, and the experiment. Each method yields valuable information that may be pertinent to documenting a media effect. Content analysis reveals what content the media contain. Surveys can reveal valuable descriptive information as well as important relationships between variables. They are capable of meeting two of the three criteria for causal relationships: documenting the presence of a relationship and documenting time-order.

Relationships between variables are often documented using the technique of correlation. Correlation coefficients can range in value between -1.0 and $+1.0$. Coefficients that are unlikely to occur by chance any more than 5 times in 100 are declared to be statistically significant. Although correlation coefficients can be computed from survey data, and time-order between two variables can often be established, surveys always measure a finite set of variables. Consequently, they are incapable of eliminating all possible third variables that might be responsible for a relationship. The third research method, the experiment, has the advantage of being able to meet all three of the criteria for causal relationships. Taken together, these three research methods constitute an invaluable set of tools for exploring the effects of the mass media. Epidemiological approaches to the study of media effects can add even further insight to the discoveries made using the other three methods.

KEY TERMS AND CONCEPTS

Content analysis 20

Coder 21

Manifest content 22

Latent content 22

Random sample 23

Unit of analysis 23

Category scheme 23

Coding reliability 24

Sample survey 25

Cross-sectional 28

Longitudinal 28

Trend study 28

Cohort study 29

Panel study 29

Causal relationships 29

Correlation 30

Correlation
coefficient 30

Positive correlation 30

Negative correlation 30

Statistical significance 32

Time-order 32

Coefficient of
determination 33

Statistical importance 33

Third-variable
explanations 34

Experiment 35

Independent variable 35

Dependent variable 35

Random assignment 35

Manipulation of the
variable 36

Control group 37

Pre-test, post-test
design 37

Pre-test, post-test,
control group
design 37

Post-test-only design 38

Mood-management
theory 38

Replication 40

Convergence 40

Epidemiological
approach 40

To learn more about the topics in this chapter, enter the Key Terms and Concepts found in this chapter as subject and keyword searches on your InfoTrac® College Edition.

NOTES

1. Berelson, B. (1952). *Content analysis in communication*. Glencoe, IL: Free Press.

2. Glantz, S. A., Kacirk, K. W., & McCulloch, C. (2004). Back to the future: Smoking in movies in 2002 compared with 1950 levels. *American Journal of Public Health, 94,* 261–263.

3. Hu, F. B., Li, T. Y., Colditz, G. A., Willet, W. C., & Manson, J. E. (2003). Television watching and other sedentary behaviors in relation to risk of obesity and type 2 diabetes mellitus in women. *Journal of the American Medical Association, 289*(14), 1785–1791.

4. Tucker, L. A., & Bagwell, M. (1991). Television viewing and obesity in adult females. *American Journal of Public Health, 81,* 908–911.

5. Alter, J. (1995, November 6). Next: "The revolt of the revolted." *Newsweek,* 46–47.

6. Ibid.

7. Davis, S., & Mares, M. L. (1998). Effects of talk show viewing on adolescents. *Journal of Communication, 48,* 69–86.

8. Zillmann, D. (1988). Mood management through communication choices. *American Behavioral Scientist, 31,* 327–340.

9. Knobloch, S., & Zillmann, D. (2002). Mood management via the digital jukebox. *Journal of Communication, 52*(2), 351–366.

3

■

A Brief History of Media Effects Research

uring the summer of 2003, a few months after the initial invasion of Iraq by the United States, I was asked to consider writing an essay for a new book about the media coverage of the conflict. Although most of the essays in the book focused on new journalistic techniques applied in the war or new dimensions of the media environment that had never been present in past wars, I (along with my coauthor, Dr. Will Miller) decided to emphasize aspects of the media situation and environment that hadn't changed much.[1] My decision was influenced in part by the results of public opinion polls taken during the initial months of the conflict. In one poll by the Gallup organization, respondents were asked, "Do you favor or oppose the U.S. war with Iraq?" The results of this poll revealed that the percentages of people who either favored or opposed the war remained virtually constant during the entire month of the most intense news coverage of the conflict (March 22 through April 23, 2003). At the war's beginning, 72% of the respondents favored the war and 25% opposed it. One month later, these percentages were 71% and 26%, respectively. During the entire month-long period, opposition remained between 25% and 28%, and support remained between 68% and 72%. Despite hours upon hours of news coverage, special reports, and journalistic accounts broadcast live from the battlefield, public opinion about whether the war was a good thing or a bad thing didn't change much at all.

This stability of public opinion reminded me of the research findings that you'll read about in this chapter, which come from a study conducted back in 1940.[2] When researchers studied the effects of political advertising on attitudes toward the presidential candidates during the 1940 campaign, they found very little evidence that people changed their minds after being exposed to the ads. There have been many occasions like this one when I have been reminded that current research findings often echo findings that have long since found their way into dusty corners of journal stacks in university library basements. When I started out as a graduate student in mass communication, I never regarded the history of media effects as very interesting or important. Now, however, I recognize that it is very important for us to read this past research so we don't run the risk of "reinventing the wheel"—duplicating research that has already been done.

It is also enlightening to see how research interests change over time and interact with the technologies that are available. I am now convinced that a solid understanding of any research area must include an understanding of its development over time. As it turns out, the history of media effects research is a fascinating field of study in its own right. An understanding of that history will give you an appreciation of the scholarly tradition reflected in later chapters of this book. The questions that you will raise about the study of media effects will almost certainly be different as a result of knowing some of the history behind the topic.

With that in mind, the rest of this chapter takes you on a quick tour through the history of research on media effects. What follows is not complete in any sense. It will highlight some of the most important moments and provide a basic framework for thinking about past studies on media effects—especially those that occurred before television came into its own. It also provides you with some names and citations that could take you further along the road back into the past, if you ever decide to take that journey in a more leisurely fashion.

SETTING THE STAGE

In the wake of the tragic shootings at Columbine High School in Colorado in the spring of 1999, a number of social and political commentators observed that the country would never be quite the same. The incident seemed to crystallize a number of issues that were already on the public agenda (for example, debate about the easy availability of guns, parental responsibility, social isolation, the effects of violent video games, and incivility). Perhaps, years from now, scholars will look back and identify this event as a significant one that helped to shape a particular research agenda in sociology or family studies. Today, in mass communication, scholars have identified a number of early events that seem to have set the stage for public and scholarly concern about the impact of mass media. Although there is no universal agreement about these precipitating events, most would acknowledge that each of the situations outlined below played a role in stirring interest in the study of media effects.

1898—Congress Declares War on Spain

Why did Congress declare war on Spain in April 1898? Although a complete answer to this question would require reading through several book-length manuscripts, many historians would point to the famous newspaper publisher William Randolph Hearst as a prominent player in the decision to go to war. When Hearst's illustrator, Frederic Remington, wrote him a memo from Havana that there was no trouble there and there would be no war, Hearst responded with the now infamous words, "Please remain. You furnish the pictures and I'll furnish the war."[3] The fact that Congress eventually did declare war may have had something to do with the newspaper coverage in Hearst's *New York Journal;* many believe that Hearst stirred up public opinion in favor of war and helped to provide Congress with a public mandate.

1917—Propaganda in World War I

President Woodrow Wilson certainly recognized the potential of newspapermen like Hearst to influence public opinion. He appointed one of those men, George Creel, to lead the **Committee on Public Information.** This committee helped to advise President Wilson on how public relations could be used to influence public opinion about the war. As one scholar in mass communication noted, "It [the Committee on Public Information] engaged in public relations on a scale never before seen, using movies, public speakers, articles in newspapers and magazines, and posters."[4] The use of **wartime propaganda** sensitized the public to the fact that mass media might be used to influence public opinion on a large scale.

The 1920s—Movies Explode
as Mainstream Entertainment

If you ever try to imagine what life was like in the United States nearly 80 years ago, you probably think of the daily routine then as being very different from your own routine today. Certainly life is different in many respects. In one respect, however, it might be similar. If you go to the movies regularly for your entertainment, you are no different than millions of people who lived in the 1920s. Shearon Lowery and Melvin DeFleur characterize the situation with respect to movies in their book, *Milestones in Mass Communication Research:*

> Going to the movies was a frequent event for most families—they were great fun. Also, there were very few alternatives for inexpensive recreation. Homes had neither radios nor television sets. Some had pianos and windup Victrolas; a few even had books. But for the majority of families with limited means, taking in a motion picture was an enjoyable and affordable evening out. . . . Data on movie attendance were not systematically gathered before 1922. During that year, some 40 million tickets were sold every week in the United States. By the end of the decade, the figure had more than doubled to 90 million! Among the moviegoers in 1929 were

an estimated 40 million minors, and among those were approximately 17 million children under the age of fourteen. (p. 32)[5]

With so many people visiting the cinema every week, it was inevitable that people would begin to think about the effects of movies on attitudes and behaviors. Parents undoubtedly became aware that their children were picking up certain behaviors from the movies they saw on Saturday afternoons. With movies as the primary source of public entertainment, researchers started to become interested in documenting the effects of movies toward the end of the 1920s. Fortunately, the development of social science research techniques converged with the appearance of movies, and researchers were able to launch a series of studies that focused on the effects of film.

1929–1932—THE PAYNE FUND STUDIES

In 1928, in response to the growing public concern about the effects of movies on children, a private foundation known as the Payne Fund agreed to fund a series of studies that were conducted by the leading researchers of the time. The purpose of the **Payne Fund studies** was to discover the real impact of movies on children and adolescents. The studies represent the first systematic attempt to discover media impact scientifically. A total of 13 studies were published in 10 volumes on various topics pertaining to the impact of movies. One interesting aspect of these studies is that they introduced many themes that persist in the media effects literature to this day.

What Was the Content of Movies?

A researcher named Edgar Dale studied the content of 1,500 films made between 1920 and 1930.[6] Although Dale did not have the advantage of today's more sophisticated techniques of content analysis, he did attempt to categorize the films in different groups according to their major themes. Imagine that you were to do such a study on today's movies and had to use the 10 categories that Dale used in 1930. His categories were children, comedy, crime, history, love, mystery, sex, travel, social propaganda, and war. Which categories do you think would see the most use today? It might be interesting to repeat Dale's study with current films to see what changes, if any, have taken place. His results revealed that over 75% of all the films he studied could be classified using only 3 of the 10 categories: crime, love, and sex. If this result were released for current films, it probably wouldn't surprise many people. These same themes often provoke controversy in today's entertainment market, yet they remain prominent and readily available to consumers.

The Emotional Impact of Movies

Of course, the *effects* of movies cannot be gauged just by looking at content. Researchers involved with the Payne Fund studies wanted to collect information about how these themes actually affected viewers. In one line of investigation, children and adults were monitored with physiological electrodes to see how they reacted to romantic or sexy content.[7] One measure that was used in this investigation was **galvanic skin response.** When a person has an emotional reaction to an event, the reaction is often reflected in a sweat response. Perhaps you have discovered that before you are called upon to give a speech or visit your professor to talk about your grade, your fingers and palms get sweaty. Because moisture conducts electricity, researchers are able to measure the intensity of the emotional reaction by shooting a small (undetectable) electric current through two electrodes that are typically attached to the inner pads of two fingers. The more moisture coming off the skin, the better the conductivity in the electric circuit. The conductivity can be measured precisely in units called **micromhos.** When the researchers involved with the Payne Fund studies employed this technique, they found that young children were not much affected by romance movies. But older adolescents showed dramatic increases in their physiological responses. This research fore-shadowed two ideas that are clearly present in current research. First, as you will discover in chapter 7 on media that stir emotions, today's media scholars make important theoretical distinctions between younger and older children in their attempts to predict and explain the effects of media messages. Second, measuring physiological responses to media messages, including skin conductance responses, is an integral technique employed in many current studies of media impact.

Does Watching Movies Affect Behavior?

One of the key questions addressed in the Payne Fund studies dealt with the impact of movies on actual behavior. Again, this emphasis on the impact of movies seems just as relevant today as it was in the late 1920s when the studies were done. Public discussion about the V-chip and the possible effects of violent video games is just a contemporary version of the same concerns that were voiced 70 years ago. One study that addressed the issue was conducted by a prominent scholar named Herbert Blumer. Blumer collected responses from questionnaires and interviews with children, adolescents, and young adults. In these questionnaires and interviews, the respondents were encouraged to reflect on how exposure to media messages had affected their behavior. Many of the responses indicated that people definitely believed that they had been influenced by the media. For example, one 19-year-old male said:

> In my childhood it was common for one to imitate consciously heroes of the screen. For instance, I would climb the lone tree that was in the yard of the Catholic school near us and hang by one hand or hammer my chest shouting, "Tarzan" and the like. Jumping over fences on a run as did the heroes of the screen was usual in my young life. Fighting with one another, and after conquering him, placing one foot on his chest and raising our arms to the sky as Tarzan did was also common. (p. 22)[8]

Responses like these were typical in Blumer's study and, in retrospect raise a number of interesting issues. First, the behavior described by the 19-year-old male fits very nicely with the **theory of social learning,** which you will encounter in chapter 5. According to Albert Bandura, the author of this theory, children are more likely to imitate characters who receive rewards for their behavior and are perceived as attractive. Certainly, Tarzan fits the bill.

Second, as appealing as it might be to embrace Blumer's results and take the autobiographical comments at face value, it is important to recognize that his technique would come under criticism today (as it did in the 1930s) as a valid technique for assessing media impact. The technique assumes that people are aware of how media affect them. Although this assumption might be valid in some instances, it turns out to be misguided in many others. There are at least two kinds of problems. One problem is that people may be mistaken about the effects on their own behavior that they attribute to the media. Perhaps the young man in Blumer's study heard some of his friends talking about the impact of the media on children and used this idea to selectively reconstruct his past experiences. Maybe he did engage in the behavior described, but he may have been imitating other friends who were playing with him more than he was copying the actual behaviors on the TV show. A person's own introspection into the causes of behavior may or may not be accurate. Another problem is that by relying on people's own reports about media impact, researchers run the risk of missing effects that occur quite unconsciously. As you will see in later chapters, most of the effects of the media that are well documented in research studies are not ones that people are capable of reporting on a conscious level. People are not necessarily aware when media messages affect their attitudes and behavior. If researchers relied exclusively on introspective reports, they would miss a rich world of very significant media impact.

One example that shows the potential problems of relying on self-reports for assessments of media impact comes from the recent annals of criminal behavior. Ted Bundy was an infamous serial killer who raped and killed women. He was eventually brought to trial and executed. Before his death, he issued a public statement containing his own analysis of his actions. What had caused him to engage in such atrocious behavior? According to Ted, it was the mass media—specifically, exposure to volumes and volumes of pornography. As you will read in chapter 6, pornography certainly has been studied and associated with antisocial effects. But to what extent should we rely on Ted Bundy's own assessment of what caused his behavior? According to Paul Wilson, former research director at the Australian Institute of Criminology, it probably isn't a good idea to indict pornographic media as the culprit on the basis of Bundy's own self-analysis. Wilson noted:

> In Ted Bundy's case, no serious social scientist or law enforcement officer takes the explanation that "pornography made me do it" seriously. Well before Bundy turned the pages of a sexually explicit magazine or watched an adult video he was exhibiting bizarre behavior. Dr. Dorothy Lewis, who conducted multiple interviews with the killer just after his arrest, reported that Bundy was a highly disturbed child at the age of three.

When Bundy was first arrested in 1978, early interviews with police and psychiatrists reveal that the killer referred to popular sexually explicit magazines as "normal healthy sexual stimuli." It was only in the 1980s, when a court refused to certify him insane and to save him from the electric chair, that Bundy became a born–again Christian and reiterated the party line on pornography. (p. 40)[9]

The Bundy case illustrates that in addition to being unaware of media impact on themselves, people may deliberately articulate a view of media effects for personal reasons. In the final analysis, although Blumer's work on the Payne Fund studies was crucial for its time and helped to launch the formal scientific examination of media effects, scholars are reluctant to attach too much weight to the introspective self–reports that Blumer's methodology generated.

The Aftermath of the Payne Fund Studies

The Payne Fund studies played a huge role in the development of the study of media effects. In terms of the public consciousness, Lowery and DeFleur noted that the conclusions of the studies helped to establish a **legacy of fear**— widespread beliefs that the media were dangerous and that the effects of media messages might pervert and upset the proper social order.[10] Earlier concerns about propaganda and the role of newspapers in shaping political events helped to reinforce the attitude of public concern following the publication of the Payne Fund studies. Subsequent events in American life only tended to fuel the fire of concern about the pernicious impact of the media. In the end, one thing that inevitably impresses the student of media effects about the Payne Fund studies is how many of the themes and rhetorical tidbits from the 1930s resonate with those of the modern day. As Lowery and DeFleur point out in their excellent review of the studies, a summary document of the major findings concluded that "the commercial movies are in an unsavory mess," and "the producers ought to have heart" over their bad influences on children.[11] The current Hollywood film industry has endured many similar attacks that call upon filmmakers to exercise a greater sense of social responsibility.

THE INVASION FROM MARS

In the late 1930s, the dominant communication medium in America was radio. If there was any doubt about the potential of radio to influence people quickly and in large numbers, those doubts ended on the night of October 30, 1938. On that particular evening, the CBS radio network broadcast a radio drama as part of its *Mercury Theatre on the Air*. A young man by the name of Orson Welles narrated a radio adaptation of "War of the Worlds," a science fiction story written by H. G. Wells. An estimated audience of about 6 million listeners tuned in. Of all the programs that the producers at CBS might have thought would have an impact on the audience, "War of the Worlds" was not one of them. In an article written for *Harper's* by John Houseman, one of the cofounders of *Mercury Theatre* along with Orson Welles, we learn that virtually no one thought that this production was going to be anything special. In the week preceding the broadcast, the production crew even contemplated scrapping the whole idea.[12] But they didn't. The show went on as planned—and stirred the public as nothing before it ever had.

The premise of the show was very simple. Listeners would be lulled into a sense of relaxation and even boredom as the show began with classical music. Then, a radio announcer would interrupt and refer to an atmospheric disturbance that had been reported over Nova Scotia. Listeners would then be returned to the light music until the announcer interrupted again. Over the course of the one-hour program, what started as an atmospheric disturbance turned into an alien invasion by Martians who had landed their invading craft in Grover's Mill, New Jersey. In retrospect, one would think that the discerning listener would easily recognize that the reported events were nothing more than a fictional drama. But the realistic format of cutting away from the music to feature what sounded like live news reports apparently fooled about one million people in the show's audience.

In some cases, random events helped to promote the illusion of reality. In the town of Concrete, Washington, a power failure occurred while the radio announcer was informing Americans that the Martians were disrupting power and communications across the country. Needless to say, the residents of Concrete didn't need any more reason to believe the broadcast was true. But even without such events, people up and down the eastern seaboard went into a panic. CBS eventually apologized to the public for its miscalculation. The morning after the broadcast, a bewildered Orson Welles was shown fielding questions about the incident from a crowd of reporters that must have seemed to him like an attack mob. Welles was still trying to figure out exactly what had happened.

The Research at Princeton

Orson Welles was not the only one who wondered what had happened on that October night. A research team at Princeton University led by Hadley Cantril did a quick postmortem of the whole affair in a study that included an analysis of newspaper accounts of the incident as well as data from surveys and personal interviews.[13] Lowery and DeFleur summarized the findings of the research.[14] As for why so many listeners found the show believable, the Princeton research team cited the fact that most Americans had tremendous confidence in radio as a news medium. They never expected that their most trusted medium would mislead them into a hoax. They noted, too, that the show used the brilliant creative technique of on-the-spot reporting and sounded convincing in introducing various scientific experts to the public. Also contributing to the panic was the fact that many listeners missed the announcement at the beginning of the show that told the audience that the program was a dramatic adaptation.

The Princeton research also focused on the characteristics of people who believed the program was real. According to the results, these were people who had less critical ability, less self-confidence, and less emotional security than those who recognized that the program was only a dramatization. People with strong religious beliefs were also more likely than others to believe that earth was being invaded by Martians. These results may not be particularly surprising, and they didn't exactly startle the scholarly community. But the broadcast and the subsequent research were important in the history of media effects. The broadcast itself demonstrated that the media could trigger widespread, intense responses in the audience. The research pointed the way to future studies that would employ a variety of personality and demographic variables to predict media impact. In terms of the legacy of fear, the "War of the Worlds" broadcast did little to dispel the notion that media messages were potentially dangerous for society. As the 1940s began, this assumption was widespread.

EARLY THEORY OF MEDIA EFFECTS:
THE MAGIC BULLET MODEL

In the wake of the Payne Fund studies and Cantril's study of the "War of the Worlds" broadcast, the view among scholars was that the mass media were indeed powerful agents for change and influence. The studies that were done were typical of investigations in a new area of research. They were essentially exploratory studies that attempted to discover any new information. The studies were not characterized by well-developed theory and the testing of specific hypotheses.

Contemporary scholars often look back on this early period of media effects history and see a general theoretical view that seemed to prevail, even though it wasn't stated formally. This view has come to be known as the **magic bullet model** or the **hypodermic needle model of mass communication.** According to this view, the communication of a message in a mass medium can be compared to shooting a gun that contains a magic bullet or to injecting someone with a hypodermic needle. Once the message reaches the audience, it will exert powerful, relatively uniform effects on everyone who processes it. It would probably be difficult to find a single scholar in 1940 who articulated this particular view of media impact. It seems too extreme and simplistic. Nevertheless, it does capture something of the general outlook that many scholars held at the time regarding the media's tremendous power.

Part of the explanation for this outlook had to do with the psychology of the time, with its emphasis on the uniform physiological mechanisms common to all human beings. Little consideration was given to the possibility that people might respond differently to the same message. The theoretical framework that allowed for individual differences in responding was not yet in place. The public tended to concur with the view of great media impact. The Orson Welles affair was still fresh in their minds, and the public debate about movies in the aftermath of the Payne Fund studies had resulted in an attitude of self-censorship on the part of Hollywood that only served to highlight the power of movies.

The convergence between the scholarly and public views of media impact, though, was about to change. In 1940, a team of researchers from Columbia University undertook an exhaustive study of the role of radio messages on voter behavior in the presidential election. Their results had a great impact on how scholars came to think about the theoretical underpinnings of media effects. More than any other study up to that point, *The People's Choice* advanced the study of media effects both theoretically and methodologically.[15]

THE PEOPLE'S CHOICE STUDY:
THE LIMITED-EFFECTS MODEL

The 1940 presidential election was between Wendell Willkie, the Republican, and the Democratic incumbent, Franklin D. Roosevelt. As the two candidates prepared to do battle at the polls, a team of researchers from Columbia University, Paul Lazarsfeld, Bernard Berelson, and Hazel Gaudet, set out to study "how and why people decided to vote as they did." The study took place in Erie County, Ohio, using a sample based on visitations to every fourth house in the county. The researchers decided to employ a longitudinal panel study design (see chapter 2). That is, they followed a main panel of 600 people throughout the campaign and interviewed them repeatedly (seven times). One of the methodological innovations of this very ambitious study was the use of large **control groups** of 600 respondents each.

Why Use Control Groups?

On reflection, it is easy to see why control groups were used. Imagine that you were one of the 600 people selected for repeated interviewing during the campaign. The fact that you knew ahead of time that you were likely to be interviewed again about your voting preferences and behavior might cause you to modify your behavior or your answers in the next round of questions. That is, the panel design itself might have an effect on the data collected—an effect quite separate from the responses that people might make if they were untarnished by the repeated interviews. In order to determine if this was actually happening, when the researchers went back to the main panel of 600 people to interview them for a third time, they also interviewed a separate group of 600 people for the first time. Theoretically, if interviewing the main panel three times had no impact on their responses, then there would be no difference between them and the control group of 600 people that had been interviewed for the first time. The researchers selected another control group of 600 people to interview when the main panel was interviewed for the fourth time. They repeated this procedure on the sixth interview. In general, the main finding from this procedure was that the responses of the control groups did not differ significantly from the responses of the main panel. This was a very important finding. It indicated that the longitudinal panel design was a viable method for studying change. Concerns that multiple interviews would alter the nature of people's responses proved to be unfounded in this case. The longitudinal survey design is still a very important technique in research today.

Media Impact in the 1940 Campaign

One of the surprising results of *The People's Choice* study was that the impact of media exposure to campaign messages was rather negligible in terms of **conversion**—changing voters from an intention to vote for one candidate to an intention to vote for the other. A more significant effect of media exposure was **reinforcement**—assuring voters that their current intention was worthwhile and correct. The data showed that half of the voters had already decided by the time of the first survey whom they were going to vote for. It was important that media messages over the coming months keep these people in the fold. Although the effect of reinforcement doesn't appear in the data as a great change, it is nonetheless a very important media effect.

In today's modern age of computing technology, it is a little tough to appreciate the monumental task that faced the researchers from Columbia after they had gathered their data. They had no personal computers on their desktops. There was no large mainframe computer at Columbia that could be called upon for number crunching. It is little wonder, then, that it took the researchers nearly 8 years to synthesize their data and bring it to publication. Consequently, the theoretical impact of *The People's Choice* study did not appear to take hold until the end of the 1940s or the beginning of the 1950s. Combined with several other significant studies of media impact in the 1950s,[16] *The People's Choice* served to usher in a new perspective on media impact. Far from the view that media effects were powerful and comparable to a magic bullet, the newer research seemed to indicate that the media had only limited effects.

Experiments on World War II Movies

During the years when the researchers were preparing their data from *The People's Choice* study for publication, the United States was involved in World War II. One of the weapons that Germany took very seriously as part of its arsenal was propaganda in the form of movies. During the war years, the Germans produced hundreds of films that were seen regularly in movie theaters and were designed to convince people that the German war machine was invincible and that Germany's occupation of the countries of Europe was a great thing for the people of those countries.

The U.S. government took notice of how effectively the Germans were using film and, in response, called upon Hollywood to fight back. Specifically, they asked director Frank Capra, maker of such film classics as *It Happened One Night, It's a Wonderful Life,* and *Mr. Smith Goes to Washington,* to make movies that would convince audiences that the German empire was evil and that the United States needed to achieve ultimate victory in the war. At first, Capra was overwhelmed by his task. But after studying the German films, he decided that he could effectively use the film footage that the Germans had used in their movies and turn it back against them. Capra actually shot very little new film footage. This allowed him to make seven films in a very short period of time. These films, which are now known as the *Why We Fight* film series, were shown to thousands of people during the war years—particularly to military recruits, who saw these movies as part of their standard initiation and training.

If you have never seen any of these movies, it might be worth your while to try to obtain a copy of either *Prelude to War* or *The Battle of Britain*. Even after 60 years, you can still appreciate the masterful job of filmmaking that Frank Capra achieved in putting these movies together. One day, after I had shown *The Battle of Britain* to one of my media classes, an exchange student from England, whose grandfather had fought in the battle, approached me as I was leaving class. Tears filled her eyes as she thanked me for showing this movie. She told me that until she saw the film, her grandfather's war stories had always seemed distant and unreal. The movie images brought those stories to life for her, and she told me that she left that class feeling as though she had captured an important part of her family history. It was an emotional moment.

After Capra made these movies, the U.S. government hoped that everyone who saw them would have the sort of emotional response that my student reported. More specifically, the government hoped that these movies would improve people's understanding of the facts of the war, and would change their opinions and interpretation so that they would adopt a position favorable to the United States, improve attitudes toward the Allied forces, and motivate the soldiers to fight a tough war. How could the government find out for certain if the films were really effective in bringing about these results?

From your reading in chapter 2, you might recognize that the experimental method would be a good way to test the effects of these movies. The government assembled a team of researchers to do the experiments, and these studies are noteworthy as the first sophisticated set of experiments in media history. The results were summarized in a book published just one year after *The People's Choice* called *Experiments on Mass Communication*.[17] What did these experiments find? Were the movies effective? Unfortunately for the U.S. military leaders who were hoping to see evidence of profound effects, the actual evidence was somewhat disappointing. Although the movies were definitely educational and increased people's factual knowledge about the war, there was very little evidence that they changed the essential motivation of the soldiers who were fighting the war. Of course, some argued that what these studies really showed was a **ceiling effect**. The levels of motivation of most of the soldiers who saw the movies may already have been about as high as they could go—they had "hit the ceiling." After all, prior to their military service, many of the recruits had probably seen portions of the movies in newsreels that were presented at the nation's movie theaters. Perhaps the films had already had their intended effect, and their levels of motivation couldn't go any higher. Although this was one possibility, the relatively meager effects observed in these experiments tended to reinforce the view of limited media effects that emerged after the publication of *The People's Choice.*

Carl Hovland, the main author of the book that summarized the experiments on the *Why We Fight* movies, went on to conduct numerous communication experiments at Yale University during the 1950s that focused primarily on how messages might change attitudes and behavior. Although many of these experiments did not directly test the effects of media messages, this tradition of experimental research had a significant impact on media effects studies by encouraging researchers to use the techniques of the carefully controlled experimental approach. Despite the fact that some of these experiments showed that communication variables had a great impact on attitude change, the prevailing evidence about media effects in the early 1950s was still in favor of the limited-effects model.

The Limited-Effects Perspective

One of the chief spokespersons for the new **limited-effects perspective** was a communication consultant who worked for the General Electric Company, Joseph Klapper. In 1958, Klapper published a book that had wide influence. It argued that the effects of the mass media ranged from small to negligible.[18] Klapper's position is captured in remarks that he made as part of a program on mass media presented in New York City by the Child Study Association of America on March 21, 1960. He said:

> I think it has been pretty well demonstrated that the mass media do not serve as the primary determinant or even as a very important determinant of any of the basic attitudes or the basic behavior patterns of either children or adults. This is not to say that they have no influence at all, but only that their influence seems to be incidental to other forces; or if it is not incidental, to pertain to rather superficial aspects of attitude or behavior rather than to basic attitudes and behavior. (p. 48f)[19]

Ironically, Klapper's comments about the minimal influence of the media came at just the time when scholars were starting to explore the impact of the new medium that had virtually exploded on the scene in the 1950s: television. Just as the limited-effects perspective was starting to take hold in the scholarly community, a new wave of research would call this perspective into question. As it turned out, the advent of the limited-effects model of mass communication is a good example of how theories about social phenomena can change as society changes. In an era of relatively high political stability, strong party identification, and straight-ticket voting, it isn't surprising that the Columbia researchers found that radio messages didn't change many votes. Today, however, political scientists work with a concept called **voter volatility.** The political system is more unstable. There are fewer people who identify strongly with a single party, more people who call themselves independents, and more people splitting their ticket at the polls. In such a volatile climate, scholars expect that the media might have more impact on the political process than they did in the 1940s. One important principle to emerge from the limited-effects

**STUDY BOX 3-1   The Principle of Selective
                   Exposure to Communication**

In an amazing interview captured on videotape (Episode 9 of *A Walk through the 20th Century with Bill Moyers*), the well-known journalist Bill Moyers interviewed Fritz Hippler, one of the men who helped produce Nazi propaganda films during World War II. As Moyers listened attentively, Hippler explained that the Germans had discovered a very important principle of mass propaganda: **People only want to see things that they find to be agreeable.** The Germans capitalized on the principle by showing the mass audiences images of military might, but never focusing on the problems associated with warfare. They were busy practicing a powerful principle of communication even before that principle had been formally uncovered in the annals of communication research.

Today, the principle of selective exposure is so well known and well documented that in 1985, Dolf Zillmann and Jennings Bryant edited an entire book on the subject, *Selective Exposure to Communication*. Their volume contains overviews of how the dynamic of selective exposure enters into the mass-communication process at multiple points. People are motivated to expose themselves to messages with which they already agree or to messages that make them feel good. Similarly, they are motivated to avoid messages that they find disagreeable or messages that make them feel bad.

One interesting line of research on selective exposure reported in the volume by Zillmann and Bryant is described by Jacob Wakshlag. Wakshlag reports how the principle of selective exposure should inform the work of TV producers who work on educational TV programs. In a study with first- and second-grade children, Wakshlag and his colleagues made different versions of an educational TV program available on different channels. The children were free to watch whichever channel they wished for as long as they wished. They were also free to turn the TV off. The researchers discovered that the children strongly preferred to watch the educational programs that contained humorous content. Wakshlag summarized the implications of this research in the following way:

> [T]he findings suggest that non-entertaining educational television programs are not likely to compete very well with other educational programs, such as *Sesame Street*, which contain humor and other embellishments. Furthermore, when faced with programs whose principal function is entertainment, such as those typically available from the networks, non-entertaining educational programs would probably fare even worse. (p. 194)

In today's competitive media environment, programmers would undoubtedly do well to consider carefully the wisdom of media effects research on this point of selective exposure. In general, audiences will not voluntarily expose themselves to messages that they find to be unpleasant.

SOURCES: (1) Wakshlag, J. (1985). Selective exposure to educational television. In D. Zillmann & J. Bryant (Eds.), *Selective exposure to communication* (pp. 191–201). Hillsdale, NJ: Erlbaum. (2) World War II: The propaganda battle. *A walk through the 20th century with Bill Moyers* (Episode 9). Alexandria, VA: Public Broadcasting Service. (3) Wakshlag, J. J., Day, K. D., & Zillmann, D. (1981). Selective exposure to educational television programs as a function of differently paced humorous inserts. *Journal of Educational Psychology, 73,* 27–32.

perspective that remains important today is the notion of **selective exposure to communication.** According to this idea, people are motivated to expose themselves voluntarily to messages with which they already agree. Likewise, they will tend to avoid messages that they find disagreeable. Study Box 3-1 focuses on this principle and discusses some of the research over the years that supports the principle. The statistics that I mentioned at the beginning of this chapter from the Gallup poll taken shortly after the U.S. invasion of Iraq are consistent with the principle of selective exposure. If people simply watch the things with which they already agree, then we shouldn't expect many attitudes to change over time.

THE EVILS OF COMIC BOOKS

During the 1950s, the public's view of media effects probably didn't change very much from the one reflected by the phrase "legacy of fear." One reason that public attitudes didn't change was because of the research of Frederic Wertham, a famous psychiatrist. Wertham took his case right to the people in the form of articles in popular magazines like *Collier's* and the *Ladies' Home Journal*. His book *Seduction of the Innocent*[20] was a virtual diatribe against the evils of comic books. (If you are lucky enough to find a genuine 1954 edition of this book, it might make sense to buy it. The book is becoming somewhat rare and is highly valued among comic book enthusiasts.) Wertham's research was based on selective analyses of comic book content—not random samples. He tended to highlight the most offensive material and then to characterize the entire comic book industry on the basis of the material he examined. He also studied a variety of young people who had been referred for behavioral difficulty. Wertham was convinced on the basis of his interviews and testing that comic books played an important role in corrupting the behavior of the adolescents he studied. One of the more incredible claims that Wertham made in his analysis of comic books was that the heroes Batman and Robin were homosexual lovers. He wrote:

> Only someone ignorant of the fundamentals of psychiatry and of the psychopathology of sex can fail to realize a subtle atmosphere of homoerotism which pervades the adventures of the mature, "Batman" and his young friend "Robin." (pp. 189–190)[21]

Wertham also warned the public about Superman. Apparently, he was concerned about the large "S" that Superman wears on his shirt. According to him, this symbol was uncomfortably close to the famous Nazi "SS." Wertham believed that exposure to the messages of these comic books could corrupt juvenile behavior and lead young people into a life of reckless crime and self-abuse. Many lawmakers and ordinary citizens agreed. On the basis of "research" procedures that were hardly scientific, Wertham managed to convince many people that comic books had powerful effects on young people. His content analysis procedures were not systematic and did not rely on random samples.

And the youth on whom he based his conclusions were members of a population that had already been referred for problems of various sorts. They did not represent the larger population of comic readers in any sense.

THE DAWN OF TELEVISION

As the public became worked up over comic books, a new medium was exploding on the scene. In 1950, only about 10% of American homes had a TV set. Neither the scholarly community nor the public could have imagined how the next 10 years would change the media effects landscape. By the end of the decade of the 1950s, 90% of homes had a TV. From the very beginning, it seemed that something new had started to take place on a regular basis. Reports of imitative crimes, particularly among young people, proliferated. Robert Liebert and Joyce Sprafkin documented some of these crimes in their book about the effects of television on children.[22] One example that they cite from the *New York Journal-American* was reported in the following way:

> [P]olice arrested an 11-year-old who admitted having burglarized Long Island homes for more than $1,000 in cash and valuables. His accomplice was identified as a 7-year-old friend. The boy said he learned the technique of burglary by seeing how it was done on television. (p. 8)

This type of report tended to stir public and government concern. A number of government reports in the mid-1950s and 1960s called attention to the large amount of violence on TV, but the reports also noted that scientific studies that would establish a cause–effect relationship between exposure to violence and aggressive behavior were lacking in the literature.

As the government continued to keep media violence in the spotlight, it also started to make grant money available for scientists who wanted to study the media's impact on human behavior. The 1960s and 1970s were years of new theories and research about media impact. The limited-effects perspective started to give way to a new paradigm based on more sophisticated scientific techniques. In particular, the laboratory experiment was a critical method that was used repeatedly to study the issues surrounding the impact of media violence. Chapter 5 provides a closer look at that research.

MANY TYPES OF MEDIA EFFECTS

Today, media scholars understand **media effects** as being more complicated than either the magic bullet or the limited-effects view would imply. Depending on the message, the medium, the audience, and the type of effect focused on, researchers have found the effects of media to be either strong or weak. In one of the classic essays written on media effects, Jack McLeod and Byron Reeves outlined a number of ways to think about media effects.[23]

Their analysis reveals that there is no simple answer to the question of whether the media affect people. It depends on what type of effect you may be talking about. According to McLeod and Reeves, media effects can be classified in many ways using some of the category schemes that follow. The appearance of their essay in 1980 signaled a major move toward conceptualizing media effects in a much more sophisticated way than had been typical only 20 years earlier. Today, research on media effects makes use of all the distinctions alluded to by McLeod and Reeves.

Micro-Level or Macro-Level Effects Micro-level effects involve effects on individual media consumers. Studies that rely on the experimental method might be classic examples. Studies that monitor physiological arousal while viewers watch a horror movie are concerned with how media messages affect individual body physiology. On the other hand, research on **macro-level effects** might examine media impact on large communities. Some researchers are concerned that in an age of media mergers and large corporate ownership of media outlets, the quality of news coverage in a given area might suffer and communities might not have adequate exposure to certain issues. Researchers may want to investigate the pattern of media ownership in a given community and attempt to relate it to general community awareness by studying the kinds of social programs or political action groups that citizens have available. Notice that in this case data are not gathered from individuals. Instead, the data are gathered on communities.

Content-Specific or Diffuse-General Effects One way to think about media effects is to ask whether they might result from exposure to particular kinds of content. People who watch media violence may adopt very different attitudes or behaviors than people who watch nature programs. Researchers who study this type of effect are interested in how **specific content** affects viewers. But another possibility is that the media bring about very general effects, quite apart from the content of the messages. In chapter 4, you will read about research that links TV viewing to obesity. The presumed effect in this case doesn't arise from exposure to any particular content; it is a much more general effect of time spent with the medium. Watching TV may replace physical exercise and give rise to more frequent eating. Such an effect would be referred to as a more **diffuse or general effect** than the effect of media violence on aggressive behavior.

Attitudinal versus Behavioral versus Cognitive Changes In 1980, when McLeod and Reeves wrote their article, they indicated that the history of media effects research "is very nearly the history of attitude change research." Up to that point, the main focus of study was the extent to which exposure to the media produced **changes in people's attitudes.** Certainly, this is an important effect to study. However, attitude change does not always produce **behavior change.** And sometimes changes in what people think about (that is, **cognitive changes**) might also be of great interest. Since McLeod and Reeves published their essay, the study of media effects has moved beyond the narrow focus on attitudes to include more studies on the media's impact on people's behavior and thoughts. You will encounter some of this newer research in chapters 8 and 9.

Alteration Versus Stabilization Most people think of media effects in terms of change. Exposure to media messages might produce an **alteration** in public opinion or in a decision about whether to buy a particular product. In contrast to an emphasis on change, another way to think about media effects is to emphasize how media messages reinforce the status quo and exert a powerful force for **stability.** *The People's Choice* investigation discussed earlier in the chapter revealed that exposure to radio commercials tended to reinforce prior voting dispositions. People tended to listen closely to the ads for their own candidates and became even more committed in their intent to vote for those candidates. The absence of dramatic change might not indicate the lack of media impact. Instead, it might indicate that the media exert a force for maintaining things as they are. In the chapters that follow this one, you will learn about the results of current research in a number of important areas. This research reflects a number of different types of media impact, including some of the varieties that are mentioned by McLeod and Reeves.

SUMMARY

Examples of media effects extend back to the 19th century, when the impact of newspapers on political affairs seemed obvious. With the Payne Fund studies, the research community generated the first systematic attempt to investigate the impact of media. These studies revealed that exposure to movies did have various effects on children. These results, combined with the obvious impact of the infamous "War of the Worlds" radio broadcast, introduced the "legacy of fear"—the idea that media were extremely powerful and could bring about effects that were often harmful. The research on comic books in the 1950s tended to reinforce the legacy of fear and the magic bullet model of mass communication. A study of voting behavior, *The People's Choice,* revealed a much more limited impact of mass media and ushered in the limited-effects perspective. As this perspective took hold in the 1950s, television exploded on the scene and attracted research attention in the 1960s and 1970s. This early research led to a more sophisticated view of media effects that prevails to the present day. Part of that sophistication is reflected in the number and different types of media effects that scholars now recognize.

KEY TERMS AND CONCEPTS

Committee on Public Information 45

Wartime propaganda 45

Payne Fund studies 46

Galvanic skin response 47

Micromhos 47

Theory of social learning 48

To learn more about the topics in this chapter, enter the Key Terms and Concepts found in this chapter as subject and keyword searches on your InfoTrac® College Edition.

NOTES

1. Sparks, G. G., & Miller, W. (2004). News coverage of the war in Iraq: Cognitive and emotional consequences for viewers. In R. D. Berenger (Ed.), *Global media go to war: The role of news and entertainment media during the 2003 Iraq war* (pp. 305–312). Spokane, WA: Marquette Books.

2. Lazarsfeld, P. F., Berelson, B., & Gaudet, H. (1948). *The people's choice.* New York: Columbia University Press.

3. Straubhaar, J., & LaRose, R. (2000). *Media now: Communications media in the information age.* Belmont, CA: Wadsworth.

4. Baran, S. (1999). *Mass communication: Media literacy and culture.* Mountain View, CA: Mayfield.

5. Lowery, S. A., & DeFleur, M. L. (1983). *Milestones in mass communication research.* New York: Longman.

6. Dale, E. (1935). *The content of motion pictures.* New York: Macmillan.

7. Dysinger, W. S., & Ruckmick, C. A. (1933). *The emotional responses of children to the motion picture situation.* New York: Macmillan.

8. Blumer, H., & Hauser, P. M. (1933). *Movies, delinquency, and crime.* New York: Macmillan.

9. Wilson, P. (1995). *Dealing with pornography: The case against censorship.* Sydney, Australia: University of New South Wales Press.

10. Lowery, S. A., & DeFleur, M. L. (1983). *Milestones in mass communication research.* New York: Longman.

11. Charters, W. W. (1933). *Motion pictures and youth: A summary.* New York: Macmillan.

12. Houseman, J. (1948). The men from Mars. *Harper's, 168,* 76.

13. Cantril, H. (1940). *The invasion from Mars: A study in the psychology of panic.* Princeton, NJ: Princeton University Press.

14. Lowery, S. A., & DeFleur, M. L. (1983). *Milestones in mass communication research.* New York: Longman.

15. Lazarsfeld, P. F., Berelson, B., & Gaudet, H. (1948). *The people's choice.* New York: Columbia University Press.

16. See the following for some of the most important studies during this time period: (1) Katz, E., & Lazarsfeld, P. F. (1955). *Personal influence: The part played by people in the flow of mass communication.* Glencoe, IL: Free Press of Glencoe. (2) Lewin, K., & Grabbe, P. (1948). Conduct, knowledge, and acceptance of new values. *Journal of Social Issues, 1,* 53–64. (3) Stauffer, S. A. (1948). *The American soldier: Studies in social psychology in World War II* (Vols. 1 and 2). Princeton, NJ: Princeton University Press.

17. Hovland, C. I., Lumsdaine, A. A., & Sheffield, F. D. (1949). *Experiments on mass*

communication. Princeton, NJ: Princeton University Press.

18. Klapper, J. T. (1960). *The effects of the mass media.* Glencoe, IL: Free Press of Glencoe.

19. Klineberg, O., & Klapper, J. T. (1960). *The mass media: Their impact on children and family life.* Comments presented to the Study Association of America. New York: Television Information Office.

20. Wertham, F. (1954). *Seduction of the innocent.* New York: Rinehart.

21. Ibid.

22. Liebert, R. M., & Sprafkin, J. (1988). *The early window: Effects of television on children and youth.* New York: Pergamon Press.

23. McLeod, J. M., & Reeves, B. (1980). On the nature of media effects. In S. B. Withey & R. P. Abeles (Eds.), *Television and social behavior: Beyond violence and children* (pp. 17–54). Hillsdale, NJ: Erlbaum.

4

■

Time Spent with Mass Media: Reasons and Consequences

I n a documentary about the history of radio that was made for Home Box Office,[1] a young child's fascination with listening to radio drama was captured with a question that he directed to his parents: "Gee, Mom and Dad, what did people do before the days of radio?" The parents hesitated as they reflected on their past and finally answered, "Well, we *talked*." As the young child started to express his incredulity at how boring life must have been before radio, the parents ordered him to stop talking so they could listen to the radio. In the 1970s, this same conversation might easily have taken place with respect to television. When I was a teenager, I might well have been tempted to ask my own parents, "What did you ever do before the days of TV?" For my generation, growing up without TV was simply unimaginable. Today, the question I am likely to get from my own children is "What in the world did you ever do before the days of computers, mobile phones, and the Internet?"

One thing that these parent–child conversations reveal is that, quite apart from the effects of media content, the mass media have had a profound impact on the way people use their time. In the 1940s, children spent time listening to their favorite radio heroes. In the 1970s, they were glued to the TV screen watching all sorts of shows, from sporting events to sitcoms. Today, they are surfing the Internet, downloading MP3s, and chatting online with their friends across town or across the country. They have been integrated into a more complex media environment. And radio and TV are not gone; they still occupy significant amounts of our time. Most of the chapters that follow this one will deal with the effects of particular kinds of media content. But this chapter deals with a different issue. Quite apart from the actual content of the media, why do we elect to spend so much of our time with media messages, and what are some of the consequences of those decisions?

Before we take a look at the research on how much time we spend with the media and how that time influences who we are as human beings, this is a good place to take a step back from the idea that the media influence people. Can we gain any insights from reversing the typical logic of media impact? Instead of thinking about the media first and their impact on people second, what happens when we start with people and move to the media? It is certainly true that media messages influence us, but this influence does not take place in some sort of static environment of one-way communication. The time that people spend with mass media is often the result of a deliberate choice. Before we study the impact of the media messages that we consume, it is important to understand what leads people to the media in the first place. Why would people choose to spend their time going to a movie, watching a TV show, or reading a magazine or newspaper?

THE USES AND GRATIFICATIONS PERSPECTIVE

Recall from chapter 3 that in the 1950s and 1960s, there was a shift among scholars about how to think about media effects. The idea of limited effects became popular. This perspective emphasized that audience members are not all the same. Because individuals react to media content in very different ways, the idea that the media have uniform, powerful effects on a wide audience fell out of favor. It was only natural that the limited-effects perspective, which emphasized individual differences, would spawn a new interest in why individuals use media in the first place. This new emphasis, the **uses and gratifications perspective,** was formalized in an article by Elihu Katz, Jay Blumler, and Michael Gurevitch.[2] This perspective was designed to lend insight into the ways that people use media to meet their needs. It focused heavily on individual motivations for media use. Since the time of the article by Katz, Blumler, and Gurevitch, an entire tradition of studies in uses and gratifications has grown up and matured in the mass-communication literature. We now know a great deal about the various reasons people have for choosing media exposure of particular kinds.

Why Do Children Watch TV?

You might want to pause before you read the following paragraphs and take out a pen and paper. Why do *you* think children watch TV? Jot down as many reasons as you can think of, using your own childhood as an example. How many reasons were you able to come up with? How does your list compare with the one that follows? This list of **motivations for media use** was developed

---

STUDY BOX 4-1   Jordan's Reasons for Using the Internet

Glenn: Hi. I have a question for you.

Jordan: shoot

Glenn: List as many reasons as you can for why you use the Internet.

Jordan: Okay . . . It's a form of communication between my family members and me [COMPANIONSHIP]

Jordan: It's a way to express some things I "hold dear" to the rest of the world, or views I am interested in.

Jordan: It's a source of information for school. [LEARNING]

Jordan: It's a source of information for other "facts." [LEARNING]

Jordan: It provides things to do, like play card games. [RELAXATION]

Jordan: It's a hobby . . . like, my homepage . . . something to do when I'm bored [PASS TIME] (Note: Jordan's homepage is at http://www.geocities.com/. She learned how to write her own HTML code when she was 12 years old.)

Jordan: It's "vast" . . . it won't get boring easily. [AROUSAL]

Jordan: It's a way to stay informed about issues in the world. [LEARNING]

Jordan: It's a way to stay informed about ANYTHING, I guess . . . music, TV, etc. [LEARNING]

Jordan: It's a way to meet people—chat, email pen pals, blah blah. [COMPANIONSHIP]

---

by Bradley Greenberg in one study of British children[3] and was replicated by Alan Rubin in a study of children from the United States.[4]

Learning Not surprisingly, children turn to TV to learn things. Occasionally, I hear a very small minority of students say that when they have children, they won't permit TV in their homes. Inevitably, the rationale for this intention is that there is simply too much objectionable material on TV today. I am somewhat sympathetic with the position of these students, but having raised three children in a home with multiple TV sets, I also usually ask about the missed opportunities to use TV for **learning.** Cable TV has expanded the number of possible programs to object to. But it has also expanded the opportunities for learning that could never have taken place years ago. In our family, we love PBS, the Discovery Channel, and the History Channel. The data from the uses and gratifications research suggest that children do use TV deliberately to learn things. Perhaps not much has changed in terms of children's motivations for media use, even in the age of the Internet. In Study Box 4-1, I have reprinted the text of an Internet chat that I had with my daughter Jordan (when she was 14 years old) about why she uses the Internet. As you will discover, learning things is an important motivation. Remember, though, that the scientific approach does not permit me to make any generalizations about children from just one child. If I really wanted to introduce evidence for this point, I would have to do a formal study with a random-sample survey of many children. Going back to the Payne Fund studies reviewed in the last chapter, there is no shortage of scientific evidence for the notion that children learn from the media. Researchers who study uses and gratifications note that some of this learning is motivated—not just an accidental by-product of media exposure.

Habit Watching television may be habit forming. The research studies reveal that children are conscious of the fact that they may view out of **habit.** If it's there, kids like to watch. Related to the habit motive is the suggestion in the literature that TV, like a drug, encourages behavior that looks like a full-blown addiction.[5] The literature on television addiction is somewhat mixed. One early survey of adults conducted by Robin Smith failed to find much evidence of a true addiction to TV.[6] But several later studies seem to indicate that **TV addiction** is a real phenomenon. One study that appeared in the journal *Addictive Behaviors* found that whereas women tend to be more addicted to caffeine and chocolate, men are more likely to be addicted to alcohol, cigarettes, gambling, and television.[7] Research by Robert McIlwraith indicates that some college students endorse the statement "I'm addicted to television," and those who do tend to be more easily bored, more introverted, and more likely to suffer from neurosis.[8] The area of television addiction, as well as possible addictions to video games, deserves more attention from scholars, especially as it pertains to children. Clearly, the current trend is for scholars to take seriously the idea that certain people can become addicted to TV. In February 2002, the prestigious journal *Scientific American* ran a cover story entitled "Television Addiction Is No Mere Metaphor." In that article, communication researchers Robert Kubey and Mihaly Csikszentmihalyi review a variety of evidence that points in the direction of TV addiction as very real. They state:

> The term "TV addiction" is imprecise and laden with value judgments, but it captures the essence of a very real phenomenon. Psychologists and psychiatrists formally define substance dependence as a disorder characterized by criteria that include spending a great deal of time using the substance; using it more often than one intends; thinking about reducing use or making repeated unsuccessful efforts to reduce use; giving up important social, family or occupational activities to use it; and reporting withdrawal symptoms when one stops using it. All these criteria can apply to people who watch a lot of television.[9]

At present, it seems safe to say that there may be a tendency for some individuals to develop a psychological dependence on TV that resembles addictive behavior in some respects.[10]

Companionship Children watch TV because it gives them a sense of connection to other people—a sense of **companionship.** As it turns out, the same is true for adults. Why should this be? Where the Internet is concerned, the concept of companionship is easier to understand. People can actually communicate with other people in chat rooms and use e-mail to keep in touch. But how does TV foster a sense of companionship? Researchers Byron Reeves and Clifford Nass may have some insight into this question. According to them, the human brain does not easily separate media images from reality. The title of their book summarizes their thesis rather well: *The Media Equation: How People Treat Computers, Television, and New Media Like Real People and Places.*[11] If Reeves and Nass are right, when children see people on TV, some primitive part of the brain is tricked into thinking that those people are physically present. Higher-order cognitive processes may tell them that the images are not real, but the images stimulate real emotional reactions just the same. A more complete confirmation of the Reeves and Nass thesis must await further testing and more complete understanding of brain functions. But the basic theoretical idea may be useful for explaining the sense that some people have of relationships with media personalities. Media researchers Elizabeth Perse and Rebecca Rubin refer to the feelings and attachments that people have toward media characters as "**parasocial relationships.**"[12] There seems to be no doubt that such relationships do exist.

Arousal Some children watch TV because it stimulates them, excites them, and increases their **arousal** level. Arousal refers to the physiological system and involves responses such as heart rate, blood pressure, sweat, and respiration rate. Back in the 1950s, Donald Hebb introduced the idea that each human being was wired with an **optimal level of arousal.** For some individuals, their natural baseline **set point** of arousal was higher than their optimum. Consequently, these people would seek out calm, boring activities. For other individuals, the natural set point of arousal is lower than their optimal level. As a result, these people would seek out stimulating and arousing activities. In support of this general notion, Marvin Zuckerman has documented the presence of a personality trait known as **sensation seeking.**[13]

Sensation seekers are individuals who tend to seek out arousing activities. Unlike individuals who are low sensation seekers, those high on sensation seeking express a much greater desire for activities such as skydiving, riding roller coasters, attending wild parties, and using drugs for recreation. Zuckerman devised a simple measure of sensation seeking that consists of a number of statements about preferred activities. Respondents simply indicate whether each statement applies to them. Several studies show that high sensation seekers prefer to watch horror films.[14] One of the reasons that some children (particularly males) seem to seek out media content that is violent or frightening may have to do with the need for arousal. For such children, reading a book is not likely to be an adequate substitute for watching a movie. Riding a roller coaster may be a better alternative.

Relaxation Just as children use TV in order to raise their arousal levels, they also use it for **relaxation.** Today, when I talk to groups of parents about using TV effectively in the home, I often take a few minutes to talk about the transitional time between afternoon and evening activities. This is often a time of chaos in the household as people shift gears and change activities. For parents, the combination of winding down from the workday and preparing the evening meal can seem like a major challenge when young children are running around at a hyper pace. A carefully selected, non-arousing TV program or video can often be the perfect remedy to ease the household tension at this time of day. In this case, the parents have control over the selection. But studies show that children do select relaxing shows themselves. Just as sensation-seeking behavior is a function of one's arousal set point, so too may be the tendency to use TV for relaxation. Of course, at any given time, any person may choose a TV program for the purpose of relaxation. But those who have high arousal set points that need to be lowered may be particularly likely to choose this kind of entertainment repeatedly.

Escape   You have probably found yourself at one time or another using the media as an **escape** from the unpleasant duties and occupations that you have in real life. This escape behavior has been documented by uses and gratifications researchers in connection with TV. It may also be related to TV addiction, discussed under the habit motive for TV use. Just as a drug addict seeks escape from reality through drug use, so the TV addict may be seeking an escape from the stresses and strains of life through watching TV programs. Although this motive has been documented by uses and gratifications researchers, not much is known about when such behavior may be healthy or unhealthy.

Passing Time   A final motive for TV use is simply for **passing the time.** It is not uncommon today to find TV screens in a variety of public places where people have to wait for things to happen. When people sit in a doctor's waiting room, watching TV helps to pass the time if the doctor is running behind schedule. I have now seen TV in three places where I had never encountered it before: in a hotel elevator, at the gas pump, and over the urinal in a public restroom. As the pace of life seems to be increasing, people are less tolerant of situations in which they are forced to wait for something (apparently even their own natural bodily functions). Waiting creates frustration. If a person can catch up on the headlines while waiting for the gas tank to fill or waiting for the elevator to make it to the 20th floor, perhaps this frustration decreases a little. Major airlines caught on to this principle years ago when they started to offer movies on longer flights. They discovered that people would pay a few dollars for the headphones and would watch a film that they might not order at home or rent at the local video store. Why? The reason is very simple. On an airplane, there is little else to do. Watching a movie helps to pass the time.

Uses and Gratifications Among Older Viewers

It would be a mistake to give the impression that uses and gratifications research is focused only on the reasons that children watch TV. In fact, researchers are actively studying how and why adolescents and adults use not only television but a host of other media, including radio, books, cell phones, video games, and the Internet. Some of the most recent research along these lines attempts to connect people's motivations for using particular media with the effects that the media might have on them.

In one recent study, Alan Rubin, Paul Haridakis, and Keren Eyal administered a questionnaire to 354 undergraduate students who were enrolled in a
communication class at a large university in the Midwest.[15] One of the main
purposes of the study was to discover whether viewers of different television
talk shows could be distinguished from one another in terms of their motivations for using TV, their personal attitudes, their emotions, and other traits. For
example, if you know someone who loves to watch Oprah Winfrey, does this
fact tell you anything about how that person is likely to be when compared to
another person who loves to watch Jerry Springer? As you might suspect, the
results of the research did show some differences. Compared to the Oprah
Winfrey viewers, those who liked to watch Jerry Springer reported that TV
shows were less realistic and said that they enjoyed watching shows where people got angry, embarrassed, and hurt by someone else. They also reported that
they tended to watch TV for entertainment and excitement—not to become
better informed. Oprah viewers tended to be much more likely to be motivated to form a parasocial relationship with the host than were the viewers of
Jerry Springer. In addition to these findings, the researchers also discovered
that they could differentiate viewers on the basis of how they had responded to
a questionnaire that measured levels of trait aggressiveness. Viewers with high
levels of aggression were much more likely to enjoy watching guests being
embarrassed or hurt. They also tended to report more anger and had more
negative attitudes toward women.

Although the researchers did not attempt to study the effects that talk
shows had on these viewers, they suggested that the effects might be determined in part by the attitudes that viewers brought with them to the viewing
experience. For example, viewers who think that talk shows are not very realistic might not tend to be greatly affected by what they see. On the other hand,
viewers who think that these shows are quite realistic might tend to be influenced to adopt attitudes and behaviors that they see depicted on the screen. The
relationship between what viewers bring with them to the viewing experience
and how viewing subsequently affects them is one of the most important areas
of current research in the uses and gratifications tradition.

THE PROBLEM WITH SELF-REPORTS

One common criticism of the uses and gratifications perspective is that it relies
heavily on self-reports. Are people able to report accurately about the reasons
they use the media? Even if they are able to report accurately, are they always
motivated to do so? These are important questions that researchers can never
answer definitively for all time. That is, whenever a given study is undertaken,
these two questions must be considered. In answer to the first question, the
chances of getting accurate answers about motivations improve with the
recency of the behavior in question. You might be able to report quite accurately that the reason you watched the news last night was to find out how the

weather would be for the football game today. But if you were called upon to report on your motivations for watching the news six weeks ago, you might have to resort to a reasonable speculation about your behavior, which might or might not be accurate.

The second question concerns whether or not people might deliberately misrepresent their viewing motives. One of the principal reasons that people might do this is to make a good impression on the researchers. This sort of misrepresentation is sometimes called the **social desirability response.** That is, they may want to make themselves look good for the researchers. As a professor, I might consider it more desirable to report that I watched TV in order to become better informed, instead of simply to pass the time or escape from life's stress. Passing the time doesn't sound quite compatible with the notion that, as a professor, I should be concerned about learning things. In order to save face, I might be tempted to alter my response. Researchers can counter the tendency for people to respond out of motives of social desirability by assuring them that their responses are completely confidential or even anonymous. These promises, combined with an emphatic statement in the questionnaire's instructions that only honest answers are valuable to the researchers, can be effective tools to combat the effect of social desirability. In the final analysis, researchers need to stay sensitive to the potential problems of self-report data. But although these reports can sometimes be flawed, our knowledge about mass communication would be significantly impoverished without them.

TIME SPENT WITH MEDIA

When it comes to the topic of time spent with the media, it would be difficult to know much at all without relying on self-report data. You have probably read or heard about some of the statistics that are generated from surveys about media use. In fact, the data indicate that people spend large quantities of time processing media messages of one sort or another.

One recent large-scale survey of media use was reported by the Kaiser Family Foundation.[16] The focus of this report was on children and adolescents up to the age of 18. The survey contained questions about multiple media sources, including television, videotapes, movies, video games, print media, radio, CDs, and computers. What did the results show? First, regarding television use, it is important to note that viewing begins at a very young age. Even among children in the 2- to 4-year-old age category, average viewing totals two hours daily. Children reach the peak of their TV watching (about 3½ hours daily) by the time they reach the end of grade school. In later adolescence, viewing drops off to about 2¾ hours daily. One interesting finding that emerged from the study was that when all children (2 through 18 years old) and all media were considered together, the average amount of time spent with media was about 5½ hours. But during that 5½ hours, children were exposed to 6½ hours of media content! How is this possible? I need only to think of my own children to arrive at the answer. Too often, I have seen them surfing the Internet at the same time they are monitoring their favorite TV show. On average, children use more than one medium at the same time for about one hour each day.

One major finding to emerge from the Kaiser Family Foundation survey was that reading time pales in comparison to time spent with TV. On average, children between the ages of 2 and 18 spend only 25 minutes per day reading books, only 16 minutes per day reading magazines, and only 5 minutes per day reading newspapers. Many educators who are sobered by these discouraging reading statistics have placed their hope in the computer as the new educational tool for young people. But if this hope is to be realized, the findings from the survey will have to change radically in coming years. On average, children between the ages of 2 and 18 used the computer only 34 minutes per day. And, of those 34 minutes, 21 of them were devoted to recreational uses such as games, chat rooms, and e-mail. Only 8 minutes per day outside the classroom were devoted to schoolwork. The numbers for computer time will undoubtedly increase as more households acquire computers. But the survey showed that nearly 70% of households with children between 2 and 18 already own a computer, and nearly half have Internet access. Despite the explosive growth of computers, television is still the medium of choice for children and adolescents. During an average year, the average child spends the equivalent of nearly two solid months of 24-hour days doing nothing but watching TV.

In the spring of 2003, the Kaiser Family Foundation released another report that specifically focused on children between 6 months and 6 years of age. In a survey of more than 1,000 parents, the researchers who wrote the report (Victoria Rideout, Elizabeth Vandewater, and Ellen Wartella) revealed that half of all children in this age range live in a home with three or more TV sets, and over one-third of the children have a TV in their bedroom. The authors concluded that "the vast majority of children are growing up in homes where television is a near-constant presence."[17] They note that for over 35% of the children in this age range, the home environment is one in which the TV set is either *always* on or on most of the time. These statistics ring true. I have talked with therapists in my own community who regularly visit children's homes in order to help them with their speaking skills or motor development. Inevitably, the therapists report that, almost without exception, the homes that they visit have a TV set that is turned on when they arrive. In most cases, the family members do not even think of turning the set off for the duration of the therapist's visit. This is anecdotal evidence for the notion that TV has simply become part of our living environment.

Television is not the only medium with which young children are spending time. Over 40% of children *under 2 years old* watch a video or DVD during a typical day. And, during a typical day, about 5% of children in this same age group use a computer.

When these statistics are combined with ones from the movie business, it all adds up to a large quantity of time spent watching moving images on a screen. The National Association of Theatre Owners recently reported that about 1.6 billion movie tickets were sold during a single year in the United States and Canada.[18] The number of tickets sold annually in the United States has tended to increase steadily over the last five years, with some small dips from time to time. The general expectation is for ticket sales to increase even more. This growth comes at the same time that ticket prices are spiraling upwards. With all of this viewing time, it seems naïve to suggest that TV and movies are merely innocuous sources of entertainment that have little or no impact on viewers. Starting with the next chapter, you will read about some of the effects associated with particular kinds of media content. For now, let's focus on a different question: Apart from the content of TV and movies, does simply spending time watching the content have any unique effects that researchers have been able to document? The answer to this question seems to be yes. Let's look briefly at some of the effects that have been examined.

The Displacement Hypothesis

For a number of years, researchers have been concerned about the possibility that the large quantity of time spent with media (primarily television) was serving to displace time that would ordinarily be spent in other important activities. This general idea has become known as the **displacement hypothesis.** The basic notion is that people have a limited amount of time in their daily routines that can be allocated to different activities. If, as the data seem to show, the time spent watching TV and movies has increased over the years, then it would seem logical to suspect that the time spent in some other activities must necessarily have decreased. Depending on what those other activities might be, there could be reason for concern. The symmetric version of the displacement hypothesis would suggest that if TV viewing decreased, the amount of time spent in other activities would correspondingly increase.

Relative to other areas, there are fewer studies that examine the displacement hypothesis directly. One study that was specifically designed to investigate this idea was a survey (panel design) of children in South Africa. Its authors, Diana Mutz, Donald Roberts, and D. P. van Vuuren, examined data on nearly 2,000 children over an eight-year period.[19] Each year, they questioned the children about the way they spent their time. The results of this study show that if a displacement effect exists, it isn't very large. The study began in 1974, and TV wasn't introduced to South Africa until 1976. Consequently, the authors were able to study the direct impact of TV in a way that can rarely be done today. Initially, TV seemed to displace radio listening and movie attendance, but not other important activities. In fact, the authors reported that over 60% of children's viewing time came from activities that could be regarded as very marginal in terms of their overall importance.

Another major study that employed a longitudinal design (panel study) was reported by Tannis MacBeth Williams and A. Gordon Handford.[20] These researchers took advantage of a unique situation in Canada before the advent of TV in one of the towns they studied. Over a period of several years, the researchers studied three towns. One of the towns (referred to as "Notel") had no access to television at the study's outset. Another town ("Unitel") had access to only one TV station. Finally, a third town ("Multitel") had access to four stations. Just after the initial baseline data were collected from grade school children in all three towns, Notel received access to a single TV station. Two years later, the researchers returned to each town and collected more data. At that time, Unitel had gained a second TV signal, and Multitel still had access to four stations. By studying the same children two years later as well as the kindergarten children who had subsequently moved into grade school in the interim, the researchers could see if changes had occurred in the towns that increased their access to TV (Notel and Unitel). The results of the study revealed that television definitely had an impact on other activities. The authors concluded the following:

> Television apparently has little if any impact on the number of community activities available, but it has a noticeable negative effect on participation in those activities. Involvement in community activities, summing across the categories, was greatest in the absence of television and fell significantly following its arrival in Notel. . . . Television's negative impact was greatest for sports, and the effect was stronger for youths than for adults. There was also reasonably clear evidence to implicate television in decreased attendance at dances, suppers, and parties, and again, the effect was stronger for youths than adults. (pp. 182–183)

Displacement of Important Activities Of course, what constitutes a marginal activity as opposed to an important activity may be debated. Should the effects from the Canadian study be regarded as ones that implicate TV in displacing important activities, or marginal ones? You may not tend to think that attending suppers and dances is very important. Sometimes, however, activities that seem trivial may not be so trivial when examined more closely. If TV viewing has a tendency to decrease opportunities for social interaction, perhaps people will lose the many benefits that come from close social ties. A psychologist, David Myers, has recently noted that, in the United States, a number of disturbing social trends seem to point toward a decline in close connections between people.[21] For example, he discusses the decline in marriage, the reduction of social networks, the increase in individualism, a decline in civility, and so forth. Could these symptoms in society be related to increases in time spent with mass media? For the most part, these issues have yet to be explored by researchers.

Despite the lack of research in some areas related to the displacement hypothesis, researchers have examined certain issues. Child psychologists argue that developing children need to engage in a proper amount of fantasy play in order to maintain an optimum level of stimulation that encourages healthy growth. Does watching TV encourage such fantasy play or discourage it? In a major review on the research pertaining to this question, two researchers, Tom van der Voort and Patti Valkenburg, concluded that the best evidence suggests that TV viewing discourages fantasy play through a displacement effect.[22]

The effect may depend on the type of content viewed. In some rare cases, educational programs may actually stimulate fantasy play. Programs with high levels of violence reduce fantasy play, while nonviolent programs appear to have little impact either way.

One of the chief concerns among educators is that watching TV disrupts academic learning by displacing important educational activities such as reading. A team of researchers studied this issue by collecting diaries from preschool children over a three-year period.[23] Once completed, the diaries contained information about the amount of time spent in a variety of different activities. In one sense, the results from this study show some support for the displacement hypothesis. As children spent more time watching TV, they tended to spend less time on activities related to education, talking to others, or playing video games. But the general relationship between TV viewing and these activities depended on a number of other factors, including the type of content viewed and the overall quality of the home environment. For example, watching educational TV programs did not result in any decrease in educational activities.

From these data, it appears that the displacement hypothesis may not be a simple phenomenon. In a study conducted by W. J. (James) Potter, more data emerged in support of the idea that the displacement hypothesis probably didn't operate in a simplistic fashion.[24] Although Potter did uncover a negative relationship between TV viewing and academic achievement (as viewing increased, achievement decreased), the relationship did not appear to kick in until TV viewing had reached at least 10 hours per week. This kind of relationship is referred to as a **threshold effect.** In this case, no negative impact from TV viewing was observed until the 10-hours-per-week threshold had been crossed.

Educators generally agree that one of the most important skills learned during the educational process is reading. How does television viewing affect the acquisition of reading skill? Is there a negative impact, and, if so, is that impact due to a displacement effect? Do children read less because they watch TV more? The available data on these questions do not permit a strong conclusion. The issue was examined extensively by the researchers who conducted the study of Notel, Unitel, and Multitel in Canada. They concluded that there was a small negative correlation between TV viewing and reading skill, but they argued that this relationship was probably not evidence of a direct impact of TV viewing. Instead, in the opinion of these authors, "[C]hildren who are more fluent readers tend to be more intelligent, to read more, and to watch television less." Consequently, it may be that the negative relationship between television viewing and reading skill has more to do with the fact that both of these things are related to intelligence, amount of reading, and other third-variable explanations.

One particularly interesting question about displacement effects has to do with the impact of computers and the Internet. In one recent longitudinal study of children who lived in Singapore, Waipeng Lee and Eddie Kuo discovered that increased use of the Internet did tend to be associated with reductions in the amounts of time that children spent watching TV. It also tended to be associated with increases in the amounts of time spent reading newspapers, listening to the radio, and talking with friends.[25] The possibility that time spent watching television may be gradually displaced by time spent on the Internet and using other newer media technologies is also suggested in several recent surveys published in the communication literature.[26]

Television Viewing and Obesity

Before I began writing this section of the chapter, I noticed that there was an exciting football game on TV. I also noticed that it was getting late in the afternoon and that I had not yet gone out for my 30-minute jog around the neighborhood. As I became more involved in the game, I found myself thinking that I might put off my jog until the next day. Fortunately, I resisted this temptation—partly because I knew that if I jogged, I would find it easier to read through the research for this section when I came back. The notion that television viewing might lead to obesity seems like a pretty reasonable conjecture. If TV displaces other activities, then perhaps it displaces activities like jogging and other forms of physical exercise that help keep extra pounds off. TV viewing may also encourage extra eating, which could also lead to additional pounds. Obesity has recently attracted public attention as a health problem. On October 27, 1999, the *Journal of the American Medical Association* devoted an entire issue to obesity, which, the editors noted, is a major risk factor for heart disease. At that time, an estimated 97 million American adults (over half the population) were considered to be overweight. According to the American Obesity Association (easily accessed on the web), that number has now increased to 127 million. The trend is even more startling. The percentage of *overweight* Americans (defined as those with a body mass index between 25 and 30; see Study Box 4-2 for more on the body mass index) increased from 46% to 65% over the last 25 years. During that same time period, the percentage of *obese* Americans (those with a body mass index of 30 or higher) doubled, from about 15% to 30%. Is it possible that the large amount of media use documented earlier in this chapter has something to do with the national proclivity toward being overweight? Is there any evidence that watching television may be playing a negative role in this national health problem? The current evidence is pretty intriguing.

More than 20 years ago, a sample of 1,000 respondents solicited through a questionnaire in the *National Enquirer* answered questions about their weight and their TV viewing.[27] The results of the study revealed that TV viewing was indeed positively correlated with snacking behavior. When the sample was broken down into subgroups, the results showed that 52% of the people who watched more than 28 hours of TV each week were overweight, compared to only 33% of those who watched fewer than 28 hours of TV. In another study of nearly 400 adolescent males whose average age was around 16, it turned out that those who watched less TV were not any less obese than those who watched more TV, but, on average, they were in much better physical condition.[28]

**STUDY BOX 4-2   Compute the Relationship Between
Body Mass Index and Daily TV
Viewing for Your Class**

You can calculate the correlation between body mass index (BMI) and daily TV viewing for your own class. Have your instructor coordinate the following exercise. First, have each student estimate the number of hours spent watching TV on a daily basis. Second, have each student compute his or her own BMI, using the following formula:

1. Multiply weight in pounds by 700 (e.g., 190 lbs × 700 = 133,000)
2. Divide that number by height in inches (e.g., 133,000/66 in. = 2,015)

3. Divide the result by height in inches again (e.g., 2,015/66 in. = 30.53). The resulting BMI = 30.53.

Your instructor can take the average hours of TV viewing and the BMI from each member of the class and compute a correlation coefficient using some statistical software. (If the class is relatively small, a hand calculator could be used after consulting any statistics text for the computational formula for the correlation coefficient.) What did you find? Were TV viewing and BMI related for your class? What do you think these results mean?

The most recent evidence on TV viewing and obesity establishes a positive relationship between these two variables. In a large-scale survey of nearly 5,000 women over the age of 19, those who watched three to four hours of TV per day were compared to those who watched less than one hour per day.[29] Those who watched three to four hours each day had twice the rate of obesity. It is important to remember that any correlation like this one could be the result of some other variable that is related, in this case, to both obesity and TV viewing. But the authors of this study considered several variables, such as age, level of education, and weekly amount of exercise, and, even controlling for the impact of these variables on the relationship, TV viewing was still positively correlated with obesity levels.

In the study that included a large number of respondents, a team of researchers studied over 20,000 males in the health profession who were between the ages of 41 and 78.[30] The results of this study showed a clear relationship between TV viewing and obesity. Some of the men reported watching TV more than 41 hours per week. Others reported watching a maximum of only 1 hour per week. The men in the first group were over four times more likely to be obese than the men in the second group. The authors of the study concluded that watching TV (or videotapes on the VCR) contributed to men's obesity.

Another study of interest in this area was conducted on nearly 2,500 Pima Indians.[31] The researchers in this study concluded that physical activity and watching TV were both related to body mass index, a standard measure of obesity (see Study Box 4-2). Finally, in another large study that involved over 50,000 women, a team of researchers who published their findings in the

Journal of the American Medical Association found that TV viewing was associated with greater levels of obesity and the likelihood of having type 2 diabetes.[32] Clearly, the preponderance of the evidence on the relationship between TV viewing and obesity shows that the two variables are related. Many researchers have concluded that the relationship is causal in that TV viewing displaces physical activity and consequently leads to more obesity. Although this may well be true, recall from chapter 2 the cautions about interpreting correlations as evidence for causality. What we really need is an experimental-type design that manipulates TV viewing and measures its impact on obesity.

One study by Thomas Robinson did attempt this type of design with third- and fourth-grade children. Some of the children who participated in the study were randomly assigned to a media intervention that included a period of 10 days during which the children were encouraged to limit TV viewing and video game playing to just one hour each day. Compared to the control group who didn't receive the intervention and who tended to spend about triple the time with TV and video games, the children who had the intervention treatment had significant decreases in their BMI, on average, over the term of the study. Although this experiment does tend to support the causal link between TV viewing and obesity, we still must be careful about stating the relationship in strong causal terms. Part of the intervention treatment included a variety of different types of instruction that encouraged children to modify their TV habits. In the final analysis, we can't be sure which parts of the intervention directly produced the decreases in BMI. It could be that the instructional portions of the intervention sensitized children to the importance of physical activity and played a direct role in the final results of the study. Without more carefully controlled experiments, however, we have to settle for the knowledge that TV viewing and obesity are related, and that there is good reason to suspect that the relationship is partly due to the fact that TV viewing displaces physical activity.

SUMMARY

This chapter started by reviewing some of the reasons that people have for using the media. With so many different reasons, it isn't surprising to find that daily media use is quite substantial. With people spending so much time with mass media, questions about the effects of all this time have occupied the attention of researchers for years. Apart from the content that people are processing, some research has focused on the impact of the time spent in and of itself. The major focus of this research is on the displacement hypothesis—the idea that time spent in media use displaces other activities. Some research does indicate that TV viewing displaces social activities, reduces children's fantasy play, and leads to obesity by reducing physical activity. In the final analysis, mass-communication researchers need to study this topic with renewed vigor. The possibility that heavy media use decreases social interaction and contributes to higher levels of social isolation is one hypothesis that deserves to be taken seriously. The consequences of such a possibility are profound. Perhaps your course instructor may want to lead a classroom discussion on this topic and provide you with an opportunity to express your views.

KEY TERMS AND CONCEPTS

Uses and gratifications perspective 64

Motivations for media use 64

Learning 65

Habit 66

TV addiction 66

Companionship 66

Parasocial relationships 67

Arousal 67

Optimal level of arousal 67

Set point 67

Sensation seeking 67

Relaxation 67

Escape 68

Passing the time 68

Social desirability response 70

Displacement hypothesis 72

Threshold effect 74

To learn more about the topics in this chapter, enter the Key Terms and Concepts found in this chapter as subject and keyword searches on your InfoTrac® College Edition.

NOTES

1. Cohn, B. (Producer), & Barry, M. (Writer). (1981). *Remember when*. Home Box Office.

2. Katz, E., Blumler, J. G., & Gurevitch, M. (1973). Uses and gratifications research. *Public Opinion Quarterly, 37,* 509–523.

3. Greenberg, B. S. (1974). Gratifications of television viewing and their correlates for British children. In J. G. Blumler & E. Katz (Eds.), *The uses of mass communication: Current perspectives on gratifications research* (pp. 71–92). Beverly Hills, CA: Sage.

4. Rubin, A. M. (1979). Television use by children and adolescents. *Human Communication Research, 5,* 109–120.

5. Winn, M. (1977). *The plug-in drug*. New York: Bantam.

6. Smith, R. (1986). Television addiction. In J. Bryant & D. Zillmann (Eds.), *Perspectives on media effects* (pp. 109–128). Hillsdale, NJ: Erlbaum.

7. Greenberg, J. L., Lewis, S. E., & Dodd, D. K. (1999). Overlapping addictions and

self-esteem among college men and women. *Addictive Behaviors, 24,* 565–571.

8. McIlwraith, R. D. (1998). I'm addicted to television: The personality, imagination, and TV watching patterns of self-identified TV addicts. *Journal of Broadcasting & Electronic Media, 42,* 371–386.

9. Kubey, R. W., & Csikszentmihalyi, M. (2002). Television addiction is no mere metaphor. *Scientific American*, February [Online]. Available: http://www.sciam.com/article.cfm?chanID=sa006&colID=1&articleID=0005339B-A694-1CC5-B4A8809EC588EEDF

10. Kubey, R. W. (1996). Television dependence, diagnosis, and prevention: With commentary on video games, pornography, and media education. In T. M. MacBeth (Ed.), *Tuning in to young viewers: Social science perspectives on television* (pp. 221–260). Thousand Oaks, CA: Sage.

11. Reeves, B., & Nass, C. (1996). *The media equation: How people treat computers, television, and new media like real people and*

places. Cambridge: Cambridge University Press.

12. Perse, E. M., & Rubin, R. B. (1989). Attribution in social and parasocial relationships. *Communication Research, 16,* 59–77.

13. Zuckerman, M. (1979). *Sensation seeking: Beyond the optimal level of arousal.* Hillsdale, NJ: Erlbaum.

14. Zuckerman, M. (1996). Sensation seeking and the taste for vicarious horror. In J. B. Weaver III & R. Tamborini (Eds.), *Horror films: Current research on audience preferences and reactions* (pp. 147–160). Hillsdale, NJ: Erlbaum. Lawrence, P. A., & Palmgreen, P. C. (1996). A uses and gratifications analysis of horror film preference. In J. B. Weaver III & R. Tamborini (Eds.), *Horror films: Current research on audience preferences and reactions* (pp. 161–178). Hillsdale, NJ: Erlbaum.

15. Rubin, A. M., Haridakis, P. M., & Eyal, K. (2003). Viewer aggression and attraction to television talk shows. *Media Psychology, 5,* 331–362.

16. Roberts, D. F., Foehr, U. G., Rideout, V. J., & Brodie, M. (November, 1999). Kids & media @ the new millennium. Henry J. Kaiser Family Foundation [Online]. Available: http://www.kff.org/content/1999/1535/KidsReport%20FINAL.pdf

17. Rideout, V. J., Vandewater, E. A., & Wartella, E. A. (2003). Zero to six: Electronic media in the lives of infants, toddlers and preschoolers. Henry J. Kaiser Family Foundation [Online]. Available: http://www.kff.org/entmedia/loader.cfm?url=/commonspot/security/getfile.cfm&PageID=22754

18. Madigan, N. (1999, November 18). Moviegoers to hit 1.6 billion in 1999. Entertainment Headlines [Online]. Available: http://dailynews.yahoo.com/h/nm/19991118/en/film-admissions_1.html

19. Mutz, D. C., Roberts, D. F., & van Vuuren, D. P. (1993). Reconsidering the displacement hypothesis: Television's influence on children's use of time. *Communication Research, 20,* 51–75.

20. Williams, T. M., & Handford, A. G. (1986). Television and other leisure activities. In T. M. Williams (Ed.), *The impact of television: A natural experiment in three communities.* Orlando, FL: Academic Press.

21. Myers, D. G. (1999). Close relationships and quality of life. In D. Kahneman, E. Diener, & N. Schwarz (Eds.), *Well-being: The foundations of hedonic psychology* (pp. 374–391). New York: Russell Sage Foundation.

22. van der Voort, T. H. A., & Valkenburg, P. M. (1994). Television's impact on fantasy play: A review of research. *Developmental Review, 14,* 227–251.

23. Huston, A. C., Wright, J. C., Marquis, J., & Green, S. B. (1999). How young children spend their time: Television and other activities. *Developmental Psychology, 35,* 912–925.

24. Potter, W. J. (1987). Does television viewing hinder academic achievement among adolescents? *Human Communication Research, 14,* 27–46.

25. Lee, W., & Kuo, E. (2002). Internet and displacement effect: Children's media use and activities in Singapore. *Journal of Computer-Mediated Communication, 7*(2) [Online]. Available: www.ascusc.org/jcmc/vol7/issue2/singapore.html

26. Ferguson, D. A., & Perse, E. M. (2000). The World Wide Web as a functional alternative to television. *Journal of Broadcasting & Electronic Media, 44*(2), 155–174. Kayany, J. M., & Yelsma, P. (2000). Displacement effects of online media in the socio-technical contexts of households. *Journal of Broadcasting & Electronic Media, 44*(2), 215–229.

27. Forrest, D. V., & Ryan, J. H. (1977). The *National Enquirer* TV poll. *Journal of Biological Psychology, 19,* 16–20.

28. Tucker, L. A. (1986). The relationship of television viewing to physical fitness and obesity. *Adolescence, 21,* 797–806.

29. Tucker, L. A., & Bagwell, M. (1991). Television viewing and obesity in adult females. *American Journal of Public Health, 81,* 908–911.

30. Ching, P. L. Y. H., Willett, W. C., Rimm, E. B., & Colditz, G. A. (1996). Activity level and risk of overweight in male health professionals. *American Journal of Public Health, 86,* 25–30.

31. Fitzgerald, S. J., Kriska, A. M., Pereira, M. A., & DeCourten, M. P. (1997). Associations among physical activity, television watching, and obesity in adult Pima Indians. *Medicine & Science in Sports & Exercise, 29,* 910–915.

32. Hu, F. B., Li, T. Y., Colditz, G. A., Willet, W. C., & Manson, J. E. (2003). Television watching and other sedentary behaviors in relation to risk of obesity and type 2 diabetes mellitus in women. *Journal of the American Medical Association, 289*(14), 1785–1791.

5

■

Effects of Media
Violence

Most people know Rod Serling's name because of his brilliant creativity in the hit TV series *The Twilight Zone.* Fewer people know about Serling's unfortunate venture into the world of made-for-TV movies. In a way, Serling's movie *The Doomsday Flight* (1966) was his own journey into the Twilight Zone. The premise of the film was a sure winner for the NBC network. It promised to be a suspense-packed adventure from beginning to end. After a routine passenger jet took off and established its flight path, a report came in that the plane was carrying an altitude bomb. A terrorist had set the bomb to explode if the plane descended below 5,000 feet.

As planned, the movie was a ratings success. In the end, the plane managed to land in Denver, which was barely 5,000 feet above sea level. The plane averted disaster and everyone lived happily ever after. Well, almost everyone. Those who were working in the airline industry on the evening that *The Doomsday Flight* made its debut were not so happy. Even before the movie ended, a bomb threat was phoned in to one of the major airlines. Four more threats were phoned in during the next day, and eight more were reported by week's end. In some cases, the callers threatened to use exactly the same kind of altitude bomb depicted in the movie.

Fortunately, none of these threats turned out to be real. Still, it was a time of tension and high anxiety for airline pilots, crew members, executives, and family members waiting for loved ones. They had been the victims of what media researchers know as the **copycat phenomenon.** People sometimes imitate the exact behaviors that they see depicted in the media. When those behaviors are violent or illegal, this translates into a significant social problem. Rod Serling felt such regret at this unanticipated effect of his movie that he issued a public apology to the nation and requested that the film never be shown again.[1]

Rod Serling was not the first person—or the last—to feel the unanticipated consequences of the copycat effect. Several years before the O. J. Simpson trial turned a spotlight on domestic violence, the ABC network aired a movie depicting spouse abuse. *The Burning Bed* (1984) starred Farrah Fawcett Majors as a battered housewife who felt so desperately trapped by an abusive husband that she did the unthinkable. In what she believed was her only avenue of escape, she soaked her husband's bed in gasoline while he slept. Then, she set the bed—and her husband—ablaze.

In this drama, based on a real-life occurrence, the wife escaped a murder conviction. The court held that she had acted in self-defense. Many experts recognize this movie as one that encourages battered women to seek shelter in the professional help community. Unfortunately, researchers also recognize that the film triggered some rather nasty copycat consequences. In the days following the broadcast, several women around the country who were victims of abuse decided to copy the behavior of the main character in the televised drama. They murdered their husbands. In a few cases, the scenario for the crime was exactly the same as depicted in the movie. Women doused beds with gasoline and set their sleeping husbands on fire.

Scholars have documented the phenomenon of copycat crime regularly since the dawn of TV. Survey results indicate that as many as one-third of the males convicted for felonies admit that they have imitated crime techniques shown on TV. Newspaper reports of early copycat incidents back in the late 1950s helped to trigger a massive effort to investigate the effects of television and movie violence. The controversy over media violence has raged ever since. One of the most recent incidents hit the news in February 2001 and stirred up the controversy anew. According to one report, a young teen set his friend on fire after seeing the same stunt acted out on the MTV program *Jackass*. His friend suffered second- and third-degree burns over most of his body. Another ongoing concern about copycat violence centers on the potential effects of televised wrestling events. At least four children have died as victims of violence that may have been linked to exposure to professional wrestling. In the case of Lionel Tate, a 13-year-old boy convicted in 2001 for killing a 6-year-old girl by lifting her in the air and dropping her onto a table, the legal defense specifically sought to place some responsibility for the incident on televised wrestling events. As you might suspect, the World Wrestling Federation denied any culpability in the girl's death and maintained that Tate's defense was simply a "contrived hoax." Although it can certainly be difficult to document conclusively whether a TV show, movie, or video game actually inspired a copycat incident, this difficulty has not prevented scholars from studying media violence. Of the hundreds upon hundreds of studies that scholars have published on the effects of television and movies, violence is, by far, the most frequent topic of investigation.

The government's threat in 1996 to introduce a rating system for television programs designed to protect children from the unwanted effects of violence and other objectionable content spurred the networks to act. A new rating system went into effect amid great controversy. Manufacturers now produce TV sets with a V-chip that permits parents to block out programs that contain unwanted violence.

Should we be making all of this fuss over media violence? Are the murder and mayhem on television really to blame for the increased violence in society? Would copycat criminals eventually commit their crimes even if a TV program or movie never inspired them to act? The answers to these questions are not simple. The researchers who have conducted the studies over the years sometimes disagree among themselves. Nevertheless, if one examines the research carefully, it is possible to make some sense of the mountain of data.

What exactly do we know today about the effects of media violence? In this chapter, I have tried to provide brief, accurate summaries of the many dimensions of this complicated body of research.

THE PRESENCE OF VIOLENT CONTENT

George Gerbner, professor emeritus at Temple University in Philadelphia and former dean of the Annenberg School of Communication, has directed a series of studies over the years that he designed in order to tell us something about how much violence there is on television. In short, Gerbner's finding was that there was a large amount of violence on prime-time TV and that, despite public controversy over the years, the level of violence had remained fairly constant.[2]

It isn't difficult to understand why our entertainment media contain a steady staple of violence. Good drama revolves around conflict, and violence is one of the common consequences of conflict. In the early days of the TV medium, however, the notion that people in the average home would have their television set on for more than 7 hours per day would have been incomprehensible. As recently as 1950, only 1 home in 10 even had a TV. A decade later, only 1 home in 10 was without one. The idea of having more than 50 channels to select from—24 hours a day—would have been laughable in 1950. By the 1990s, it had become a reality.

As the statistics on TV viewing changed, the sheer amount of violence being beamed into the average American household went beyond what anyone could have imagined. Today's estimates of viewing time, combined with what we know about how much violence is present, produce some very sobering numbers.

Newton Minow, former chairman of the Federal Communications Commission (FCC), noted in his recent book,[3] "By first grade, most children have spent the equivalent of three school years in front of the TV set." By age 18, time spent with TV exceeds time spent in school, time talking with teachers, time talking with friends, and time talking with parents. By age 70, today's average child will have invested more than 7 years in TV viewing. Total viewing time varies with age, but the average child, regardless of age, spends more than 3 hours each day in front of the tube. How much of that viewing time contains violence?

According to George Gerbner, children's shows contain more violence than any other type of programming. He estimates that shows designed for kids average about 32 violent acts per hour. On the basis of a study that spans 15 years, Gerbner estimates that crime is about 10 times more prevalent on TV than it is in the real world. According to the American Psychological Association (APA), the typical child will view more than 8,000 murders and over 100,000 acts of TV violence in the course of a lifetime. These are conservative estimates.

So, there is little question about whether violence saturates our TV screens. No one can dispute this fact. The most recent studies have attempted to capture more than just the number of violent acts. In the recent *National Television Violence Study,*[4] researchers examined the context of violence. These data help to give us an even deeper understanding of what is happening on the screen.

According to these most recent content studies, nearly 60% of all television programming contains some violence. One-third of all programs contain nearly 10 violent interactions. These statistics confirm what we knew from earlier research. Violence is prevalent on the tube. But how is it depicted? In nearly 75% of all of the scenes depicting violence, no punishment is given for the violent actions. This finding takes on real significance when we consider it in the light of Albert Bandura's theory of social learning, which I discuss later in this chapter.

How realistic are the portrayals of violence? The newest data show that in over half of all violent interactions, no character is depicted as experiencing pain. And fewer than half of the violent interactions result in negative consequences for the perpetrator of aggression. There is ample room for concern about the lessons that media violence might be teaching to TV audiences.

But at this point we have to be careful. Although the content studies clearly show that there is a lot of violence on TV, the studies have *nothing* to say about how that violence may be affecting people. Remember from chapter 2 that it isn't possible to make inferences about media effects from the content alone. It is at least theoretically possible that all of that TV violence amounts to a kind of warning about how we ought *not* to behave. Maybe the best way to deal with the violent urges inside all of us is to turn on the tube and purge these impulses by indulging our wildest violent fantasies. Over the years, a few scholars have suggested that this idea might have some merit. We will look at this idea in a later section of this chapter. The important point here is that we must resist the temptation to look at the content of the media and assume that it must be having a particular effect on people. People can react to the very same content in a number of different ways. A person might react by walking away from a program and forgetting that it existed. No matter how strong the tendency to think otherwise, it is important to recognize that **content does not equal effect.**

One of my favorite illustrations of the difference between content and effect comes from the world of TV advertising. Several years ago, a clever person who was working on the ad campaign for Domino's Pizza invented a strange little cartoon character to star in the pizza commercials. This character was named the "Noid," probably because his name sounded like the word *annoy*. The sole purpose of the Noid's existence was to find ways to make pizza cold before people could eat it. Domino's boasted fast delivery times and a special packing method that guaranteed the delivery of hot pizza. Their ad slogan was very simple: One could "avoid the Noid" by ordering from Domino's.

The people at Domino's loved the concept and the ads went on the air. Based on the content of the ad, it seemed easy to speculate about the effect: People would buy more pizza. And that probably was one of the effects of the campaign. But the people at Domino's could not possibly have imagined in their worst nightmare what was to happen next. Out there in the vast urban sprawl lived a little man named Mr. Noid. Mr. Noid was a troubled person, likely suffering from paranoia, who had not yet figured out what TV was all about. When Mr. Noid slouched back on the couch one evening and saw the pizza commercial that told the whole world to "avoid the Noid," he was furious. He couldn't believe the audacity of a major pizza chain taking out national advertising in order to tell the people of the world to avoid *him*. What could he possibly have done to deserve such treatment? He searched his memory long and hard to try to remember if he had done something to make his local Domino's Pizzeria mad at him. He just couldn't understand why he was under personal attack. He had to do something drastic.

The next thing the people at Domino's knew, one of their pizzerias was making national news. A hostage crisis was under way. A man whose last name happened to be Noid was holding hostage the customers and employees at one of their stores. Mr. Noid's demand was simple: Discontinue the "avoid the Noid" advertising. Mr. Noid didn't kill anyone in the hostage crisis, and I haven't seen the Noid on a Domino's commercial for several years. Things could have turned out far worse than they did.[5]

The example of Mr. Noid is one of my favorites because it is so unusual. And in fact this sort of case is not likely to happen often. A more common example of the principle that media effects cannot be inferred accurately from an analysis of content comes from research on attitudes toward AIDS. Joy Berrenberg and her colleagues wanted to know whether an educational film on AIDS prevention actually brought about positive effects in viewers. In a simple experiment, the researchers discovered that undergraduate students who watched the film expressed increased fear and dislike of a hypothetical person with AIDS. The film also increased viewers' perceptions that AIDS was a preventable disease. After studying their data, the researchers concluded that films that emphasize disease prevention may actually create a tendency for viewers to "blame the victim" when they confront others with the disease. In this case, an educational film with "positive" content may actually create some undesirable and unanticipated effects in many viewers.[6]

One lesson to be learned from these examples is that the human capacity to react in unanticipated ways to media messages must be carefully respected. For this reason, we have to be cautious about looking at any media content, including violence, and jumping to conclusions about how that content is affecting the viewers. The number of possible effects may be large. Of course, it is also possible that there are no significant effects at all. In order to find out whether violent content really affects viewers, carefully designed research studies are the most trustworthy sources.

THE CAUSAL LINK BETWEEN VIEWING
VIOLENCE AND BEHAVING AGGRESSIVELY

The Research of Albert Bandura

Since the late 1950s, researchers have attempted to answer the question of whether viewing media violence actually causes people to behave more aggressively. Albert Bandura, a Stanford University psychologist, designed some of the earliest studies with children. He developed a theory of how TV viewing might cause people to act in particular ways. This theory, known as **social learning theory,** emphasized the importance of **rewards** and **punishments.**

According to Bandura, if a child watched a person on TV who seemed very attractive and who received rewards for acting aggressively, then the child would be more likely to imitate that character's behavior. On the other hand, if a child saw a character who received punishment for acting aggressively, then the child might refrain from acting out any aggressive impulses in real life. Bandura's theory did not just apply to TV. It was a general theory about the way people learn behaviors. The basic principles could explain how children learn to help people as well as hurt them. Many of Bandura's experiments used TV and violence to test the theory because the government was giving out grant money to do research on that topic.

In a typical experiment designed by Bandura, he randomly assigned children to watch one of two different videos. In one version, one of the leading characters acted aggressively and received rewards for his actions. In the other version, the same aggressive behavior received punishment. When the video was over, Bandura permitted the children to play freely in a room where his assistants could carefully monitor what happened. They counted the number of times each of the children imitated one of the acts of aggression that they had seen in the video.

The results of these studies are consistent. Children who saw aggressive behavior rewarded were more likely to imitate the aggression than were the children who saw it punished. Critics complained that some of Bandura's early studies used videos that didn't come from actual TV shows. In addition, Bandura considered it "aggressive" when children smacked a large "bobo" doll that toymakers had specifically designed for that purpose. Bandura overcame these early problems in later studies, and scholars around the world now accept the basic principle of social learning.[7]

The results of Bandura's studies should come as no surprise to most parents. When my own children were young, I can remember them tuning in religiously to the popular animated series *He-Man*. When the neighborhood children would come over to play afterwards, they often pretended to be the characters from the show. I watched many a heated argument over who was going to take the role of the hero, He-Man, and who was reluctantly going to accept the evil role of his archrival, Skeletor. If I ever needed to intervene once the play began, it was usually because the person playing He-Man was busy performing his heroic—yet very aggressive—actions. The person who was He-Man had a license to be aggressive. He-Man was a good guy who received rewards for his aggressive acts.

Bandura's studies helped researchers to understand a number of things about TV violence and children. First, viewing TV violence could cause children to behave more aggressively, particularly if the violent characters were attractive and received rewards for their actions.

Second, in many of these studies, the effects emerged most strongly for boys, not girls. Many researchers interpret this finding in the context of biological differences between the sexes. Throughout the animal kingdom, nature has programmed the male of the species with a predisposition to behave more aggressively than the female. The researchers thought that perhaps this aggressive predisposition resulted in boys being more sensitive to the impact of media violence. As it turns out, some studies on media violence show that the effects do extend to females as well as males. For a brief description of a recent study that found both sexes affected by media violence, see Study Box 5-1.

A third conclusion that can be drawn from Bandura's social learning effect is that the effect is quite general. It doesn't matter whether researchers make up the videos used in these experiments or borrow them from standard TV programs like old *Batman* and *Superman* cartoons. The principles remain the same. The presence of attractive TV characters who receive rewards for acting aggressively seems to promote more aggressive behavior in children.[8]

Finally, in studies of this type, it is important to understand that differences between the two experimental groups do not necessarily imply anything about a particular child. Not every child who saw the aggression being rewarded behaved aggressively after the video. Some of the children who saw the aggression punished acted aggressively just the same. In fact, as in most experiments of this type, *most* of the aggressive behavior that researchers observed after TV viewing was not the result of watching one of the two videos at all. Many other factors are important in determining aggressive behavior at any given instant. Probably one of the most crucial factors has to do with the years of modeling and teaching that children receive from parents and the other important adults in their lives. Still, although the effect of video violence observed in these experiments is statistically small, it is predictable and reliable.

Although Bandura's studies offered initial insights into the effect of TV violence, many questions remained. One of the most important ones had to do with the type of aggression that researchers were measuring in these studies. Children were doing more hitting, kicking, biting, scratching, and so on in the context of playing with other children. What about more serious acts of aggression? When the government started funding Bandura's research, strong

---

STUDY BOX 5-1   Prolonged Exposure to Media Violence

Dolf Zillmann and James Weaver reported an experiment with college students that was designed to test the impact of prolonged exposure to media violence. They recruited 93 students (53 males, 40 females) to participate in the study. These students were randomly assigned to one of two film-viewing groups. In the "innocuous film" condition, they watched *Little Man Tate, Driving Miss Daisy, Rich in Love,* and *Postcards from the Edge* on successive days. In the "violent film" condition, students watched *Universal Soldier, Under Siege, The Hitman,* and *Excessive Force.* The day after they watched the last movie, the participants were told that they were needed to help identify emotional expressions on the faces of people in photographs. After each participant completed this task, he or she was provided with either positive or negative feedback that was given randomly. Some of the participants were told that they had done a good job. Others were told that their ratings were terrible. After completing this task, each participant was brought to a professor's office and given a form to complete about the experimenter

who had provided the feedback. The form asked the participant to rate how deserving the experimenter was of receiving financial support as a research assistant. It also asked the participant, "If you had to make a Yes or No decision [for financial support], what would it be?" These measures were taken by the researchers as an opportunity for the participants to express hostility toward the assistant. The results indicated that both male and female participants who had watched the violent films earlier in the week were much more likely to express hostility in their ratings of the assistant. Of great interest to the researchers, this effect held regardless of the nature of the feedback the assistant had delivered in the ratings task. The researchers concluded that "the findings support the proposal that repeated, prolonged exposure to exceedingly violent drama is capable of facilitating hostile behavior for extended periods after exposure" (p. 159).

SOURCE: Zillmann, D., & Weaver, J. B. III. (1999). Effects of prolonged exposure to gratuitous media violence on provoked and unprovoked hostile behavior. *Journal of Applied Social Psychology, 29,* 145–156.

---

interest was expressed in the possibility that media violence causes an actual increase in the crime rate. Could violence in the media really cause more beatings, robberies, assaults, and murders? This is a more difficult question to answer confidently. A number of researchers have tried to gather data that might help us to provide an answer. What about the possible relationship between media violence and more serious acts of aggression among adults?

The Long-Term Studies of
Leonard Eron and Rowell Huesmann

One of the most impressive lines of research in the area of media violence comes from two psychologists, Leonard Eron and Rowell Huesmann. Working together with other researchers (Lefkowitz and Walder) back in the 1960s, the team studied over 800 children under the age of 10. There were two things that were of particular interest. First, Eron and Huesmann wanted to know how much violence these children watched on TV. Second, they wanted to know how aggressive each child was in daily life activities. Through conversations and questionnaires given to parents, teachers, and the children themselves, they were able to assign a number to each child that indicated the quantity of violence in that child's daily diet of TV. Higher numbers indicated more violence. They also were able to assign another number to each child that indicated how aggressive the child was in day-to-day situations. After they gathered this information, they looked at the relationship between these two numbers across the entire group of children.

What did they find? Eron and Huesmann found that there was a tendency for those children who watched higher levels of TV violence to also have higher scores on the ratings of aggressive behavior. Researchers now recognize this finding as one that appears again and again in the literature. It might seem straightforward to conclude from this data that children are more aggressive because of their TV diet. Unfortunately, it isn't quite that easy. For one thing, since the researchers measured everything at the same time, there is no way to tell which came first—the TV viewing or the aggressive behavior. Maybe children who behave aggressively like to watch more violent programs because they want to see people who act the way they do.

Even though the researchers found it intriguing that children who watched more violence were also more aggressive, they understood the need for more information. So, they waited. In fact, they waited until the children reached the age of 19. After collecting data on the 19-year-olds, they waited another 11 years, until the children were 30. At each of these two later ages, they gathered some new information about the criminal records that had accumulated over the years. What kinds of crimes and how many crimes did each person commit? How long were the prison sentences that the court assigned? After gathering these data, the researchers went back and examined how much violence these adults had watched on TV when they were children. The findings were interesting, to say the least. The children who had the higher numbers on TV violence also tended to be the adults who became involved in more serious crimes! Huesmann summarized the findings of the study when he wrote:

> Aggressive habits seem to be learned early in life, and once established,
> are resistant to change and predictive of serious adult antisocial behavior.
> If a child's observation of media violence promotes the learning of aggressive habits, it can have harmful lifelong consequences. Consistent with this
> theory, early television habits are in fact correlated with adult criminality.
> (pp. 129–130)[9]

In a recent study published in 2003, Huesmann, Eron, and their colleagues reported more results from a longitudinal investigation that followed children into adulthood. The findings are the same. Specifically, the authors noted that boys and girls who were in the upper 20% on TV viewing were significantly higher on the measures of adult aggression than were the rest of the study's participants.[10]

Do these findings guarantee that if a child watches TV violence, a life of crime will result? Not at all. First, it is important to understand that, just as in the experiments done by Bandura, not every child who watched large amounts of TV violence ended up getting involved in crime. There was simply a *tendency* for this to be the case. As in Bandura's research, this tendency, although it was definitely present, was small. Knowing the amount of TV violence children viewed enabled the researchers to account for less than 10% of the crimes committed by the children as they matured over the 22-year period. Depending on your perspective, you may believe that we should view this small percentage as an alarming and important statistic, or that we should view it as evidence that TV is not a very strong determinant of criminal behavior. One way to think about these two views is to consider a group of 10 children in your neighborhood. If these 10 children collectively committed 20 acts of aggression over some period of time, then the data indicate that perhaps two of these acts might be safely attributed to media violence. On one hand, this sounds like a small and insignificant effect. On the other hand, if this effect is multiplied for the total number of aggressive acts committed in society, it is easy to see reason for concern.

Second, even though the researchers could predict a certain number of crimes based on childhood viewing of TV violence, we can't be absolutely sure that the childhood viewing was a causal factor in the later commission of crimes by these adults. Perhaps there was something else about the families of the children that predisposed them to watch either violent or nonviolent programs. This same factor may have helped lead the children to either a life of crime or a life of civic responsibility. The researchers tried to measure as many of these other factors as possible. After using some sophisticated statistical analyses, they still concluded that the children's early TV viewing very likely did contribute to criminal activity later in life.

Eron and Huesmann's research is important because it potentially links media violence with real-life violence. One of the criticisms made of many of the studies in this area is that we cannot extrapolate the results from laboratory studies to the real world. What other evidence might there be that television violence is a culprit in increasing real-life violence?

The Research of Brandon Centerwall

Dr. Brandon Centerwall graduated from Yale in 1975. He is a medical doctor and teaches at the University of Washington as a psychiatrist in the behavioral sciences. His analysis of crime statistics paints a very disturbing picture. In 1945, just before TV emerged on the scene in the United States, statistics show 3 homicides per 100,000 people. By 1974, that figure had doubled. Similar data emerged for Canada. One could argue that during these years, many changes occurred in addition to the introduction of TV. Centerwall agrees. In an exhaustive series of studies, however, he claims that the data really do point to TV as the major culprit in the rise of homicides.[11]

Centerwall selected other countries that were very similar to the United States in a number of ways. South Africa was one such country. When Centerwall examined the homicide rate in South Africa between 1945 and 1974, he discovered that the rate actually dropped by 7% during that time. Centerwall argues that one of the only major differences between South Africa and the United States during those years was the ban on TV imposed by the South African government. What happened in South Africa when the government lifted the ban in 1974? By 1983, the murder rate had increased by 56%. By 1990, the increase registered 130%—the rate had more than doubled in less than 20 years. The pattern of data strongly resembles those for the United States and Canada. In order to avoid getting a distorted picture of the data in South Africa due to racial tensions, Centerwall excluded all homicides against Blacks in his analysis of that country. Apparently, when racial tension resulted in homicide in South Africa, Blacks were typically the victims.

Although we can't be absolutely certain that Centerwall's analysis is correct, it is difficult to explain his findings without taking TV into account. Centerwall claims that roughly half of all homicides in the United States are a direct result of television-watching. Given that Centerwall is not in a position to make a clear causal claim from the type of data he has analyzed, many media scholars conclude that his claim is too extreme. But even if we adopted a more conservative estimate, the numbers would still need to be taken seriously.

The Catharsis Hypothesis

Even though the research considered so far has tended to indict media violence as a cause of aggression, some researchers were slow to accept this idea. One of the most popular alternative views was advanced by Seymour Feshbach very early in the violence controversy (1960s). Feshbach thought that viewing TV violence could actually be therapeutic for a person filled with anger or frustration. TV could help purge those pent-up emotions. He borrowed this idea from the ancient Greeks. The idea of **catharsis** (meaning "to cleanse or purge; to get rid of") goes back to the Greek culture, which thrived on good drama. The Greeks believed that a person could get rid of grief and misery by going to a play that featured other characters who were grieving.

Feshbach simply extended the idea of catharsis to media violence. He reasoned that a person could cleanse pent-up feelings of anger by watching other people act aggressively. In this view, media violence was actually a positive thing. It could tend to lower the amount of aggressive behavior that might occur if angry people couldn't release their frustrations by watching others act out violence on TV.

Feshbach reasoned that watching TV would tend to calm angry people, making them less likely to react with intense anger. He also believed that watching violence would enable the angry people to engage in aggressive fantasies. If people could act out anger in their heads, they might have less need to act it out in real life. The network executives loved this theory. After all, if Feshbach was right about the effects of media violence, then the networks were actually providing an important public service by serving up a steady diet of TV violence. The crucial task for Feshbach was to prove that his idea had some merit.

The initial evidence that Feshbach offered in support of his theory looked convincing. First, he located a detention facility for boys; he reasoned that the boys who lived in this place would be angry and frustrated about their situation. After gaining the cooperation of the authorities who ran the facility, Feshbach randomly assigned the boys to watch either a violent TV diet or a nonviolent TV diet for several weeks. Feshbach carefully monitored the behavior of each boy during the experiment. He relied on reports made by the house-parents of any incidents involving aggressive behavior. At the end of the study, the results were clear: The boys who had watched TV violence behaved *less* aggressively than the boys who had watched no violence. The results seemed to support the theory of catharsis.[12]

The lesson from Feshbach's research is that we should be slow to arrive at definitive conclusions from any single study. Other researchers who examined what Feshbach had done were quick to criticize his conclusion. Imagine that you were a boy in this detention facility. Watching TV was one thing you could do to pass the time and entertain yourself. If you were like most of the boys of this age, your favorite programs were the ones packed with violence and suspense. One day, Feshbach's research team arrives and tells you that you can no longer watch your favorite programs because you are participating in a study. To make matters worse, you notice that the researchers permit some of the other boys to watch those shows for no apparent reason. How do you react? Perhaps you feel like hitting someone! If most of the other boys deprived of viewing violence felt like you did, it could easily explain why the boys who watched violence behaved less aggressively than the boys who watched nonviolence.[13]

Feshbach's findings demonstrated that people will act more violently if they can't watch their favorite TV programs than they will if they can watch them. Most researchers now agree that this is the best interpretation of the results of Feshbach's study. The results do not support the catharsis hypothesis.

A Priming Analysis of the Effect of Media Violence

Over the years, many studies show that viewing media violence does not calm people down. In fact, a series of experiments by Leonard Berkowitz and his associates at the University of Wisconsin–Madison shows that angry people and media violence make for an especially volatile mix. Quite the contrary to Feshbach's idea of catharsis, if angry people watch media violence, they are *more* likely to behave aggressively.

Recently, Berkowitz and his colleague, Eunkyung Jo, have offered an explanation for how this **facilitating effect** of media violence might operate.[14] The key word in their explanation is **priming.** Priming is a process that can be understood simply in terms of associations. If you read a news story about an airplane crash, the story might "prime" thoughts associated with airplanes that you already have in your mind. You might start thinking about an upcoming trip that you have to take. The story might also prime thoughts about where you will choose to sit on the plane. You might remember that you haven't made your seat reservation yet, so you decide to make a phone call to your travel agent. In short, priming is a process whereby one thing that you think about reminds you of other things in your mind that you associate with the first thing. Berkowitz and his colleagues believe that the mass media are potent sources of images or ideas that can prime our thoughts and actions. According to these researchers, when

> . . . people witness, read, or hear of an event via the mass media, ideas having a similar meaning are activated in them for a short time afterwards, and . . . these thoughts in turn can activate other semantically related ideas and action tendencies. (p. 45)

According to this analysis, several things appear likely to happen when people view images of media violence. First, the violence can prime thoughts that are related to hostility. At least for a short period of time, such thoughts might affect the way we see other people and interpret their actions. I was reminded of this process recently when I was out jogging for my daily exercise. As I ran by a parked car, a woman sitting in the driver's seat let out a loud shriek. I had startled her as I ran by the car. As I circled back around toward the car to offer an apology, the woman explained that she was in the middle of reading a newspaper story about a serial killer. The thoughts and feelings that this story had evoked may have primed her to react in a very different way to my presence than she would have otherwise. Second, in addition to priming violence-related thoughts, media violence might prime thoughts that lead one to believe that aggressive behavior might be warranted in certain situations and might bring about certain benefits.

Finally, media violence might prime action tendencies that cause people to be more inclined to act violently. My brothers, who recently retired from their jobs in a state prison system, reported to me that the prison inmates are almost always more unruly and violent immediately after they have watched a violent movie. I expressed some astonishment that the prison administration actually supplied such films for weekend entertainment and was told that this practice is common in many prison systems.

Despite the many studies by Berkowitz and others that clearly show evidence for priming and a facilitative effect of media violence on aggressive behavior, catharsis theory became very popular. This probably had something to do with the TV networks, who had a lot to gain in the violence controversy if the theory was viable. Catharsis is an idea that has died hard. There are still many who espouse this idea in discussions of the effects of media violence. But if the research over the last 30 years tells us anything conclusively, it tells us that we should allow the theory of catharsis to rest in peace.

DESENSITIZATION TO VIOLENCE

The research summarized here points to the reasons that there is such a strong consensus among scientists that media violence causes aggressive behavior. We shouldn't conclude our look at this area of research without discussing another powerful effect that seems to be emerging from current studies. Media violence may have a **desensitizing effect,** making us numb to violence in real life so that we don't react to it as we would if we had never seen it on the screen. What evidence is there for this effect?

The first type of evidence is anecdotal. Researchers who have taken the time to examine Hollywood movies have noted something very interesting about the ones that have sequels. Inevitably, when producers make a sequel to a violent movie, they pack it with more violence than they did the original film. If one looks only at the number of people killed by violent actions, the statistics are revealing. The first production of *RoboCop* featured 32 dead bodies. The second version featured 81. In *Deathwish,* the body count climbed from 9 in the first version to 52 in the second. Rambo killed off 62 people in the initial *Rambo* film. By the time *Rambo III* rolled around, that number had soared to 111. George Gerbner, the researcher who took the time to chart these statistics, noted that the trend is even evident in the critically acclaimed *Godfather* movies. In the first film, 12 people were killed. The second film depicted 18 deaths, and the third installment featured 53![15]

One way to explain the increased violence in movie sequels is that Hollywood is attempting to satisfy the people who bought tickets to the first movie. Producers may intuitively realize that when they keep the same level of violence in the sequel, viewers won't get as great an emotional charge as they did the first time around. As a result, they provide more blood and gore. If this intuition is correct, it points to the possibility that some of our entertainment is actually getting more violent over time. The desensitization idea suggests that there is no easy way to go backwards. The entire momentum is toward an ever-increasing level of violence.

Is there any research to suggest that exposure to media violence may actually desensitize people to violence in real life? To answer this question, two researchers, Ronald Drabman and Margaret Thomas, set up an interesting study.[16] They randomly assigned children to watch either a violent or a non-violent TV show. After each child finished watching the show, the experimenter drew attention to another TV monitor in the room and told each child that this monitor was displaying pictures of two children who were interacting in an adjacent room. The experimenter also explained that he had to leave the room and would return shortly. Just before leaving, the experimenter instructed the child to watch the TV monitor in case any trouble broke out between the children in the other room. If trouble did break out, the experimenter instructed each child to leave the room and go around the corner to notify him. Actually, the monitor was displaying a videotape in which the two children began fighting. The fighting grew more severe and, eventually, the screen went black. Drabman and Thomas wanted to know if watching a violent video just before receiving these instructions would cause children to be less sensitive to the fighting that they witnessed. The answer they got was clear: Children who had watched the violent video were far less likely than the other children to actually make an attempt to notify the experimenter about the fight that they observed on the monitor. These results support the idea that watching media violence can desensitize one to violence in real life.

The discussion of desensitization to violence goes beyond movies and TV shows. Before we leave the topic of media violence, it is important to recognize that the controversy about violent content extends to new technologies as well.

WHAT ABOUT VIDEO GAMES?
ARE THEY TRAINING KIDS TO KILL?

It doesn't seem like too long ago that my son and I carefully unpacked the newest and hottest toy in all the land—an Atari video game system. Together, we sat transfixed at the TV set and played game after game of *Pong*. We weren't sure that life got any better. What we couldn't have foreseen at the time was that *Pong* was the beginning of a video game revolution that seems to have no end in sight. Over the years, the graphics have become so advanced that it is sometimes difficult to tell whether the person on the screen is an animated image or a real human character from a TV show. The game characters now move in ways that are so close to human movement as to seem almost miraculous.

Although video games have provided hours of enjoyment and entertainment for those who own them, in the past few years the video revolution has shown a darker side. Many of the games seem to be little more than exercises in virtual killing. These games, known as "first-person shooters," equip the player with a video gun. The object of these games is to rack up the highest score by blasting various characters to smithereens. The improved graphic technology of these games has enabled the manufacturers to create scenarios that seem quite realistic. The games have fantastic appeal to adolescents— particularly males. They are so much a part of our culture that, as you read these words, you are undoubtedly able to think of specific games and images that perfectly illustrate what I am describing. In fact, video game producers take in *billions* of dollars each year. Recent titles that feature lots of violent action are *Quake, Doom, Mortal Kombat, Resident Evil, Grand Theft Auto,* and *Carmageddon*—but by the time you read these words, there will probably be others. Some of these games are actually banned for sale in countries such as Brazil, New Zealand, and Germany.

Although violent video games generated a certain amount of controversy in the public arena, things really started heating up after the killings at Columbine High School in Littleton, Colorado, in 1999. Eric Harris and Dylan Klebold, the two teens who attacked their classmates and teachers, were supposedly quite fond of playing Doom. By this point, you should be able to recognize that a preference for playing a violent video game does not necessarily constitute a cause for violent behavior—even though the individuals who prefer the game and those committing the violent acts are the same. It is quite possible that playing *Doom* had no impact at all on the Columbine murderers. But, once this controversy had started, researchers began to pay more attention to the issues surrounding the incident. Before we look at the academic research, let's briefly look at the rhetoric of Lt. Col. Dave Grossman, a military man who has gone on the record to express his views in the controversy about violent video games.

An Opinion on Video Games
from an Expert on "Killology"

In the 1950s, Dr. Frederic Wertham, a psychiatrist, became convinced that comic books were the ruination of the youth of America. He took his case straight to the public, shunning the peer review process of scholarly research articles. Wertham wrote for popular magazines and published his own book, *The Seduction of the Innocent*[17] (see chapter 3). Although Wertham's analysis of the tremendous negative impact of comic books was never accepted or validated by the research community, he still played a significant role in the public arena and helped to shape standards in the comic book industry itself. When one reads the writings of Lt. Col. Dave Grossman, the similarities with Wertham cannot be ignored. It is almost as if the same basic story is being played out again, 50 years later. Like Wertham, Grossman has a professional credential that gives him some authority with the public and government policymakers. Just as Wertham had a popular book in which he articulated his thesis, so Grossman is the author of his own book on the subject of killing.[18] Whereas Wertham published in popular magazines like *Colliers,* Grossman has had a series of articles in the *Saturday Evening Post*.[19] Most important, Wertham's claims about the effects of comic books were based more on his own private convictions than on solid scientific evidence. Likewise, Grossman seems to be convinced that violent video games are transforming young people into "homemade sociopaths who kill reflexively," a proposition that, as yet, scientists have been unable to confirm. Let's look briefly at Grossman's claims about violent video games.

Grossman claims that the urge to kill is unnatural. He explains that the whole purpose of the military is to use brutalization and desensitization techniques to overcome the natural aversion to killing. He insists that through desensitization, the media have trained children to associate violence and killing with pleasure. Video games that require the player to shoot a gun and react reflexively with the shooting response are, he claims, teaching an entire generation of children to associate shooting with pleasure. Grossman argues that the increases in murder and assault around the world are due largely to violent mass media—and especially to violent video games. You may have heard from news reports over the past few years that violent crime is actually decreasing. Grossman counters that this is only an illusion. Modern medical technology is now so efficient that thousands of assaults that would have ended up as murders years ago never make it into the murder column of today's statistics. Grossman contends that violent assault is increasing because of the increasing violence in our media.

As a good student of media effects, how should you respond to Grossman's contentions? Is it really true that violent video games are transforming our youth into a culture of sociopaths? Grossman is so convinced that this is the case that he has even given a name to what he considers a psychological epidemic. Instead of AIDS (acquired immune deficiency syndrome), Grossman calls this epidemic **AVIDS** ("acquired violence immune deficiency syndrome").

What Does the Research Say?

In attempting to evaluate Grossman's position, the first thing that we need to know is whether there are published scientific studies on the effects of violent video games. Although the literature at this point would certainly have to be described as limited, some published studies do exist. Back in 1988, Nicola Schutte and her colleagues reported the results of a very simple study that was reminiscent of the early research of Albert Bandura on social learning theory.[20] Working with young children between 5 and 7 years old, she randomly assigned them to play either a violent or a nonviolent video game. The violent game, called *Karateka,* involved a protagonist who was controlled by the player and had a mission to hit, kick, and kill enough villains so that a damsel in distress would be saved. The nonviolent game, *Jungle Hunt,* involved a character who would swing from vine to vine in such a way that he would not fall and perish.

After the children had played one of the two games, the researchers observed the children's free play in a large room that was equipped with several toys. One of the toys was a jungle swing with small men attached to vines; another toy was a "bobo" doll that was dressed in a karate-type robe that resembled the garb of characters in the violent video game.

The study produced two main findings. First, the children who had played *Jungle Hunt* tended to play with the jungle swing toy, whereas those who played *Karateka* tended to play with the karate bobo doll. Second, as the authors had predicted, the children who had played *Karateka* tended to play in a more aggressive fashion than the children who had played *Jungle Hunt.* They had significantly higher scores on pushing, hitting, and kicking another child in the playroom as well as higher scores on hitting or kicking the bobo doll.

Considering the results of Bandura's studies, these results really shouldn't surprise you very much. They are consistent with some of the first studies on the effects of televised violence. The results also suffer from some of the same limitations as those of the early studies. We have to be careful about generalizing the results broadly from a single study that used one particular violent game. We also have to be careful about drawing too much from the fact that the children who played the violent video game acted more aggressively toward a bobo doll. Play aggression may have little to do with aggression toward real people. However, the authors did note that these same children were also more aggressive toward other children who were playing in the room.

Two other researchers who study video games, Craig Anderson and Catherine Ford, reported the results of an experiment in which college students played either a high-aggression game (*Zaxxon*) or a mild-aggression game (*Centipede*).[21] Other students were randomly assigned to a no-game control group. Instead of measuring aggressive behavior, the researchers had the students assess their feelings by checking off words that described how they felt after playing the games. The results showed that both of the video games produced higher feelings of hostility than were seen in the control group. In addition, the group that played the high-aggression game reported significantly higher levels of anxiety than either of the other two groups. The authors concluded,

"The results indicate that playing aggressive video games can have short-term negative effects on the game-player's emotional state."

An important limitation in Anderson and Ford's study was that aggressive behavior was not measured directly. Placing check marks next to adjectives may have little to do with what someone actually does after playing a violent video game. Anderson tried to address this limitation in a more recent study that he authored with Karen Dill. The authors actually conducted two different types of studies and reported them together in an article in one of the leading journals in psychology, the *Journal of Personality & Social Psychology*.[22]

In their first study, Anderson and Dill had college students respond to some questions about the extent to which they played video games of various types as well as the extent to which they had been involved in aggressive delinquent behaviors in the past. They found that these two variables were significantly related. Students who reported more playing time with violent video games also reported more aggressive delinquent behaviors. Of course, once again, we must be careful in interpreting this evidence. A relationship of this sort does not necessarily mean that playing the games caused increases in aggression. Perhaps some unmeasured variable was causally related to both playing aggressive video games and the tendency to commit acts of delinquent aggression. In fact, the authors gathered some evidence for this possibility. They also had students respond to a number of items that formed a measure of trait aggressiveness. For those students who scored high on trait aggression, the relationship between playing aggressive video games and delinquent acts of aggression was even stronger. One way to interpret these results is that some people are, for whatever reasons, inclined to behave aggressively. They score high on the trait of aggression. These people are also more likely to play violent video games, and they are also more likely to be involved in acts of delinquent aggression when compared to people who do not possess the trait of aggression.

Although the kind of survey data that Anderson and Dill gathered in this first study is certainly informative, it still doesn't help very much in gaining an understanding of the impact of playing violent video games on actual aggressive behavior. To address this issue more precisely, the authors set up a second study, which used an experimental design. Some college students were randomly assigned to play a violent video game (*Wolfenstein 3D*), and some were randomly assigned to play a nonviolent game (*Myst*). These two games were chosen because in laboratory pretests, they both generated the same amount of physiological arousal during playing even though they differed significantly in terms of their levels of violence. After the game-playing sessions, the students participated in another phase of the experiment that they thought was unrelated to the video game session. They were placed in a situation where they had to react to a stimulus faster than their opponent. If they won the reaction-time test, they could blast their opponent with a loud noise. Not only that, they got to choose, within a certain range, how loud the noise could be and how long the noise would blast.

Imagine that you are a participant in this study and have just lost one of the reaction-time competitions. In the next competition, you win and are now allowed to blast the person who just beat you the time before. You might sus-pect that under these circumstances, you would send out a particularly loud blast of noise for a relatively long duration. In this respect, the students in the experiment reacted the same way regardless of which video game they had played. All students tended to blast their opponent louder and longer after having lost a reaction-time competition just before winning one. But those who had played the *Wolfenstein 3D* game blasted louder and longer than those who had played *Myst*. To the extent that this blasting behavior can be regarded as aggressive, the results of this experiment might be interpreted as evidence that playing a violent video game actually causes more aggressive behavior. Anderson and Dill certainly believe that these two studies, taken together, pro-vide some insight into the relationship between playing violent video games and actual aggression. They stated:

> In the laboratory, college students who played a violent video game behaved more aggressively toward an opponent than did students who had played a nonviolent video game. Outside the laboratory, students who reported play-ing more violent video games over a period of years also engaged in more aggressive behavior in their own lives. Both types of studies . . . have their strengths and weaknesses. The convergence of findings across such disparate methods lends considerable strength to the main hypothesis that exposure to violent video games can increase aggressive behavior.

Of course, the technology improvements that are constantly being made on video game hardware and software create a special challenge for researchers to keep up with the latest innovations. Most recently, Ron Tamborini and his col-leagues reported the results of an experiment that made a distinction between people who watched another person play a violent video game and those who actually played either a standard violent video game or one that featured a virtual reality experience.[23] Consistent with past results in this area, those who played the virtual reality version of the game had increased levels of hostility compared to those who only watched the games being played. Future studies will undoubt-edly test the ways in which the virtual reality experience might lead to different consequences or effects compared to other types of game formats.

John Sherry has recently attempted to summarize all of the known studies on violent video games.[24] Using the technique of **meta-analysis,** Sherry was able to estimate the statistical effects uncovered across the entire published lit-erature on this topic. As he notes in his analysis, the sample of studies to draw from is actually pretty small—only about 30 independent investigations—so we should be careful about drawing firm conclusions. Nevertheless, he reports that the data do show "a small but significant overall effect of video game play on aggression." However, he also notes that this effect is smaller than the effect of violent television on aggression. Sherry also concludes that one important variable in the relationship is the type of violence contained in the game. When the violence is related to sports or fantasy, the effect on aggression is smaller than when the violence involves virtual depictions of aggression toward human beings. In another attempt to summarize the literature on violent video games, Craig Anderson reports a meta-analysis that was published in 2004.[25] According to his analysis, studies like Sherry's may tend to underestimate the effects of violent video games. Anderson contends that the studies with better methodological designs tend to find stronger effects, whereas the studies with more problems tend to show weaker effects.

If you are like me, by this point you might be asking what we are to make of the research. That question may still be a bit premature. One thing we can say for certain is that we need more studies. This is inevitably the case with almost any question about the effects of a new communication technology. But we might be able to say a little more. At this point, the existing data on violent video games look pretty familiar to researchers who have carefully studied the pattern that emerged with TV more than 30 years ago. Although the effects might not be quite as strong, it is beginning to appear that there may be a causal relationship between playing violent video games and behaving aggressively—just as there is between viewing TV violence and committing aggressive acts.

Of course, the question that we would really like to answer is how worried we should be about violent video games. Should we let our children play any violent games? Which ones are OK and which should be avoided? Definitive answers to these questions will emerge more clearly as researchers continue to report the results of new studies during the next several years. For now, it looks as though there is some reason to be concerned that playing violent video games might be associated with the same sorts of effects that are well documented with movies and TV shows. Remember that these effects are definitely causal effects—but they are modest from a statistical standpoint. There are a host of other variables that contribute to aggressive behavior in the real world. It would be a mistake to focus exclusively on any type of media as the sole cause or even the primary cause of aggression in society. Human behavior is complicated and caused by hundreds of factors, only some of which we know about. Given this state of affairs, we shouldn't expect to be able to find easy solutions to the causes of a behavior like aggression.

Some reports out of Littleton, Colorado, have noted that Eric Harris was fond of playing a modified game of *Doom* that had extra weapons, more than one shooter, and a special feature that rigged the game so that the characters on the screen could not shoot back. Some observers suggested that when Harris played the game, he was actually acting out the sort of attack on his classmates that he eventually implemented on that fateful day in April 1999. No amount of evidence from media effects studies will permit us to conclude that the specific acts of a given individual were caused by exposure to violent media. But given what we know so far about the effects of playing violent video games, it surely seems as though Harris's video game habits could have placed him in a high-risk category for translating some of those habits into real-world behavior.

In terms of evaluating the rhetoric of Col. Grossman, it seems that the current research evidence would hardly support the sweeping claims that he makes about the impact of violent media. His rhetoric may be successful in motivating politicians to pay attention to the problem of media violence, but ultimately, the sorts of "magic bullet" claims of media impact that he suggests are not likely to be supported by scientific research. His claims are probably best regarded as rather gross exaggerations.

WHY DO PEOPLE LIKE MEDIA VIOLENCE?

As you have made your way through this chapter, perhaps you have wondered about why people even watch media violence. There wouldn't be so much controversy about it if people weren't somehow attracted to it. What are they attracted to? This is not a very easy question to answer. Researchers who study media effects have devoted much more of their energies to understanding the impact of media violence than they have to the question of the appeal of this sort of entertainment. One thing that we do know is that the assumption that people generally enjoy media violence should not be taken for granted. In one essay, Joanne Cantor pointed out that anyone studying the Nielsen ratings will be struck by the unpopularity of televised violence. The ratings for 1995 showed that among children between the ages of 2 and 11, situation comedies were much more popular than violent cartoons that were broadcast on Saturday morning.[26] One researcher, Jeffrey Goldstein, devoted an entire book to the appeal of media violence. At one point, he observed: "It is worth remembering that violent entertainment is the preferred form of entertainment only for a minority of the general audience. Most viewers appear to prefer comedies and sitcoms to violent entertainment."[27] Still, the minority of the audience that does prefer violence is a sizable one. What can we say about why they are drawn to this form of entertainment?

Recently, my wife, Cheri Sparks, who has her doctorate in social psychology, and I tried to analyze the appeal of media violence.[28] We came up with three general reasons why people are attracted to this type of entertainment. First, it does seem that violent entertainment may hold inherent appeal for some individuals. There may be some who literally experience a kind of sensory delight when they view mayhem and destruction on the screen. These images may be novel, exciting, and attractive in their own right. Second, some people may experience post-viewing gratification from viewing events, characters, and themes that tend to appear in violent contexts—while not necessarily enjoying the violence itself. For example, one researcher, Dolf Zillmann, has suggested that viewers form alignments with the characters in a movie or program. That is, we decide very quickly whom we like and whom we dislike. When good things happen to the characters we like, we find it enjoyable. Similarly, when bad things happen to characters we dislike, we also experience pleasure. Since a good deal of violent entertainment encourages the viewer to form alignments with different characters, viewers will enjoy violent films to the extent that their favored characters have good outcomes and their disfavored characters have bad ones.[29] Finally, violent media may contain other themes that viewers tend to enjoy. Perhaps violent films tend to contain more sexuality or more suspense. Viewers may be attracted to this sort of media for these factors, rather than for

---

STUDY BOX 5-2   Is It *Violence* That People Enjoy?

I became so interested in investigating the appeal of media violence that I decided to team up with my colleagues and study the question using the experimental approach. We randomly assigned college students to watch one of two different versions of the movie *The Fugitive,* starring Harrison Ford. One group watched the movie in its original form. But for the second group, we showed them a version of the movie that we had edited. The original version of the film included almost 15 minutes of on-screen violence. Using our digital editing lab, we removed almost all of this violence from the movie in such a way that the casual viewer could not detect that any editing had taken place. We pre-tested this version to make sure that students couldn't detect that the film had been altered. Even students who had seen the movie in years past and saw the edited version in our experiment didn't recall that the movie was any different from the version they had seen before. After participants in each group watched the movie, they responded to a post-viewing questionnaire that contained several questions about their reactions to the film—including a number of items about the extent to which they enjoyed the movie. We also asked them to estimate the number of scenes of violence that the movie contained and asked them to rate the level of violence in the film. The group who watched the edited version of the movie rated it as significantly less violent. But they also reported that they enjoyed the film to the same extent as the group who saw the film in the original, violent version.

Although this finding is limited to only a single movie and needs to be replicated with other films if possible, we still raised the general question of the extent to which violence is an essential ingredient for a film's success. Perhaps Hollywood should examine the common assumption that violence is a popular film commodity. What do *you* think about the extent to which violence, in itself, contributes to the appeal of a movie?

SOURCE: Sparks, G. G., Sherry, J., & Lubsen, G. (2005, in press). The appeal of media violence in a full-length motion picture: An experimental investigation. *Communication Reports.*

---

the violence. Although there is some research evidence to support all three of these explanations for the appeal of violent entertainment, researchers need to study these issues much more carefully in order to come to a better understanding of why violence is so attractive to some people (see Study Box 5-2).

CONCLUDING COMMENTS

This chapter provides an overview of the research on media violence. This is a challenging task because there are many studies to consider in this literature. When all is said and done, what should you take out of all of the research?

First, the researchers who conduct these studies agree strongly that viewing violence does cause an increase in aggressive behavior. But it is also important to note that, from a statistical point of view, the effect is not very large. People behave aggressively for many reasons. The contribution that media violence makes to aggressive behavior is only one small piece of the puzzle.

Second, even though the statistical contribution of media violence to aggressive behavior is small, this does not mean that the effect is unimportant. In today's media environment, millions of people may view the same violent program or movie. Even very small statistical effects will translate into large social problems when this many viewers are involved.

Third, the idea that viewing media violence can reduce aggressive behavior is no longer viable. Results from dozens of studies refute this idea. When network executives argue for symbolic catharsis or declare that media violence has no effect, we should believe them to the same extent that we would believe the major tobacco companies if they told us that smoking does not cause lung cancer. In short, we shouldn't believe them at all.

Finally, even though most of the research on media effects deals with violent content, there are many other important effects that scholars have studied. Our picture of media impact would be woefully incomplete if we did not consider these other areas as well.

SUMMARY

This chapter began by encouraging you to think about copycat crimes and the prevalence of violence in today's media content. In raising the question of the possible causal connection between media violence and aggressive behavior, the chapter reviewed some of the important surveys and experimental research relevant to this issue. It discussed some of the key theoretical concepts, such as priming and desensitization. Finally, you were encouraged to think about why people like media violence.

KEY TERMS AND CONCEPTS

Copycat phenomenon 81	Punishments 86	Desensitizing effect 94
Social learning theory 86	Catharsis 91	AVIDS 96
Rewards 86	Facilitating effect 92	Meta-analysis 99
	Priming 92	

To learn more about the topics in this chapter, enter the Key Terms and Concepts found in this chapter as subject and keyword searches on your InfoTrac® College Edition.

NOTES

1. Liebert, R. M., Neale, J. M., & Davidson, E. S. (1973). *The early window: Effects of television on children and youth.* New York: Pergamon Press.

2. Gerbner, G., Gross, L., Morgan, M., & Signorielli, N. (1994). Growing up with television: The cultivation perspective. In J. Bryant & D. Zillmann (Eds.), *Media effects: Advances in theory and research* (pp. 17–41). Hillsdale, NJ: Erlbaum.

3. Minow, N. (1996). *Abandoned in the wasteland: Children, television and the first amendment.* New York: Hill and Wang.

4. Smith, S. L., Wilson, B. J., Kunkel, D., Linz, D., Potter, W. J., Colvin, C. M., & Donnerstein, E. (1998). Violence in television programming overall: University of California, Santa Barbara Study. In Center for Communication and Social Policy, University of California, Santa Barbara (Ed.), *National television violence study* (Vol. 3, pp. 5–220). Thousand Oaks, CA: Sage.

5. I can't remember exactly where I first heard the story of Mr. Noid, and I have had difficulty verifying all of these details since I read the initial account of the incident. As a result of searching on the term "Noid" on a news website (http://www.wweek.com), I have at least been able to verify that the incident happened. Another website (http://tvacres.com/admascots_noid.htm) provides a brief account of the incident that is consistent with mine and cites a story from *Advertising Age* (February 6, 1989).

6. Berrenberg, J. L., Rosnik, D., & Kravcisin, N. J. (1990). Blaming the victim: When disease-prevention programs misfire. *Current Psychology: Research & Reviews, 9,* 415–420.

7. Bandura, A. (1994). Social cognitive theory of mass communication. In J. Bryant & D. Zillmann (Eds.), *Media effects: Advances in theory and research* (pp. 61–90). Hillsdale, NJ: Erlbaum.

8. Stein, A. H., & Friedrich, L. K. (1972). Television content and young children's behavior. In J. P. Murray, E. A. Rubinstein, & G. A. Comstock (Eds.), *Television and social behavior: Vol. 2. Television and social learning* (pp. 202–317). Washington, DC: U.S. Government Printing Office.

9. Huesmann, L. R. (1986). Psychological processes promoting the relation between exposure to media violence and aggressive behavior by the viewer. *Journal of Social Issues, 42,* 125–139.

10. Huesmann, L. R., Moise-Titus, J., Podolski, C. L., & Eron, L. D. (2003). Longitudinal relations between children's exposure to TV violence and their aggressive and violent behavior in young adulthood: 1977–1992. *Developmental Psychology, 39*(2), 201–221.

11. Centerwall, B. S. (1989). Exposure to television as a cause of violence. In G. Comstock (Ed.), *Public communication and behavior* (Vol. 2, pp. 1–58). San Diego, CA: Academic Press.

12. Feshbach, S., & Singer, R. (1971). *Television and aggression.* San Francisco: Jossey-Bass.

13. Liebert, R. M., & Sprafkin, J. (1988). *The early window: Effects of television on children and youth.* New York: Pergamon Press.

14. Jo, E., & Berkowitz, L. (1994). A priming effect analysis of media influences: An update. In J. Bryant & D. Zillmann (Eds.), *Media effects: Advances in theory and research* (pp. 43–60). Hillsdale, NJ: Erlbaum.

15. Jhally, S. (1994). *The killing screens: Media and the culture of violence* [video]. Northampton, MA: Media Education Foundation.

16. Drabman, R. S., & Thomas, M. H. (1976). Does watching violence on television cause apathy? *Pediatrics, 57,* 329–331.

17. Wertham, F. (1954). *Seduction of the innocent.* New York: Rinehart.

18. Grossman, D. (1996). *On killing: The psychological cost of learning to kill in war and society.* Boston: Little, Brown.

19. Grossman, D. (1999, July/August). We are training our kids to kill. *The Saturday Evening Post,* 64–71.

20. Schutte, N. S., Malouff, J. M., Post-Gorden, J. C., & Rodasta, A. L. (1988). Effects of playing videogames on children's

aggressive and other behaviors. *Journal of Applied Social Psychology, 18,* 454–460.

21. Anderson, C. A., & Ford, C. M. (1986). Affect of the game player: Short-term effects of highly and mildly aggressive video games. *Personality and Social Psychology Bulletin, 12,* 390–402.

22. Anderson, C. A., & Dill, K. E. (2000). Video games and aggressive thoughts, feelings, and behavior in the laboratory and in life. *Journal of Personality & Social Psychology, 78,* 772–790.

23. Tamborini, R., Eastin, M. S., Skalski, P., Lachlan, K., Fediuk, T. A., & Brady, R. (2004). Violent virtual video games and hostile thoughts. *Journal of Broadcasting & Electronic Media, 48*(3), 335–357.

24. Sherry, J. L. (2001). The effects of violent video games on aggression: A meta-analysis. *Human Communication Research, 27,* 409–431.

25. Anderson, C. A. (2004). An update on the effects of playing violent video games. *Journal of Adolescence, 27*(1), 113–122.

26. Cantor, J. (1998). Children's attraction to television programming. In J. H. Goldstein (Ed.), *Why we watch: The attractions of violent entertainment* (pp. 88–115). New York: Oxford University Press.

27. Goldstein, J. (1998). Why we watch. In J. H. Goldstein (Ed.), *Why we watch: The attractions of violent entertainment* (pp. 212–226). New York: Oxford University Press.

29. Sparks, G. G., & Sparks, C. (2000). Violence, mayhem, and horror. In D. Zillmann and P. Vorderer (Eds.), *Media entertainment: The psychology of its appeal* (pp. 73–91). Mahwah, NJ: Erlbaum.

29. Zillmann, D. (1998). The psychology of the appeal of portrayals of violence. In J. H. Goldstein (Ed.), *Why we watch: The attractions of violent entertainment* (pp. 179–211). New York: Oxford University Press.

6

■

Sexual Content
in the Media

HUMAN SEXUALITY BRINGS
OUT PASSIONATE OPINION

Recall back in chapter 3 when you read about Edgar Dale's content analysis of movies in the late 1920s. About 75% of the film content he examined could be classified as either crime, love, or sex. This should tell us something at the very outset about sexual content in the media. It is not a recent phenomenon. Although it may have seemed that the "wardrobe malfunction" during the half-time show of the 2004 Super Bowl game touched off a unique firestorm about sex in the media, this sort of controversy was really nothing new. In fact, if we wanted to go back centuries into human culture, we would find that media dealing with human sexuality in some way are never far from the cultural scene. This should hardly be surprising. The sexual appetite is basic to human existence and future survival. Therefore, it seems reasonable that human sexuality would show up constantly in art and entertainment.

When we consider sexual content in the media and the impact of that content, we enter a highly charged arena that is populated with a number of interest groups. First, more than with any other area of media content, people with religious concerns have historically expressed their views about sexual content with fervor. Back in 1977, when the sitcom *Soap* hit the airwaves, the National Council of Churches launched a vigorous campaign that resulted in many letters of complaint being filed with the ABC network and the advertisers who sponsored the program. Several advertisers withdrew their ads and several affiliate stations decided not to air the first program of the series. Other stations decided to run the program later in the evening in order to protect children who might have been in the audience during the earlier time slot.[1] This kind of pressure strikes many as an insidious kind of censorship, even though no laws prohibiting expression are involved. The passion that many bring to this topic based on their religious convictions is matched by the fervor of those who seek to protect free expression under the First Amendment at all costs. The resulting clash of values and voices can make a hotbed (pun intended) of rhetoric. As you might imagine, the TV networks and Hollywood studios want no part of government censorship. They want to be free to produce the content that will make them the most profit—regardless of who might be offended on the grounds of an inappropriate or excessive sexual depiction. They also fear a government that can restrict the flow of any type of information by legal decree.

Despite the fears of Hollywood, U.S. law does permit the government to restrict the flow of certain messages. Complicating the rhetorical scenario is the fact that law enforcement officials tend to have strong opinions about sexually explicit media. **Obscenity** is not protected under the First Amendment. If media content is judged as fitting the legal definition of obscenity, it can theoretically be restricted from circulation. Fortunately or unfortunately, depending on your viewpoint, the legal test for obscenity is very rigorous, and few judges or courts have been willing to declare many media messages to be obscene. Essentially, in order to win an obscenity case, a plaintiff must establish that the media message in question was designed primarily to stimulate or appeal to sexual or prurient interests, that it has no redeeming artistic value, and that it violates contemporary community standards. Because all three of these criteria must be met, the history of efforts to declare media legally obscene shows little consistent success. Because of the community standard criterion, it is theoretically possible to have a movie or magazine declared to be obscene in one community but not in another. Despite the legal nightmare involved in tests of obscenity, the legislative branch of government has always had some stake in the issues surrounding sexual content in the media.

A variety of competing political interests are evident in the debates about sexual content in the media. Many feminists have been quite outspoken about the dangers for women of certain types of sexual depictions. Their early voices of concern have been joined by others. Sometimes, strange bedfellows (pun intended again) join together in debates about sexual content. For example, feminists and members of the religious right often find themselves opposing the same sorts of sexual content in the media. This may be one of the few political issues that they agree on, and they typically find this agreement to be an uncomfortable state of affairs. Other groups have children's interests at the forefront of their campaigns. Believing that early exposure to explicit sexuality can induce various psychological harms in children, these groups fight against public displays of sexually explicit magazines at convenience stores and call for strict enforcement of the MPAA movie code that prevents children from being admitted to watch some movies without a parent or adult guardian.

Unwary scientific researchers often fail to realize that, in conducting research on the effects of media sex, they enter into a volatile mix of religion, law, and political agendas. It is important to understand at the outset that regardless of the findings of any given study, the researcher who studies sexual content in the media is probably more vulnerable to criticism than in any other area of media studies. There are simply too many passionate voices expressing too many passionate opinions.

A few years ago, I had the chance to talk with one media researcher who had published some results that showed negative effects of being exposed to pornography. He was struggling with the fact that some people had interpreted his results as little more than a political statement from the religious right. They accused him of being a "Bible thumper." The researcher told me with a tone of frustration that he was simply trying to report the results of his study in an objective, scientific fashion. Theology was the last thing on his mind. Some media researchers are unwilling to conduct studies on the effects of sexual content because they fear having to deal with the controversial political fallout that might arise from a study's findings. Fortunately, there is still an abundance of good research in this area that helps to inform us about the impact of sexual media content.

SORTING OUT DEFINITIONS AND TERMS

The area of sexual content is fraught with definitional ambiguities. Sexual content is a general label that can refer to something as innocuous as a kiss between two married adults or as horrifying as a brutal rape in a XXX-rated pornographic video. Researchers have struggled with the choice of terms they use to describe the content that is the focus of their investigations. Over time, the term **pornography** seems to have become associated with material that features explicit sexual behavior and nudity in a context frequently characterized by depictions of one character exerting physical or psychological dominance over another. Often, this type of material contains explicit violence that is shown at the same time as explicit sexuality. The term **erotic media** seems to be associated more with material that features explicit sexual content in the absence of violence and without the overt power dynamics that appear in pornography.

One way to think about media content is to classify media messages according to the quantity and explicitness of both sex and violence. TV soap operas may contain lots of sexual content and low to moderate levels of violence. But on each of these dimensions, the content is not very explicit compared to what is offered in movies. Hard-core pornographic films typically contain large amounts of very explicit sexuality and violence. Erotic films are filled with explicit sexuality but little or no violence, and typically do not show coercive behavior where one character dominates another. Before we can gain an accurate picture of the effects of sexual content in the media, we need to

understand what type of content we are talking about. Because the government has been greatly concerned with the effects of pornography, much of the
research has concentrated on studying the impact of very explicit sexual material that also features images of dominance, coercion, and/or violence. The
research history of this material is tied closely to government-funded efforts.
Let's turn our attention to that history and to the research findings that have
emerged over the last few decades.

THE COMMISSION ON
OBSCENITY AND PORNOGRAPHY

In 1967, the U.S. Congress established the **National Commission on
Obscenity and Pornography.** Formed under the presidency of Lyndon B.
Johnson, the commission was put in place because of growing concern about
the role of pornography in crime and juvenile delinquency. Part of the charge
of the commission was to study existing laws pertaining to pornography and
to arrive at a better understanding of the distribution of this material. Media
effects scholars were most interested in another aspect of the commission's
charge—to study the effects of pornography on the public.[2] On the basis of
what was found, specific recommendations for legislation were to be formulated. In order to meet this charge, the commission sponsored several research
projects that examined the impact of sexually explicit materials. University
researchers were commissioned to undertake new research designed to answer
the question about impact.

It is important to note here that the term *pornography* as it was used in 1967
did not carry the same connotations as it does today, particularly with respect
to violent content. Much of the material studied by the commission was sexually explicit but not violent. It is also important to note that much of the material was not nearly as explicit as some of the mainstream material available in
today's neighborhood video stores. Nevertheless, the report that was issued in
1970 was the most comprehensive document on the topic up to that time, and
it did include study of a wide diversity of sexual content.

Major Finding

By the time the commission published its report in 1970, Lyndon B. Johnson
was no longer president. Richard Nixon had assumed this position, and he was
not prepared to hear the findings that were published. The following is a key
passage from the report itself:

> The Commission believes that there is no warrant for continued govern-
> mental interference with the full freedom of adults to read, obtain or view
> whatever such material they wish. Extensive empirical investigation, both
> by the Commission and by others, provides no evidence that exposure to
> or use of explicit sexual materials play a significant role in the causation of

social or individual harms such as crime, delinquency, sexual or nonsexual deviancy or severe emotional disturbances.[3]

Essentially, the commission report stated that there were no known harms caused by pornography for any population studied. President Nixon didn't buy it. He rejected the commission's report—an act that was probably made easier by the fact that the commission had been formed under his Democratic predecessor. But for today's scholars and students of media effects, the important question is this: "Does the conclusion of the Commission Report accurately reflect the state of affairs regarding the effects of pornography?" Clearly, Richard Nixon didn't think so, but what about the scholarly community?

A Reexamination of the Commission's Findings

Two theoretical notions that were widely discussed in the aftermath of the commission report were the **trigger hypothesis** and the **safety valve theory.** The trigger hypothesis essentially claims that exposure to sexually explicit materials will cause a response in some individuals that will provoke them in such a way that it may lead them to commit a sex crime such as rape or indecent exposure. The safety valve theory, in contrast, claims that exposure to sexually explicit material will satisfy whatever urges might cause a person to commit a sex crime. If this second idea has merit, then we might actually see a *decrease* in sex crimes in communities that have ready availability to these materials. Of course, in today's electronic environment, virtually anyone can have access to sexually explicit materials via the Internet, making the concept of availability more difficult to assess for any given community (see Study Box 6-1).

One aspect of the research findings that led the commission to conclude that pornography is not harmful had to do with the findings pertaining to the rate of sex crimes in Denmark following the relaxation of legal restraints on the flow of sexually explicit materials. This evidence could be interpreted as support for the safety valve theory. However, subsequent analysis of this data by one researcher, Berl Kutchinsky, reveals that the decrease in some of the sex crimes may be attributed to the fact that public attitudes became more lenient, resulting in fewer reports to the police. Although this explanation for the decrease could not be applied to every sort of sex crime (it doesn't seem to account for a decrease in molestation of young women), it does seem to call into question the strength of the evidence in favor of the safety valve theory.[4] Following the publication of the commission report, another researcher, J. H. Court, collected data showing inconsistent results across the world in the analysis of sex crimes. Sometimes these crimes seem to decrease with the spread of pornography, sometimes they increase, and sometimes they remain the same.[5] One thing that seems to be relatively stable across countries, however, is that the incidence of rape does not decrease when pornography is permitted to flow freely. One recent study analyzing data from Japan over a 23-year period found that availability of pornography was definitely correlated with increases in rape and sexual assault.[6] Although the data on this issue

---

**STUDY BOX 6-1   Old Theoretical Ideas Applied
to New Content**

As you read about the trigger hypothesis and the safety valve theory, did the ideas seem to have a familiar ring? You should have been able to recognize some similarity between the trigger hypothesis and social learning theory, the facilitating effect, and the idea of priming, all of which you read about in chapter 5. If you realized that the safety valve theory sounded a bit like the theory of symbolic catharsis, then you probably have a pretty good grasp of these two ideas. In fact, scholars have a tendency to borrow the theoretical ideas that have been applied to one domain of study and apply them to another domain with some modification and a different name. This tendency is so evident that some scholars would suggest that a book like this one could be organized around a basic core set of theoretical ideas instead of being structured according to the different types of media content, as reflected in the chapter titles listed in the table of contents.

An interesting exercise to increase your understanding of the theoretical ideas applied to the study of media effects would be to take several of the ideas explored in different chapters and reflect on the extent to which they are alike or different. Because the text material is organized according to different types of *content,* the connections between theoretical *ideas* applied across the various content areas might not be immediately evident—even though definite connections do exist.

In the case of social learning theory and priming, these ideas have been used to explain a variety of different sorts of behavior. Although these theoretical ideas often tend to be associated with the effects of media violence, this is mainly because of the large volume of studies done on that topic. The same theoretical principles could be used to explain many phenomena—not just those associated with violence or sexual content. One example comes from a story that I heard reported on a CNN newscast one afternoon while I was doing my daily jog on the treadmill. The media reported that President Bill Clinton had 90% of his heart arteries clogged and would have to submit to a quadruple bypass surgery. During the period when this was being discussed in the media, health clinics and hospitals reported what they referred to as "Clinton syndrome." In some cases, the number of males in their fifties (Clinton was 58 at the time of his surgery) reporting chest pains and wanting complete exams was triple the typical number. This sort of phenomenon might be explained by appealing to the notion of priming and social learning. Clinton was rewarded for going to the hospital when he had chest pains. His doctors said that he almost certainly would have had a heart attack in a few weeks. Many men who felt some chest discomfort learned this lesson well and decided to do just as Clinton had done . . . perhaps a good example of social learning. Or perhaps when some men experienced chest discomfort, the experience primed their recent experience watching the news report about Clinton—which in turn prompted them to seek medical attention.

remain somewhat inconclusive because of their correlational nature, there appears to be sufficient reason to take the possible link between pornography and sexual assault seriously.

As it turns out, the commission noted, in its own summary of the data, a number of qualifications that serve to caution the reader about accepting the overall conclusion too readily. First, the material used in the research was collected over a very limited time period, and the findings might not generalize to other times and other types of material. Nearly 30 years after the commission report, this limitation seems potentially important. Much has happened in the interim in terms of the type of material generally available to the public and the ease of access to that material. Second, for ethical reasons, the commission could not study the impact of sexually explicit material on children. Thus, although no evidence of harm was reported by the commission, it would make little sense to conclude that children are risk-free if exposed to this kind of media. I personally remembered this point several years ago when I visited a family who lived below me in a two-flat housing unit in a large metropolitan area. Two of the young children in that household, both under the age of 10, were glued to the TV screen during my visit, watching nude women cavort across the screen in a presentation being broadcast on the Playboy Channel. This is one situation that the commission failed to study—and probably couldn't study because of prohibitions by committees concerning the ethical treatment of human subjects. I don't mean to suggest that nudity is necessarily harmful to young children. But even the programmers at the Playboy Channel would admit that its entertainment is created for adult viewers. We have little research investigating the meanings and effects that such programs might create for children.

The upshot of the Commission Report on Obscenity and Pornography was that the overall finding triggered controversy among politicians, parents, and researchers alike. As one might expect, the finding was readily embraced by media sources that had a stake in publishing sexually explicit materials. If you go back to the pages of *Playboy* magazine in the early 1970s, you will find frequent mention of the commission report and its overall finding that exposure to sexually explicit materials is harmless. I had the chance to witness first-hand the media industry's reliance on the commission report during the 1980s, when I was called on to appear on a TV talk show in Cleveland along with Marilyn Chambers, a star who appeared in many sexually explicit films. At the end of the program, Ms. Chambers retrieved a faded scrap of newspaper from her purse and proceeded to read the final commission report's conclusion about pornography's harmlessness. I had only 15 seconds to put this conclusion in a proper perspective with the research that followed the commission report. Ms. Chambers seemed uninterested and even annoyed with my response. As the controversy intensified in the 1970s, some researchers renewed their efforts to study the impact of exposure to sexually oriented media. The research that emerged out of this renewed effort served to question further the overall conclusion of the commission report. Let's take a brief look at some of the later research.

RESEARCH FOLLOWING
THE COMMISSION REPORT

The 1980s were years of rather intense scholarly study of the effects of sexually explicit materials. Many experiments were conducted that manipulated the quantity and type of exposure and studied their impact on a range of attitudes, including attitudes toward women, sexual violence, and family values. James Weaver summarized this evidence well in a recent essay.[7] His summary includes a characterization of the current content available and how that content affects the viewer's perceptions and behaviors.

Content Available

Weaver divides the available content into three categories. First, his analysis revealed that the bulk of material features standard nonviolent themes. The content of most films and videos in this category is preoccupied with sexual activity, usually from the masculine perspective. There is a heavy emphasis on heterosexual intercourse, lesbianism, group sex, anal intercourse, and oral–genital contact with visible ejaculation.[8] Weaver notes, "The predominant theme of standard-fare pornography, in other words, spotlights the sexual desires and prowess of men, whereas consistently and persistently portraying women as sexually promiscuous and obsequious."[9]

A second category of material that is much less prevalent involves coercive and/or violent themes. One of the predominant features in this type of material is the "rape myth" scenario. In this sequence of actions, a woman is taken by force against her will and raped. At some point in the sequence, the woman is shown enjoying the rape. There are many variations on this general theme, but the central idea is that the woman enjoys being dominated or abused by violence during a sexual encounter. Finally, the third category outlined by Weaver is the idealized world of sexual fantasy, sometimes referred to as "erotic." This category probably includes the smallest number of films and videos.

Perceptual Consequences of Viewing

Contrary to the Commission Report on Obscenity and Pornography, the newer research on this topic has dramatically changed the way most researchers assess sexually explicit content and its effects on viewers. One line of studies, conducted by Dolf Zillmann and Jennings Bryant, is particularly instructive.[10] The general design of these studies was to expose volunteers to weekly one-hour viewing sessions of mainstream pornography that had been carefully scrutinized by the researchers to make sure that violence and coercion were absent. Following these sessions, the researchers asked the participants questions about relationships and perceptions of women under the guise of conducting another study. Far from indicating the absence of any harmful effects, the findings of these studies show rather conclusively that people who watch mainstream pornography are more likely to think that rape is not so severe a crime, that most sexual practices are more prevalent than they really are, that their own sexual relationships are not particularly satisfying, and that trust in their own partners is misplaced.

Studies conducted by Ed Donnerstein and his colleagues tend to show that all of these perceptual effects are present after viewing sexual depictions that are accompanied by violence and coercion.[11] However, his research does not necessarily reveal these effects for nonviolent depictions. The question of whether or not these effects are typically present after viewing nonviolent material remains unresolved; it is a question that future studies will have to address more directly. At present, most of the evidence showing these effects as a result of nonviolent material comes from the research by Zillmann and his colleagues. Whatever the ultimate resolution of this issue, both research groups have agreed that depictions of the rape scenario and sexual violence promote attitudes of sexual callousness toward women and cause more lenient attitudes toward the perpetrators of rape. Donnerstein emphasizes that such images are not limited to films and videos that carry the X rating. He argues that they frequently show up in R-rated films. Although the images in these films may be less explicit than ones in X-rated material, the pairing of sex and violence in the R-rated films is often very apparent and quite capable of bringing about the effects discussed earlier.

Behavioral Consequences of Viewing

Think about what would be required to establish a clear cause-and-effect relationship between exposure to sexually explicit materials and some antisocial behavior such as rape. Researchers would need to carefully manipulate exposure to different media content and then provide an opportunity for aggressive behavior. They would then record which participants actually behaved aggressively. Of course, in the case of a behavior like rape, to set up such an experiment would be unthinkable. Researchers run into these ethical issues whenever they think about designing studies that would clearly indict pornography as a causal factor in the increase of sex crimes. For this reason, some scholars take the position that the evidence needed to make a claim for this causal proposition is simply not possible to gather. Other scholars agree but emphasize that there are certainly strong hints available in the present data about the behavioral consequences of exposure to pornography.

While it isn't possible or desirable to set up a situation where real-life sexual aggression might occur, certain types of aggressive behavior can be studied in the laboratory. Over the years in media effects studies, aggression has often been studied in the context of some sort of scenario involving the administration or *perceived* administration of electric shock. The **electric shock paradigm** goes back to the famous experiments done by Stanley Milgram on obedience to authority.[12] In these studies, the participants were ordered by the experimenter to administer electric shocks to another person whenever that person gave a wrong answer on a learning task that was part of the experiment. Real shocks were never delivered, and the person who was supposedly receiving them was actually a member of the team of experimenters. But the participants still believed that they were, in fact, administering painful electric shocks to another person. By taking note of how many shocks people were willing to give and how long they held the shock button in the "on" position, the researchers could tell which conditions would generally produce the highest levels of "obedience" to authority.

When this electric shock paradigm is used in studies on the effects of sexually explicit materials, the findings are quite revealing. In one classic study by Kenneth Leonard and Stuart Taylor, 40 undergraduate males who were in the presence of a female viewed slides that were either neutral or erotic.[13] In this case, the female was actually a member of the team of experimenters. When the erotic slides were shown, the female reacted according to one of three different randomly assigned scripts. In the "no cues" script, she showed no reaction at all. In the **non-permissive cues** script, she made a variety of disapproving comments about the slides (for example, "This is disgusting," or "Oh, that's awful"). Finally, in the **permissive cues** script, she made a variety of positive comments (for example, "That looks like fun"). After the slide-viewing session, the males were told that they were going to take part in a competition with the female that involved reaction times. Each person was given the opportunity to administer a shock to the other. The experiment was rigged such that the males would discover that the female had decided to administer a very high level of shock. The experimenters were most interested in the level of shock that the males would choose to deliver to the female once they discovered this information. Would their chosen shock levels vary as a function of their slide-viewing condition? The results of the study clearly revealed that the answer to this question was yes. Can you guess which group of males delivered the highest levels of shock to the female? Why?

The results of the study showed that the males who had watched the erotic slides in the presence of a female who displayed permissive cues were much more likely to deliver higher levels of shock. The authors reasoned that males in this condition concluded that the female would more easily tolerate inappropriate electric shocks because she had already tolerated the sexually explicit material in the slides. In short, the males adopted calloused perceptions of the female on the basis of the female's earlier tolerance.

What do we learn from this sort of experiment about the effects of sexually explicit media? It appears that males who perceive that females are tolerant of explicit sexuality will be more willing to commit aggressive acts against them if there is provocation to do so. This finding could have implications for the way women are depicted in pornographic films. If male viewers have a steady diet of promiscuous females who are tolerant of and even eager to engage in unusual sexual behaviors, calloused attitudes toward women in general might result. Such attitudes could lead to more severe treatment of women under conditions of provocation. This finding appears consistent with the results of some other studies in the literature conducted by Donnerstein and Zillmann.

One of the big issues in interpreting experimental results like the ones reported by Kenneth Leonard and Stuart Taylor is trying to figure out how the experiment might apply to behavior that takes place outside of the carefully controlled world of the experimental laboratory. This issue is referred to as one of **ecological validity** (sometimes called *external validity*). Some critics of this type of experiment would argue that it is very difficult to know for sure whether we can learn very much about the "real" world from these sorts of studies. After all, how many people have you seen carrying around portable electric shock machines that they use whenever they are angry? According to these critics, if these sorts of details (sometimes referred to as the **mundane realism** of the experiment) don't match situations encountered outside the laboratory, then we know very little about how the results inform our understanding of real-world events. Experimenters answer this criticism by arguing that the details inside the laboratory might not match the details outside the laboratory, but the meaning that people assign to those details is similar to the meaning that people assign to events in the real world. This emphasis on the meaning that is attached to responses in an experiment is referred to as **experimental realism.** Leonard Berkowitz and Ed Donnerstein discuss this issue at length in one of their articles about the effects of media violence.[14]

THE MEESE COMMISSION REPORT ON PORNOGRAPHY

The wave of research that followed the first Commission Report on Obscenity and Pornography convinced many in the government that a new report was needed on this topic. In July 1986, the attorney general of the United States, Ed Meese, released the *Attorney General's Commission on Pornography Final Report.* Although the title of this report was similar to that of the first one, the two reports diverged widely in terms of their purpose, operating procedure, and final conclusion. Unlike the early commission, the **Meese Commission** did not become involved in the conduct of new scientific research on the topic. Instead, it relied on existing studies and anecdotal data gathered from interviews and examinations of the commercial market for pornography. The purpose of this report probably had more to do with an attempt on the part of the attorney general to put some teeth into existing obscenity statutes than it did with arriving at opinion about the harms of pornography based on science. Several of the commissioners were outspoken opponents of pornography. For example, James Dobson of the organization Focus on the Family was a member of the commission. Dobson has long been known in the Christian community as a leading spokesperson for family values and a staunch opponent of pornography. Given this type of constituency, it was inconceivable that the Meese Commission would arrive at any other conclusion except one that asserted the harms of pornography.

Major Conclusion

Not surprisingly, then, the Meese Commission came to a far different conclusion than the earlier commission about the effects of pornography. In some respects, the summary it offered about the relative harms of sexually violent material, mainstream pornography depicting various degrees of domination, and purely erotic depictions was consistent with the available evidence summarized earlier in this chapter. But the report drew heavy criticism from the scientific community for a number of reasons. First, scientists objected to the weight that the commission seemed to attach to the interviews it conducted with people who were selected through a process that could hardly be called scientific. It appeared that the Meese Commission's procedures included providing an outlet for anyone who had a gripe about the pornography industry. Second, the commission seemed to be confused about how to interpret correlations. Consider this passage from the commission report:[15]

> We recognize, therefore, that a positive correlation between pornography and sex offenses does not itself establish a causal connection between the two. It may be that some other factor, some sexual or emotional imbalance, for example, might produce both excess use of pornographic materials as well as a tendency to commit sex offenses.

The commission would have been wise to stop with this statement, which shows a proper understanding of how to interpret correlations. But the report goes on:

> But the fact that correlational evidence cannot definitively establish causality does not mean that it may not be *some* [emphasis mine] evidence of causality, and we have treated it as such.

This statement is, at best, ambiguous. It is true that the presence of a correlation may be evidence of causality. But it also may *not* be. When the commission members state that they "have treated it as such," it sounds as though they may have actually treated these correlations as some evidence of causality. If they did that, then they misinterpreted the evidence. In fact, the correlations may not be evidence of causality at all.

In the end, the academic community was not pleased with the Meese Commission report because the report went beyond the scientific evidence in formulating its conclusions. It also seemed to have a very strong bias against pornography from the outset. This turned out to be unfortunate, because a strong scientific conclusion regarding the new evidence about sexually explicit materials was desperately needed. Because academic researchers could not fully embrace the Meese Commission report, much of their rhetoric was directed to revealing the scientific shortcomings of the report. Researchers found it extremely difficult to discredit the report while simultaneously emphasizing that many of the studies summarized in it were important and credible. Some of the scientists who had published findings about the harms of sexually explicit materials were seen in the news media criticizing the Meese Commission. Consequently, many of the important studies and their conclusions about the harms of sexually explicit materials got lost in a sea of controversy about the report itself.

Some researchers still describe the proposed relationship between exposure to pornography and aggressive behavior as "equivocal." In a recent summary article on the topic, Michael Seto and his colleagues argued that the multiple definitions of pornography used in the many experiments as well as a very heavy emphasis on only one type of effect (male aggression against a female) should lead to caution about the conclusions that we draw from this literature. In any case, Seto points out that the best evidence seems to suggest that the effects of pornography on aggressive behavior appear to be most pronounced with men who are already predisposed to engage in such behavior. The same argument has been made about the effects of violent media as well.[16]

SEX ON PRIME-TIME TV

To this point, the bulk of the chapter has been about the effects of pornography or highly explicit depictions of sexuality. Although these sorts of depictions are certainly prevalent in movies, videos, and Internet sites, the research on these depictions says little about the more common sexual depictions that appear on prime-time television. The fact that these images are less explicit is not a good reason to ignore their potential influence. Before you finish with this chapter, you should have a clear understanding of the research in this area as well.

One general effect of sexual material that shouldn't be overlooked is its capacity to induce elevated levels of **physiological arousal** and **sexual arousal.** Physiological arousal includes general responses such as elevations in heart rate, blood pressure, and skin conductance (for example, sweaty palms). Sexual arousal may include some of these general responses but is much more specific to the sex organs. In addition to measuring such arousal with self-report instruments, some researchers have actually measured sexual arousal in males with instruments designed to detect increased blood flow to the penis.[17] Measures designed to detect symptoms of arousal in the vaginal area have also been used for females.[18] As you might imagine, the procedures followed in studies that use these measures are scrutinized very carefully by university human-subjects committees. Typically, the instruments are self-attached in private and computer readings verify that the instruments are functioning properly. The research shows that sexual content is arousing. There are a number of questions on which researchers would like to have more data because the current understanding is quite limited. Are males and females aroused by different stimuli? Does arousal vary directly as a function of the level of sexual explicitness? Some scholars have noted that the most arousing material is not necessarily the most explicit.[19] However, there does not appear to be an abundance of research data on this topic. To the extent that low levels of explicitness can induce high levels of arousal, then, TV soap operas and other prime-time offerings that feature verbal and visual depictions of sex are potentially very arousing. What are the implications of this possibility?

The Dynamics of Excitation Transfer

According to Dolf Zillmann's **theory of excitation transfer** (which you will encounter again in the next chapter), general arousal from any source can intensify an emotional experience and make it much more prominent than it would be ordinarily without the arousal.[20] The implication of this theory is that if people become aroused as a result of watching sex on television, whatever emotions they experience immediately after viewing may be much more intense than they would be ordinarily. For example, if a person became angry right after viewing a sexually provocative show, the anger would be more intense. On the other hand, if a person experienced feelings of warmth and affection toward a viewing partner, those feelings would also be intensified.

The theory of excitation transfer is incredibly flexible. Arousal can intensify both positive and negative emotions. In addition, the source of the arousal can be almost anything. Yes, watching sexual content on television can be arousing, but so can jogging (at least in terms of the general symptoms of increased heart rate, and so on).

According to Zillmann's theory, when something produces arousal in the system, the natural course of that arousal is to decay—to return to the baseline, resting state. If you go out for a jog, your heart will begin to beat faster. But when you stop, your heart rate will gradually return to normal. When your heart rate is clearly elevated and you are aware of the source of the elevation (you jogged), an emotional experience will not be intensified as a result of the jog. Your ability to clearly identify your arousal as coming from the jog enables you to keep it separate from whatever emotional reaction you might have during this time. But as Zillmann's research has demonstrated, there comes a point during the arousal decay where a person *thinks* that arousal has returned to normal when in fact it hasn't. Arousal is still elevated. Joggers can recognize this point easily after exercise, when it feels as though the body is back to resting state but a quick check of the pulse indicates otherwise. It is during this period of time that the excitation transfer effect can occur. The arousal that is left over from the earlier activity or emotion but goes undetected in the system can transfer to a new emotion and make it more intense.

A former student of mine apparently learned this lesson well and decided to share her experience with me several weeks after the course she took from me was over. She greeted me one day by saying that the theory of excitation transfer had saved her engagement. I was more than a little curious to hear the details. Apparently, every time she wanted to discuss wedding plans with her partner, they got into an argument. Following a lecture on excitation transfer, the student had a lightbulb experience. She already knew that her partner was not particularly fond of talking about the details of the wedding. But as she thought back over their discussions, she realized that she was inevitably trying to hold these discussions immediately after her partner's daily jog. The theory predicted that his negative reaction to discussions of wedding plans would be intensified by arousal left over from the jog. Once she realized this, she changed her behavior, making sure that she discussed only pleasant topics after exercise. She saved the wedding plans for more serene moments. According to her report, this single change had made a tremendous difference. I don't know how the newlyweds are faring today, but at least in this instance, the theory of excitation transfer turned out to have a very practical edge.

Content Analyses

As it turns out, there have been many more studies about the sexual content of TV than about the effects of that content. One researcher, Bradley Greenberg, has studied the content of afternoon soap operas for many years. In one recent study, he reported that over the last decade, the number of sexual incidents per hour had increased.[21] Most of the sex centered around incidents of sexual intercourse between unmarried partners or partners who were not attached. Increases were observed in both visual and verbal depictions of sexuality. Greenberg noted that although depictions of sex on the soaps were increasing, many of the incidents of sex outside of marriage were not sanctioned by characters in the program and were portrayed as objectionable. In order to explain this paradox, Greenberg tends to favor the view that the TV networks are attempting to appease multiple audiences. Some people like sexual content. Others will not watch the shows if the attitude toward the sexuality seems to favor promiscuity. By depicting sex and then expressing moral objection, the networks can spike their ratings by appealing to both groups.

Sex on TV is hardly limited to soap operas. One of the reasons sexual content is so controversial is because of its potential impact on children and adolescents and the ready availability of TV content to those younger viewers.

In another content analysis of the most popular prime-time shows viewed by children and adolescents, Monique Ward found that nearly 30% of all the interactions that took place on an average episode contained verbal references to sexual issues.[22] On some episodes, that statistic soared to 50%. A great proportion of the messages related to sexuality emphasized the competitive nature of sexual relations and featured many comments by males about the physical appearance of females. A more recent study directed by Dale Kunkel for the Kaiser Foundation emphasized the "sobering" finding that only 10% of the programs in their study that depicted sexual intercourse included any mention of sexual risk or responsibility. The report concluded:

> In the future debate about sex on television, it may well be more important to consider *how* sex is shown rather than simply *how much* it is shown. This study confirms that sexual messages are a frequent part of the television landscape, but it also makes clear that such messages follow a pattern that poses cause for some concern. When television presents sexual content, there is scant attention devoted to sexual health issues that are essential considerations in weighing one's options for sexual activity today. By providing more balance in addressing these concerns, television could be helping young people make more informed—perhaps even life-saving—decisions about sex in their own lives.[23] [emphasis in original]

The conclusion of Kunkel's report sounds all too familiar. A decade ago, a team of researchers concluded on the basis of their content analysis that adolescents were unlikely to learn very much about contraceptives or the risk of sexually transmitted disease from watching TV depictions of sexuality.[24] Historically, the research findings of scholars have tended to have little impact on the practices of the

---

STUDY BOX 6-2   The 2000 Report on Sexual Content on TV

In February 2001, the Kaiser Family Foundation released its second major content analysis of sexual content on TV. The report was based on more than 1,100 randomly selected programs from the 1999–2000 TV season. What did the report find? Over two-thirds of all the programs that were included in the analysis contained sexual content of some sort (68%). A similar analysis done two years earlier showed that only 56% of the programs contained sexual content. Apparently, sex on TV is on the rise. If the analysis is confined to only the shows that aired on the major networks during prime time, then 75% of all the shows included sexual content—also an increase over the figures from two years before (67%).

One change that the newest study detected in sexual depictions was in the percentage of teens who were involved in sexual intercourse. In the analysis of the 1997–1998 season, only 3% of characters involved in intercourse were teens. That figure increased to 9% in the analysis of 1999–2000 programming. Although sexual depictions of intercourse among teens seem to be increasing on TV, it also seems that messages about "safe sex" are more likely. In the 1999–2000 season, 25% of all the shows that depicted sexual intercourse made some reference to sexual health issues. Two years earlier, only 10% of these depictions contained similar references.

What might be the reasons for the rise of sexuality on TV? One possibility is that as the networks have come under increasing fire for programming violence, they have turned to sex to appease audiences who might be hungry for arousing content. But there might be another principle at work that could help to explain the increase. Recall from the last chapter that the principle of desensitization predicts that once a certain level of explicitness has been crossed, it becomes extremely difficult to reverse direction. Over time, content that initially triggers an intense emotional reaction becomes commonplace. Producers may sense that in order to keep ratings high, the line needs to be pushed constantly. If this principle holds true, future content analyses of sexual content on TV will find that even more sex is turning up on TV and that the sex is more explicit. If this trend continues, the challenge for researchers of media effects will be to investigate how these changes might make a difference in terms of influencing the beliefs, attitudes, and behaviors of the TV audience.

SOURCE: The Kaiser Family Foundation. http://www.kff.org/content/2001/3087

---

entertainment industry. The report by Kunkel and his colleagues quoted above was published in 1999. However, the research program has recently been updated with a report for the year 2000. One encouraging theme in the 2000 report is that while sex on TV is increasing, so too may be the depictions of safe–sex practices. You can read more about the highlights from the 2000 report in Study Box 6-2.

Sexual Behavior and Viewing

Most of the studies on the impact of sex in the media have taken place on older populations and have dealt with content that is more explicit than what is typically seen on prime-time TV. This state of affairs is certainly easy to understand. From an ethical standpoint, it is certainly more problematic to study younger viewers in the context of a research design that requires exposure to sexual media content. From the standpoint of theory about media impact, it makes sense to study the more explicit depictions of media sexuality, since these would be the materials that one might suspect would have the most effects on viewers. Despite the fact that not much research attention has been devoted to the effects of TV sexuality, there are at least three studies that deserve mention here.

One study that was supported by ABC-TV studied how well adolescents (ages 12–16) understood sexual innuendos on prime-time TV. The findings revealed that even the youngest of these viewers understood the innuendos well and felt comfortable talking about them.[25] In a second study that used a correlational research design, pregnant and non-pregnant girls and women between the ages of 13 and 29 were studied. The results of the study revealed that the pregnant girls were more likely to have greater media exposure to those programs and movies that depicted sexual content. They also tended to be more likely to watch these programs and movies in the company of their boyfriends than did the members of the non-pregnant sample. Of course, you know from reading chapter 2 that there are various pitfalls involved in concluding from this correlation that watching the sex in the media caused these girls and women to have a greater likelihood of becoming pregnant. In this case, the researchers were not even able to establish the time sequence of the relationship (the measure of pregnancy came before the measure of media exposure), much less rule out possible third variables that may have been related to both media exposure and pregnancy status.

In one recent study, Rebecca Collins and her colleagues surveyed nearly 1,800 adolescents about their TV viewing habits, with a special focus on the shows that contained sexual content. In this case, the researchers were able to do follow-up interviews one year later. The major finding of the study was that the adolescents who, on the first survey, reported the highest viewing levels of sexual content were also the ones who were most likely to report that they had initiated an instance of sexual intercourse during the last year. This study established both the relationship between TV exposure to sex and sexual behavior and the time order of the relationship (viewing preceded behavior). In addition, the researchers attempted to eliminate numerous other variables that might have accounted for the relationship. The authors reported that adolescents in the top 10% in viewing sexual content had double the chance of being involved in sexual behavior when compared to the adolescents who were in the bottom 10% on viewing.[26] Of course, as the authors acknowledged, some of this effect could be due to the fact that adolescents who are curious about sex are more likely to watch it on TV and also to initiate sexual behavior in real life.

Although the actual amount of research evidence on the impact of TV sex on behavior is minimal, the knowledge that researchers have gained from studying other areas of media impact would certainly suggest that there is reason to be concerned about the way sex is depicted in prime time. One thing that we can be certain about on this topic is that it will remain controversial.

More than any other area of media effects, the number of angles on sexual content in the media (religious, political, scholarly, legal) will continue to make for a "hotbed" of dispute.

CONTROL OVER MEDIA CONTENT

Sex and the Internet

In the last five years, the number of sites in cyberspace has mushroomed tremendously—into the hundreds of millions. At no time in human history have sexually explicit media been so readily available as they are today. We owe that fact—good or bad—to the Internet. The significance of this easy availability is that children are part of the consuming audience in a way that they have never been before. Controversies have hit public libraries and schools about whether or not to load blocking software onto their computers to prevent children from surfing to objectionable sites. Sometimes the blocking software doesn't work properly and screens out material that isn't sexual in nature. Researchers have little to say about the effects of sexually explicit media on children because few committees on the protection of human subjects would ever approve research of this sort. The widespread assumption, of course, is that Internet pornography is harmful to children. For that reason, solutions to the problem are not typically sought in research. Advocates seeking strategies to control the flow of sexually explicit materials turn instead to **legal, social/economic,** and **education** solutions. From the looks of things, this struggle to control the material is an uphill battle.

Legal Control

One reason for the heated controversy about media sex is that obscenity does not enjoy protection under the First Amendment. Obscene speech is illegal. Consequently, the government has often attempted to restrict the flow of sexually explicit media that might be judged as obscene. As mentioned earlier, the legal battles against obscenity have not been very successful. Obscenity is a difficult thing to define. Moreover, Americans may object to sex in the media, but they simultaneously tend to defend the right of the media to produce it. The quest for censorship is almost always one that fails to enjoy popular support.

Another legal avenue that has occasionally been tried by opponents of pornography is to claim that certain sexual depictions serve to deprive some members of society (usually women) of their civil rights. These claims have usually met with failure in the courts and state legislatures around the country. One reason for the failure of these efforts is concern about the implications that such rulings would have for other kinds of media content. Do people really want to live in a world where a given group of individuals can lay waste to the media industry by claiming that certain kinds of content injure their civil rights? For now, at least, the courts have answered that question in the negative.

Social or Economic Control

Instead of passing and enforcing laws against sexual content, some groups pursue a strategy that is based on social norms and economic impact. Religious groups will often launch boycotts of advertisers who try to sell their goods on objectionable programs. Sometimes, groups will boycott particular business establishments that sell sexually oriented material. When I lived in Cleveland, one of the convenience store chains became the target of such a boycott. The stores responded by announcing an open chance for customers to vote on whether they should continue to carry sexually oriented magazines such as *Playboy* and *Penthouse*. Customers had to come into the store to cast their ballots. Since participation in the boycott meant avoiding the stores, it was no surprise when the company announced that the public had overwhelmingly voted to support its policy of continuing to sell the magazines. As a public relations ploy, the strategy worked brilliantly. The stores looked good in the public eye for having an open election. But because the boycott was going on at the same time, the results were virtually guaranteed to support the continued sale of the material—a result that the stores undoubtedly wanted. Eventually, the boycott ended and things returned to normal. Boycotts and economic pressure sometimes work in isolated cases over the short term. But history shows them to be relatively ineffective over the long haul.

Control Through Education

In a free society that protects freedom of speech and expression, the preferred form of control over media content is probably education. If people learn about media impact, they can take steps to deal with it and manage it in their daily lives. As evidence for this fact, Ed Donnerstein has shown that participating in his experiments can actually be beneficial—despite the fact that male college students who go through his experiments are exposed to violent pornography.[27] Compared to males who don't have the chance to participate in the studies, the ones who do actually become more sensitive to issues involving rape myths after they have gone through the instructional debriefing required by human-subjects committees. Research by Neil Malamuth shows similar findings.[28] In this case, education turns out to be effective. When you finish this course on media effects, you will be in a far better position to think through the issues of media impact in your own life. You will then be better able to make informed choices about your own media diet and, in the future, the media diets of your children.

SUMMARY

Few topics stir such passionate opinion as sexual content in the media. Researchers have tended to distinguish between pornography, violent sexuality, and eroticism as they have studied media impact in this domain. Early evidence from the *Report of the Commission on Obscenity and Pornography* led to the conclusion that this material was relatively harmless. Subsequent reanalysis of some of the data in the report, combined with a new wave of research that followed its publication, modified this conclusion. The Meese Commission report reversed the conclusion of the first commission report, but, for a variety of reasons, it was widely criticized by social scientists. Nevertheless, the broad consensus of the scientific community is that exposure to sexually explicit material is associated with a host of negative perceptual and attitudinal consequences. Some research also suggests that negative behaviors might also be more likely following exposure. Research on sexual content on TV has concentrated mainly on content analyses rather than studies of impact. The main concern is with *how* sex is depicted rather than with *how much* is depicted. More research needs to be done on the impact of less explicit media sex such as the depictions on soap operas and prime-time TV.

KEY TERMS AND CONCEPTS

Obscenity 107

Pornography 108

Erotic media 108

National Commission on Obscenity and Pornography 109

Trigger hypothesis 110

Safety valve theory 110

Electric shock paradigm 114

Permissive cues versus non-permissive cues 115

Ecological validity 116

Mundane realism 116

Experimental realism 116

Meese Commission 116

Physiological arousal 118

Sexual arousal 118

Theory of excitation transfer 118

Legal, social/economic, and educational strategies to control media 123

To learn more about the topics in this chapter, enter the Key Terms and Concepts found in this chapter as subject and keyword searches on your InfoTrac® College Edition.

NOTES

1. Liebert, R. M., Sprafkin, J. N., & Davidson, E. S. (1982). *The early window: Effects of television on children and youth.* New York: Pergamon Press.

2. Ibid.

3. Commission on Obscenity and Pornography. (1970). *Report of the Commission on Obscenity and Pornography.* New York: Bantam Books.

4. Kutchinsky, B. (1973). The effect of easy availability of pornography on the incidence of sex crimes: The Danish experience. *Journal of Social Issues, 29,* 163–181.

5. Court, J. H. (1977). Pornography and sex crimes. *International Journal of Criminology and Penology, 5,* 129–157.

6. Diamond, M., & Uchiyama, A. (1999). Pornography, rape, and sex crimes in Japan. *International Journal of Law & Psychiatry, 22,* 1–22.

7. Weaver, J. B. (1994). Pornography and sexual callousness: Perceptual and behavioral consequences of exposure to pornography. In D. Zillmann, J. Bryant, & A. C. Huston (Eds.), *Media, children and the family: Social scientific, psychodynamic, and clinical*

perspectives (pp. 215–228). Hillsdale, NJ: Erlbaum.

8. Hebditch, D., & Anning, N. (1988). *Porn gold: Inside the pornography business.* London: Faber & Faber.

9. Brosius, H., Weaver, J., & Staab, J. (1993). Exploring the social and sexual "reality" of contemporary pornography. *Journal of Sex Research, 30,* 161–172.

10. Zillmann, D., & Bryant, J. (1988). Effects of prolonged consumption of pornography on family values. *Journal of Family Issues, 9,* 518–544.

11. Donnerstein, E. (1984). Pornography: Its effect on violence against women. In N. M. Malamuth & E. Donnerstein (Eds.), *Pornography and sexual aggression* (pp. 53–81). Orlando, FL: Academic Press.

12. Milgram, S. (1963). Behavioral study of obedience. *Journal of Abnormal and Social Psychology, 67,* 371–378.

13. Leonard, K. E., & Taylor, S. P. (1983). Exposure to pornography, permissive and nonpermissive cues, and male aggression toward females. *Motivation & Emotion, 7,* 291–299.

14. Berkowitz, L., & Donnerstein, E. (1982). External validity is more than skin deep: Some answers to criticisms of laboratory experiments. *American Psychologist, 37,* 245–257.

15. U.S. Department of Justice. (1986). *Attorney General's Commission on Pornography: Final report* (Vol. 1). Washington, DC: U.S. Department of Justice.

16. Seto, M. C., Maric, A., & Barbaree, H. E. (2001). The role of pornography in the etiology of sexual aggression. *Aggression & Violent Behavior. 6*(1), 35–53.

17. Eccles, A., Marshall, W. L, & Barbaree, H. E. (1988). The vulnerability of erectile measures to repeated assessments. *Behavior Research and Therapy, 26,* 179–183.

18. Sintchak, G., & Geer, J. (1975). A vaginal plethysmograph system. *Psychophysiology, 12,* 113–115.

19. Harris, R. J. (1999). *A cognitive psychology of mass communication.* Mahwah, NJ: Erlbaum.

20. Zillmann, D. (1983). Transfer of excitation in emotional behavior. In J. T. Cacioppo & R. E. Petty (Eds.), *Social psychophysiology* (pp. 215–240). New York: Guilford Press.

21. Greenberg, B. S., & Busselle, R. W. (1996). Soap operas and sexual activity: A decade later. *Journal of Communication, 46,* 153–160.

22. Ward, M. L. (1995). Talking about sex: Common themes about sexuality in the prime-time television programs children and adolescents view most. *Journal of Youth & Adolescence, 24,* 595–615.

23. Kunkel, D., Cope, K. M., Farinola, W. J. M., Biely, E., Rollin, E., & Donnerstein, E. (1999). *Sex on TV.* The Henry J. Kaiser Family Foundation [Online]. Available: http://www.kff.org/content/archive/1457/

24. Brown, J. D., Childers, K. W., & Waszak, C. S. (1990). Television and adolescent sexuality. *Journal of Adolescent Health Care, 11,* 62–70.

25. Liebert, R. M., Sprafkin, J. N., & Davidson, E. S. (1982). *The early window: Effects of television on children and youth.* New York: Pergamon Press.

26. Collins, R. L., Elliott, M. N., Berry, S. H., Kanouse, D. E., Kunkel, D., Hunter, S. B., & Miu, A. (2004). Watching sex on television predicts adolescent initiation of sexual behavior. *Pediatrics, 14*(3), e280–289 [Online]. Available: http://pediatrics.aappublications.org/cgi/content/full/114/3/e280

27. Donnerstein, E., & Berkowitz, L. (1981). Victim reactions in aggressive erotic films as a factor in violence against women. *Journal of Personality and Social Psychology, 41,* 710–724.

28. Malamuth, N. M., & Check, J. V. P. (1980). Sexual arousal to rape and consenting depictions: The importance of the woman's arousal. *Journal of Abnormal Psychology, 89,* 763–766.

7

■

Media That Stir
Emotions

I will never forget the night from my childhood when my parents made a
fateful decision that they could never have known would affect me for the
rest of my life. It was a Friday evening, and my older brothers had gathered
around the TV set in keen anticipation of their favorite weekly program, *The
Twilight Zone*. Up to this point in time, my parents had insisted that I could not
watch the show because it came on after my bedtime. But on this particular
evening, for whatever reason, my parents relented and allowed me to join my
brothers in front of the set. I was 6 years old. By the end of the program, I was
certain that I would never be able to walk into a department store again. The
program depicted department store mannequins that turned into real people
and then back into mannequins. I was quite literally terrified! (After writing
these words, I went to the Internet and found the details of the particular
episode that frightened me. My memory was very accurate. The episode, "The
After Hours," was broadcast on Friday, June 10, 1960. It was the first season of
the program. Perhaps I was allowed to watch it because the school year was
ending and my parents were less concerned about bedtime.)

Despite the fact that numerous cable stations run old episodes of *The
Twilight Zone,* I have never cared to re-watch the particular episode that scared
me that night. When I have described the episode to my students, many of
them shake their heads in that knowing way. Some have even tried to fill me in
on some of the plot details that have become fuzzy in my mind over the years.
I don't really care to know. What I do know is that when I watched that program as a child, my mind could not have dreamed that a TV show could depict

such a spooky and terrifying scenario. *The Twilight Zone* may be one of the oldest classic examples of how **paranormal media content** can terrify people.[1]

Perhaps in part as a result of my intense personal experience with a frightening TV program, I ended up devoting a large portion of my research career to studying the effects of frightening media on children. This has been very rewarding. Perhaps, if I had not suffered such intense fear myself, I wouldn't have felt so drawn toward this topic. The research on frightening media really didn't get started in earnest until the late 1970s. At that time, a researcher at the University of Wisconsin–Madison, Joanne Cantor, received a major grant from the National Institute of Mental Health to study the emotional impact of frightening movies and TV programs on children. I was fortunate enough to work with Professor Cantor on this research. Cantor and I, along with a few other researchers (Barb Wilson and Cindy Hoffner), continued to study frightening media for many years and continue to have an interest in the topic today. Cantor has even published a children's book, *Teddy's TV Troubles,* which is based on key research findings and is designed to help parents deal with their children's emotional reactions to frightening media.

What has the research on this topic uncovered? In the remainder of this chapter, I attempt to provide a brief summary of the research findings in this area and in other areas concerning the emotional reactions that people experience from exposure to media. One thing clearly emerges from this research: Paranormal themes are often the most terrifying for both children and adults. After years of research, we think we know why.

☆ FRIGHT REACTIONS
TO MEDIA ARE PREVALENT

In considering the effects of media violence on aggressive behavior, the most frequently researched media effect in the literature, it is important to note that the statistical effect definitely exists, but the size of the effect is small (see chapter 5). Not many people become more aggressive because of something they see in a movie or TV show. In contrast, the emotional effects of frightening media are far more prevalent, even though they tend to receive less attention in the research literature.

Anecdotes of copycat crimes clearly support the notion that media violence sometimes affects aggressive behavior. Similarly, there are many anecdotes about the emotional impact of frightening films. When the film *Jaws* made its debut, tourism in ocean resort towns plummeted. People expressed terror at the prospect of becoming the victim of a "great white" attack. On the paranormal front, an issue of *The Journal of Nervous and Mental Disease* in 1975 carried reports of clinical psychiatric patients who had to seek hospitalization and months of treatment after viewing the movie *The Exorcist.*[2] Apparently, images of demon possession haunted these patients to the point of social and emotional malfunction. In the case of the film *Silence of the Lambs,* one graduate student in my department reported to me that she had been unable to eat meat for many weeks after viewing the film. And a remarkable number of adults report that they suffered trauma as children from viewing the Winged Monkeys and the Wicked Witch of the West in that all-time classic *The Wizard of Oz*. Anecdotes of intense fright reactions to media are common. I am almost certain that if you are reading this book, you can pause and think of at least one instance in your media experience where you found yourself frightened, anxious, spooked, or otherwise disturbed by some media image. The chances are also good that this image was part of a movie or TV show that depicted something from the realm of the paranormal. You are not alone in your experience.

As early as 1933, a researcher named Herbert Blumer found that 93% of the children in his sample reported having experienced fright caused by a movie.[3] In a classic study of the effects of television published in 1958, another researcher, Hilde Himmelweit, found that one-third of the children in her study reported having been frightened by something seen on television.[4] The most recent data from the last few years reveal that about 75% of elementary school children report fright from something seen in a movie or TV program.[5] In interviews about TV and children, parents often express concern about children's fright reactions. They frequently report that their children suffer nightmares as a result of watching frightening programs. Interviews with children confirm that this topic is an important one. In one study conducted in 1983 by researchers Palmer, Hockett, and Dean, over one-third of the children interviewed reported that there were specific scenes or programs that they were sorry they had ever seen.[6] Fortunately, the research goes beyond the documentation of the prevalence of these responses and offers some explanation and understanding of what is happening. One of the most important findings to emerge from this research is that the media content that frightens children varies, depending on the age of the child.[7]

DEVELOPMENTAL THEORY: WHAT SCARES ONE CHILD MAY NOT SCARE ANOTHER

Research on children's fright reactions made a breakthrough with the insight of Joanne Cantor. Cantor noticed that the developmental psychology of Jean Piaget helped her sort out reports of fright that she recorded from children and their parents. According to Piaget's theory, children pass through a series of stages in their cognitive development. The way they process, interpret, and think about the world around them depends on where they are in this sequence of stages. Children in the general age range of 2 to 7 years old think **perceptually.** The **concrete, visual appearance** of things tends to dominate the child's interpretation of and reaction to the world. In contrast, children older than 7 years begin to make a shift toward more **conceptual or abstract thought.**[8]

After studying these distinctions in Piaget's theory, Cantor realized that they might help explain her data on fright responses. Children in the younger age group tended to show fright in response to scenes and characters that looked grotesque and menacing (e.g., the wicked queen in *Snow White,* the Wicked Witch in *The Wizard of Oz,* or the Incredible Hulk). The fact that many of these characters appear in cartoon form and could never occur in the real world didn't seem to make any difference. The young child was not able to focus on this more conceptual or abstract observation.

In contrast to the younger children, older kids tended to report fright from movies and TV shows that featured events and characters that *could* actually occur in the real world. Their fears tended to involve scenes depicting violence or bodily harm to a character. They also included depictions of natural and technological disasters such as floods, fires, storms, earthquakes, or nuclear holocaust. Cantor reasoned that because of the older child's focus on the conceptual or abstract instead of the visual, the really scary media to them was that which depicted threatening things that might actually happen. Complicating the situation for these older children is the fact that they don't understand the low probability of many of the "real" events that they see in the media. They have a hard time telling themselves that these things won't really happen to them. They also haven't lived long enough to develop a sophisticated set of coping skills that enable them to deal with the harsh images of reality they see in the media.

Upon viewing a scene from a movie about a child kidnapping, children at 8 or 9 years of age may understand that kidnappings are real and could actually happen. They may also fail to comprehend that the probability of a kidnapping occurring in their neighborhood is very low. At the same time, they may realize all too well that kidnappings are serious business and potentially life threatening. This combination of ingredients makes it particularly likely that older children will react with emotional distress to this sort of media depiction. For an older child, this kind of depiction has much more fright potential than the wicked queen in *Snow White.* The older child simply writes off the queen as pretend or impossible. In contrast, young children, who tend to operate at the perceptual level, may find the wicked queen far more disturbing than the kidnapping movie. To them, the real possibility of a kidnapping is simply beyond their comprehension. And if the movie never actually showed physical injury, the young children would probably not react strongly to the content.

EXPERIMENTING WITH THE INCREDIBLE HULK

When I worked with Cantor on this research, I decided to do my doctoral dissertation on children's reactions to *The Incredible Hulk.* Although this may sound like an unusual topic for scholarly study, the experiment I conducted was logistically quite complex, and the findings were very important in supporting Cantor's extensions of Piaget's theory. After screening nearly every episode in the series, we elected to show children of both older and younger ages a brief segment that depicted a hospital employee becoming injured in an explosion. David Banner, played by the late Bill Bixby, witnessed the explosion and ran into a burning storage room to rescue the worker. While Banner was dragging the worker to safety, a subsequent explosion hurled him up against a wall, making him very angry. When David Banner becomes angry, he undergoes his strange metamorphosis into the huge, monstrous Hulk. Although the Hulk's transformation might not be called paranormal, it certainly falls into the more general category of "weird" or "strange." After showing the transformation (which included his eyes turning green, his shirt tearing, and his shoes ripping), the segment concluded by showing the Hulk gently lifting the worker to safety. In the closing scene, the camera followed the Hulk down a hallway and showed him jumping out of a window and growling ferociously.

Why did we show this segment to children, and what did we learn as a result? Following Cantor's logic, we reasoned that older children would show more fright than younger children during the first part of the segment. The prospect of an explosion and fire would frighten them because these were events that could really happen. Because of their appreciation for the distinction between fantasy and reality, older children would be able to understand the dangers confronted by the characters in this crisis. However, once David Banner began to transform into the Hulk, we thought that the pattern of fright reactions would change. Older children would recognize that the Hulk, despite his monstrous appearance, was really a "good" guy who would probably save the day. These children could discount the ugly visual appearance and focus on the more abstract reality that the Hulk was the answer to the problem. We reasoned that younger children would view the situation very differently. When the Hulk appeared, we thought that these children would be unable to think about very much except the fact that the Hulk's appearance was scary. We expected that the younger children would show more fright at this point in the program. We also expected that this would last until the end of the segment because the Hulk was present right up until the closing shot.

When children watched this segment, we had them come to a room in their school building that teachers had set aside for our research. Each child came separately, and we were able to monitor their heart rate and other physiological reactions as they watched. These reactions helped us interpret what the child felt during the show. The results were just as we had expected. The older children showed more fright during the explosion and fire and calmed down as the Hulk appeared. Younger children showed just the opposite tendency. They were calmer at the beginning of the show and got much more upset at the appearance of the Hulk.[9]

Perhaps you are thinking that researchers should not be going around scaring little kids. We couldn't agree more. We deliberately chose a program that most children were familiar with before the experiment. None of the emotional reactions we observed were very extreme. We also made sure that parents and children agreed to participate in the procedure and that the Human Subjects Committee at the University of Wisconsin–Madison approved of everything in the experiment. Finally, we talked with each child afterwards and made sure that no harmful emotional reactions had occurred. Actually, children seemed to enjoy these procedures. In Study Box 7-1, I detail a little more about the exact procedures

STUDY BOX 7-1   Research Procedures for Protecting Children

As you might imagine, studies of children's fright reactions must be undertaken with great care. This care is taken from the very beginning of planning a study. In getting ready to run the study that called for preschool and elementary school children to view a clip from *The Incredible Hulk,* cautious planning started with the choice of video material. Here, I detail the various steps and considerations that went into planning this experiment. As you can see, minimizing the risk to children was paramount throughout the procedure.

1. At the outset, we looked for a program that was sufficiently frightening to induce a detectable level of fear—but not one that was so intense that it would terrorize children. It was important to select a program that children were familiar with so that they wouldn't feel too frightened by some completely unknown scenario. In the case of *The Incredible Hulk,* the program was being broadcast on weekday afternoons in Madison, Wisconsin, during the time of the study. We reasoned that there was a good chance that many children had seen an episode once or twice and that they would have some familiarity with the general plot.

2. After selecting the program, we had to secure the permission of a local nursery school and an elementary school to cooperate with us in conducting the study. This meant making sure that each school facility had a room that could be dedicated to data collection during the day. More important, it meant securing the approval of school administrators to show the children the video material. The school administrators had to watch the video and give their official approval before we could move ahead.

3. In the case of the elementary school, the local school system had its own review board for all research conducted in the district. We had to submit a full proposal to this board and give the board members the opportunity to view all of the video material before we could proceed with our plans.

4. In addition to the approvals required from the participating schools, the University Human Subjects Committee had to give its own approval to our procedures and materials. Once all of these approvals were in place, we could proceed with the mechanics of the procedure. But at each step of the process, the children's welfare was paramount.

5. First, parents of all of the schoolchildren received a letter describing the research project. A permission slip was enclosed for their signature if they agreed to permit their child to participate. Parents who knew that their children might be particularly sensitive to programs like the *Hulk* simply didn't sign the permission slip, and their children were never considered for participation in the study.

that we went through to make sure that children suffered no harm from participating in this experiment with viewing clips from *The Incredible Hulk.*

What have we learned from experiments like this one? First, Cantor's ideas about the kinds of media that frighten children at different ages are confirmed. For younger kids under age 7, if it looks scary it probably will be scary. For older

6. After the permission letters were sent to parents, we set up times for parents to come to the school, preview the video material, and meet the experimenters. Parents who viewed the material and thought that it might be too intense for their children could simply refrain from turning in the permission forms.

7. Once the permission forms were submitted, the research team visited the school classroom and gave a general demonstration of the experimental procedure. We watched a few programs together with the class while one of the children wore the physiological electrodes we used in the procedure. These electrodes were attached to the fingers of one hand. We showed the class how a computer monitored the children's heart rate during the TV viewing. This was an educational time for all of the children—not just the ones who ended up participating in the study.

8. Before any individual child participated in the study, he or she had to agree to go through the procedure. In some cases, children whose parents had already given consent to participate decided on the day of the study to decline participation. Of course, if a child showed any reluctance to participate, the child was encouraged *not* to go through the procedure.

9. During the procedure, if a child showed any signs of genuine distress, the procedure would have been discontinued. Probably because of the elaborate screening procedures, all of the children who started the procedure watched the program to the end. We did not have to discontinue the viewing because of signs of distress.

10. After each child had finished viewing the video material and answering some questions, we offered that child a "scratch 'n' sniff" sticker in the aroma of their choice. The key principle in dismissing children from a study of this type is to make sure that they leave happy. Our major concern was that no child suffer any lingering distress as a result of the procedures. Parents of participating children were encouraged to contact us if they had concerns after the study was completed. As far as we know, none of the children who participated suffered any lingering reactions.

In general, guidelines followed by university human-subjects committees have grown even stricter since the time that this study was done. In the final analysis, these guidelines help to protect not only the participants but the researchers as well. No researcher would want to be responsible for inducing severe emotional trauma in a child. By following the guidelines of human-subjects committees, researchers have at least some protection from having to bear such a burden.

kids, if the depiction could really happen and the consequences are physically threatening, it probably will generate some fear. Although most fear reactions tend to be short-lived, in some cases children can suffer media fear that lasts long beyond the program. Coping with these fears can be a real challenge for the parent.[10]

WHY IS THE PARANORMAL SO SCARY?

Ironically, the seeds of understanding why paranormal media depictions are so often experienced as frightening and upsetting are contained in my early experience with *The Twilight Zone*. At the age of 6, I had come to understand the difference between reality and fantasy. At precisely the point in my life where I thought I had this distinction sorted out, along comes Rod Serling to toy with my mind. The transformation of people into mannequins looked as if it could actually happen in a real department store. I was just uncertain enough about this possibility that I found it to be terrifying.

Some of the most frightening movies that deal with paranormal themes are those that deftly juxtapose reality with the paranormal world. In a survey of college students that I did some 20 years after *The Exorcist* was first released, this film was still the most frequently mentioned as a movie that had induced enduring fright.[11] In follow-up interviews, I discovered that students often expressed the idea that the film had made them feel as if demon possession was real. And if it was real, many felt vulnerable and unprepared to deal with it. This is the nature of the paranormal world, almost by definition. If it does exist, most of us would confess to understanding it very poorly. And how can we control or protect ourselves against something we don't understand? We can't, and that's one of the things that makes us afraid. It is no wonder, then, that many a director intent on scaring the audience has turned to the paranormal for the horror film's basic ingredient. If the film can convince the viewer that it might just be possible in real life, then the rest of the task is easy. The mystery and uncontrollability inherent in the paranormal take over from there and finish the job of terrorizing the viewer. Not only is this a particularly deadly combination for young children who have just begun to sort out the difference between fantasy and reality, but it is also extremely potent for adults, many of whom carry a fair amount of uncertainty about the existence of paranormal phenomena.[12]

When I look back over the films that are mentioned again and again by college students as the ones that terrified them and caused them to experience lingering anxiety and fear, many of them depict paranormal phenomena in a context that strongly suggests the events could actually happen. There is no better way to do justice to the nature of these fear responses than to report them verbatim as they were originally reported in my research. The following descriptions are the recollections of college students from film experiences that they had in their childhood—usually around the ages of 9 to 11.

Poltergeist

[A family experiences the horror of discovering that their house is built on a burial ground. Ghosts arrive through the fuzziness of the TV screen and proceed to haunt the family in various ways.]

Respondent #1 *"This movie made me so scared that I felt like my heart froze, like I sort of went into shock. I totally remember this feeling of almost having a heart attack* *because I still get it now when I'm scared. I hate that feeling. I feel so uneasy. I'm like a basket case. Till this day that movie stayed with me. There are little things from the movie I can identify with when I see them now, and I'll get flashback feelings of how scared I felt. For example: clowns, closets, a fuzzy TV, and that little girl's voice all give me the willies. I really feel that that movie has scarred me for life."*

Respondent #2 *"I was 10 years old, and, of course, my imagination went wild. At the end of the film, I went to my room quietly . . . and being a pretty spoiled kid, I had my own black-and-white TV in my room. Well, needless to say, it was unplugged and hauled into my closet with blankets piled on top of it. To this day, I still unplug the TV every night before I go to bed . . . the idea of static in the reception magically appearing on the screen still frightens me."*

Respondent #3 *"I still get chills when I remember the part where the little girl in the movie looks at the snowy TV set and says, 'They're here!' I think the greatest effect of this experience is the fact that no one ever reassured me that events in this movie weren't real. This is probably the most important factor that shaped my belief that super-natural beings probably do exist."*

Respondent #4 *"The lingering effects of the fear I experienced that night are numerous. Because the haunting situation, in my mind, is not entirely impossible, I still find myself worrying about it at times. I feel the same fear emotions and reactions, like increased heart beat and paranoia, when I am confronted with some of the film's major symbols. Seeing a snowy TV screen at night, worrying that the tree outside my brother's window will attack him whenever it storms, thinking our house might have been built over a graveyard, clowns, and closets are all residual effects of my frightening media experience."*

The *Nightmare on Elm Street* Series

[Freddy Krueger returns from the grave to kill young children. He is only able to get them while they are sleeping. He comes to them in their dreams with sharp knives in place of fingers.]

Respondent #1 *"When the movie was over, I went home petrified to death. For about the next month and a half, I was terrified of going to sleep. I was afraid that if I went to sleep Freddy Krueger was going to kill me in my dreams. The first night I didn't sleep a wink. The next night I had trouble falling asleep and staying asleep once I got there."*

Respondent #2 *"There were many times during the movie that I thought about things such as whether or not the door was locked, or if these things could really happen. My aunt had a basement door that I continually kept an eye on to see if Freddy would come out of it. During the movie I convinced myself that I could not ever fall asleep again, because Freddy would get me. I remember this movie as being the most scary thing I have ever experienced, even to this day. To this day I seem to be afraid of dark unfurnished basements, and I do not think I will ever get over that."*

Respondent #3 *"I knew the part about the dreams was purely fiction, yet I could not make myself fall asleep that evening or for several evenings following that one. To this day, I am still especially disturbed when I hear about kids being abducted or killed."*

Respondent #4 *"This movie has a scene in it that I will never forget. It is the one where Freddy's arms stretch out to an arm span of some 30 feet and then slash someone to pieces. The reason why this scene scared me so bad is still unclear to me, but I think it might have something to do with Freddy having the superhuman ability to stretch out his arms and catch me no matter how far away I get and that it looked pretty creepy. For many nights after that I could not sleep without having a dream about Freddy reaching out and slashing me. Even now, I could do without alleys, because I am afraid if I look back I might see Freddy waiting for me with open arms, so to speak."*

The Exorcist

[A young girl is possessed by a demon and a local priest must perform an exorcism as the only remedy.]

Respondent #1 *"As I viewed this movie, I was filled with fear and terror. I had never been so frightened by a movie before. I thought that I was going to be possessed. I prayed throughout the entire movie that this would not happen to me. I tried to go to sleep, but I was too worked up to relax. By the time it was over, I was very exhausted. I finally fell asleep. That night, I had nightmares that I was possessed. When I went home the next day, I forgot all about the movie. Until I went to bed, that is. That night, I was paranoid. Every noise I heard was what I thought was the devil in my house. Every once in a while I have a nightmare still, or become a bit frightened by an unfamiliar noise. Still, to this day, I will not watch* The Exorcist.*"*

Respondent #2 *"Never in my life had I been so afraid to go to sleep. This insomnia lasted for about a week before I finally got a good night's sleep, with the assistance of a trip to church. I have yet to watch a movie that has even remotely compared to the fear I felt when I watched* The Exorcist. *To this day, I have still never seen the last 10 minutes of that movie, simply because I don't ever want to see it again. I also refuse to watch the second and third parts of this movie as well. I must also have a Bible or a crucifix in the room that I sleep in before I go to bed. I will never play with or purchase a Ouija board or even be in the same room with someone who is. All this results from my most traumatic experience in my life, watching* The Exorcist.*"*

Respondent #3 *"After seeing* The Exorcist, *I was literally afraid that if I didn't go to church every week, and do only right, this could actually happen to me."*

Respondent #4 *"The music played a tremendous part in building the evil tone of the movie. For years, whenever "Tubular Bells" would be played over the radio I would quickly switch stations or shut off the radio completely. In Indianapolis, on I-65, there was a business that had its name printed in large letters on the side of its building. Whenever we were traveling and went past this spot, I looked the other way. I knew* *exactly where this building was located and knew when to avert my gaze to the opposite side of the road. I went so far as to turn my whole body away from the building. The name of the business was "Tubular Sales." Close enough for me!"*

Clearly, based on these descriptions, one area that has been overlooked in all the controversy about paranormal media and the promotion of belief in weird things is the fact that the images and plots contained in these movies and TV shows are often very scary—particularly for children.[13]

THEORY ABOUT EMOTIONAL COPING:
✳ WHAT'S A PARENT TO DO?

Cantor's research team has also addressed the issue of what parents should do to help their children through frightening experiences that come during or after media exposure. One thing she discovered was that parents inevitably resort to what seems like a logical approach to dealing with children's fright reactions to TV and movies. They tell their children, regardless of age, that what they are seeing is "not real" or "just pretend." Actually, the research shows that this strategy can be effective with older children who have come to distinguish between **reality** and **fantasy**.[14] The problem is that parents also tend to use the strategy with younger children (under age 7) who often are not capable of comprehending why this should cause them to be less afraid.[15] If something *looks scary,* the fact that Mom or Dad is saying "it isn't real" doesn't seem to matter much. Younger children may come to understand that their **parents believe that labeling something "not real" should make it less threatening.** And they do acquire some superficial knowledge about the difference between reality and fantasy. Usually, however, this knowledge is not sufficient to make much difference in processing media images.

To illustrate the young child's difficulty with the concept of reality, I often relate a family incident that occurred when my daughter Erin was 4 years old. My wife, Cheri, wanted to demonstrate that Erin understood the difference between reality and fantasy. As we drove around the neighborhood at Christmastime, Cheri spotted a large plastic statue of Rudolph the Red-Nosed Reindeer. She called the statue to Erin's attention and asked, "Is that Rudolph *real?"* Erin answered promptly, "Of course not, Mom." It certainly appeared as if Cheri had made her point. But, just to make sure, I asked one more question: "Erin, did that Rudolph eat breakfast this morning like you did?" Erin's response was just as prompt as her first one: "Of course, Dad!"

Erin's understanding of the plastic Rudolph is typical of how young children understand their parents upon hearing that certain TV characters are not real. Children may be able to correctly label the character as pretend, but this label does not mean quite the same thing that it does to an adult. For Erin, Rudolph wasn't real, but he still ate breakfast. In the case of the Wicked Witch, young children may say that she's not real, but this doesn't tend to reduce fright reactions because the witch *looks so scary.*

The research on helping children to cope yields a number of practical conclusions. For older children, it may be very helpful to talk about the fact that media productions contain staged scenes for entertainment purposes and that the characters are not real. When the older child shows fright at viewing events that could actually happen, some attempt to work through the low probability of these events in the child's life may be helpful. Researchers refer to this approach as employing cognitive strategies. **Cognitive strategies** encourage children to think about the things they already know and relate those things to the aspects of the movie that are scary. A few years ago, a professor of chemistry at my university phoned me to seek my advice on how to handle the fears of his 10-year-old son. Apparently, his son had seen some doomsday preaching on a religious channel and had become terrified of the idea that the world would end very soon. This kind of fear—fear that something seen on TV might actually happen—is very typical for a child of this age. My advice was to tell the child two things simultaneously. First, I advised that whenever the child vocalized his fear, the parent should tell him matter-of-factly that the world was not going to end soon. Second, I advised that the child be reminded of how many days had passed since the last conversation without the world ending. Gradually, I predicted that the fear would diminish as the boy came to understand through his own experience that the world was unlikely to end very soon. That's exactly what happened. It isn't clear from the excerpts included earlier in this chapter, but most of the students who reported being scared by a paranormal depiction also noted that their fears diminished over time.

For younger children, the best strategy in coping with media-induced fears is to prevent them in the first place. To do this, parents need to heed the research findings. Hollywood is of little help here. In fact, movie advertising can be very misleading when it comes to children's fright reactions. Many of the films that carry a "G" rating and promise "family entertainment" are also films that feature characters who look very scary. Unfortunately, unwitting parents who strive to treat their young child to a movie often find that the only thing they have succeeded in doing is scaring the child. My own daughter expressed fear of the Jabberwocky in *Alice in Wonderland*—one of *Showtime*'s special Fairy Tale productions that targeted an audience of children. The research data reveal hundreds of reports from parents about scenes and characters from "family"-oriented films that scared their children. Many of these scenes are from animated classics produced by none other than the Disney studios. The key thing for parents to think about in avoiding this kind of entertainment for their young child (especially in the 2–5 age range) is *how the characters look*. Even slight variations in normal appearances (e.g., long fingernails, beady eyes, or sharp teeth) can be enough to trigger a fear reaction. Of course, parents also need to know their own children. Some kids are much more sensitive to these visual features than others. There is no substitute for spending time with a child during viewing in order to become more familiar with how emotional reactions are likely to vary.

If a young child does become scared of something seen on TV or in a movie, parents should not hesitate to turn the set off at the first sign of trouble.

As logical as this advice is, some parents become convinced that their children need to continue to watch the program in order to "conquer" their fear. But there is no research evidence to support such behavior. And it is probably better to avoid extensive discussions with a very young child about the frightening show. It is better to cuddle the child and distract him or her from the program by reading a book or playing a game. Consistent with the young child's tendency to process things perceptually, there may be some truth to the maxim "out of sight—out of mind." Researchers summarize this type of strategy with the young child as a non-cognitive strategy. **Non-cognitive strategies** refrain from trying to encourage the child to think about the source of their fear. They work instead to distract the child or avoid the object of fear altogether.

IS IT FUN TO BE SCARED?

Although the research reveals that many people regret having seen certain scenes in TV shows or movies and suffer long-term fright reactions, this is hardly the complete picture. In nearly every study conducted in which people are asked if they like to watch this type of media, the distribution of responses is similar. Roughly one-third of respondents report that they do not enjoy this kind of entertainment and will avoid it at any cost. Another one-third report that they enjoy this kind of entertainment and actively seek it out. The last group of people report that "it depends" on the content. There are certain themes that they find enjoyable and other themes that they can't take very well.[16]

Frightening Films and Roller-Coaster Rides

Researchers were intrigued by the findings on enjoyment of frightening films. *Fear is a negative emotion.* A person who feels scared is a person who is experiencing a negative feeling. Fear, by definition, is unpleasant. How can it be that people experience frightening films as enjoyable?

Actually, there are several possible answers to this question. One answer comes from Dolf Zillmann's **theory of excitation transfer,**[17] which you encountered in the last chapter. Zillmann's idea is that when people become scared while watching a movie, their entire arousal system kicks into high gear. Heart rate and blood pressure increase, as do muscle tension and other physiological indicators. During the movie, the arousal helps to intensify the negative emotion of fear. But what about after the movie is over? Recall from the last chapter that physiological arousal normally does not return to baseline levels very quickly. The arousal lingers for a while. But the fear that people experience while viewing is usually replaced with feelings of relief and even joy. The threatening scenes are over and the film's protagonist may have emerged victorious. So a person may leave the film feeling a positive emotion. Because physiological arousal intensifies any emotion that a person feels, this positive emotion at the end of the film can be very intense. There is usually a high level of arousal left over from the fright. The end result is that even a mild feeling of relief that the film is over can be experienced as a kind of euphoria. A person may leave the frightening film feeling elated—even though during the film, the only feeling was terror. Over the long run, instead of remembering the terror, a person tends to remember the last feeling experienced—euphoria.

The dynamics of excitation transfer that may take place in a scary movie are similar to what may happen during a roller-coaster ride. A person may not actually enjoy the feeling that results from thinking about the possibility that the coaster will fall from the track and plunge the riders to their deaths. But after the ride is over, the arousal generated during the terror transfers to feelings of relief and creates a kind of euphoria. There is solid evidence for the process of excitation transfer while people are viewing films.[18] And so, it may be that people don't really like feeling scared, but they do like the feeling of euphoria that follows. As in the case of roller coasters, not everyone experiences scary movies the same way. For some, the terror of the ride outweighs any feelings of relief that follow. But for others, the transfer of arousal to a feeling of relief provides an experience that outweighs the terror. Of great interest to researchers is the fact that there is a relationship between the enjoyment of scary movies and the tendency to enjoy roller coasters. People who enjoy one also tend to report that they enjoy the other.

The Sexual Dynamic in Viewing Frightening Films

One research finding that emerges over and over again is that males enjoy scary movies much more than females do. Why might this be so? According to Zillmann, it might have something to do with the ancient tribal practice of male initiation rites. For thousands of years, society has socialized males to conquer threatening stimuli and act as the protector. Modern society has discontinued this practice, but strong remnants remain. Fraternity hazing on college campuses is a constant problem. Viewed from the perspective of the tribal initiation rite, it is no wonder that colleges have been unable to eliminate this practice. College administrators are attempting to buck several thousand years of male socialization. Zillmann believes that scary movies may also serve as an informal replacement of the ancient initiation right. Males can test their masculinity by exposing themselves to the most horrible images that Stephen King can dream up. If they are able to emerge from the theater victorious, they have proved their masculinity once and for all. According to Zillmann, females also participate in this rite. By withholding affection to the males who are not able to conquer the film's threatening images, females help to contribute to the ongoing socialization pattern. Females also participate in the rite by displaying the appropriate signs of discomfort and their need for protection during a scary film. This idea is sometimes referred to as **gender role socialization.**

In order to test his idea, Zillmann and his colleagues carried out a fascinating experiment. Females who participated in the study believed that their viewing partner was just a random male participant in the study. Actually, the male participant was one of the experimenters. During the movie, the male engaged in certain behaviors that the experimenters described as either "conquering" or "escapist." For half of the female participants, the male exhibited only "conquering" behaviors. He commented on how silly the film was and how it wouldn't scare anyone. For the other half of the female participants, the male exhibited "escapist" behaviors. He placed his hands over his eyes at the scary parts of the film. He commented on how he wished the film would end soon. At the end of the experiment, the females rated their male viewing partner on attractiveness. Can you guess what happened? Females rated the male as being very attractive when he expressed conquering behaviors. When he expressed escapist behaviors, they rated him as unattractive.

The researchers repeated this same experiment on male participants using a female experimenter. The results in this case were completely opposite to the ones for the females. Males found the female more attractive when she displayed the classic fear response indicating that she wanted to escape. Males rated the female very unattractive when she showed conquering behaviors. There was one very interesting limitation to the experimental results. The pattern of findings only emerged for people who were ordinary in terms of physical attractiveness. Opposite-sex viewing partners still found those rare males and females who were judged to be gorgeous by their peers to be attractive, regardless of how they responded to the frightening film. The results of this study show that enjoyment of frightening films may reflect deeply ingrained socialized sex roles.

BEYOND FEAR: OTHER EMOTIONAL REACTIONS TO MEDIA

The possibility of feeling euphoric after a frightening movie or of feeling attracted to a viewing partner illustrate only a couple of specific emotional reactions among many that might occur when people use media. During the last two decades, more studies have been published on human emotion than were probably published in the entire century up to that point. As a result, many theoretical ideas about emotion have been tested in the context of media and have helped scholars to understand the different ways that our feelings are inextricably tied to the media we consume. Before concluding this chapter, let's consider just a few of the important ideas about emotion and the media that have helped to shape the way scholars now understand this topic.

Empathy: I Feel What You Feel

If you have ever watched U.S. television coverage of the Olympic games, you'll have no trouble recalling what has now become a familiar pattern in the way the networks put together a typical segment. Just before presenting the culminating event in a particular sport, the coverage will focus on a specific athlete's personal struggle to reach what is now the climactic moment of his or her career—or even his or her life. After learning about what the athlete has gone through to

---

STUDY BOX 7-2   Empathic Responses to Media

In a study designed to test the notion of empathy in the media context, Dolf Zillmann and Joanne Cantor wanted to see if the empathic process took place even in children. They were able to test this idea with third-grade boys and girls. Using different films, the researchers created two conditions. In one, they presented a child who was very nice in interacting with his friend, his pet, and his brother. In the second condition, they presented a child who acted in just the opposite way. After establishing that children who viewed these films expressed liking for the nice child and dislike for the mean one, the researchers presented different endings to the two scenarios. In a happy-ending film, the child received a new bicycle and was shown in a state of glee; the sad ending showed the child getting onto an old bicycle and having an accident. The camera focused on the child's face, which cringed with pain. The researchers watched the facial expressions of the children who viewed these films and also interviewed them afterwards.

What did the results show? If children viewed the film about the nice child who expressed glee at the film's conclusion, they also reported that they felt gleeful. Upon viewing the nice child who ended up in pain, emotional reactions were quite the opposite—the children felt sad and pained as well. In short, children empathized with the nice child and took on his feelings whether they were positive or negative.

Also of interest were the responses of children who watched the mean child. Their emotional reactions might be described as *anti*-empathic. When the mean child showed glee at receiving a new bike, the children felt bad. On the other hand, when the mean child was shown in pain after crashing his old bike, children felt a great sense of satisfaction. This study suggests that feelings of empathy apply across a wide range of emotions and are seen even in very young viewers.

SOURCE: Zillmann, D., & Cantor, J. R. (1977). Affective responses to the emotions of a protagonist. *Journal of Experimental Social Psychology, 13,* 155–165.

---

make it to the Olympics, it is difficult for most people to keep themselves from feeling joyful if the person featured is shown smiling in victory with a gold medal hanging around the neck. Alternatively, if the athlete fails and we see feelings of distress and pain etched on his or her face, viewers tend to experience a profound sense of disappointment. The process that occurs in both cases can be described as **empathy**—the tendency for viewers to feel the same feelings as the person they are watching on TV. One important thing to notice about the process of empathy is that viewers can experience virtually *any emotion* as a result of consuming media depictions of other people. Empathy is especially likely to occur if you have formed a positive view or bond with the person projected by the media. Once that bond is in place, whatever the media character feels, the tendency will be strong for viewers to feel the same thing. Is there any evidence that this sort of process actually takes place? You can probably think of examples from your own viewing experiences that confirm this kind of empathic process. It should come as no surprise, then, to discover that the process has been documented systematically in the research laboratory (see Study Box 7-2).

Using Media to Manage Your Mood

Have you ever found that you weren't "in the mood" to go to a particular type of movie or watch a particular TV show? According to Dolf Zillmann's **theory of mood management**, this experience is not only common—it is quite predictable.[19] According to the theory, our entertainment choices are often a function of how we're feeling at the present moment and how we anticipate that exposure to certain media content is likely to make us feel during and following that exposure. One proposition from this theory is that when people find their emotions to be at a low ebb, they will make entertainment choices designed to lift their spirits. This proposition has been tested with female viewers in a most interesting fashion. Jean Meadowcroft and Dolf Zillmann asked women to indicate their viewing preferences for different types of TV programs at the time that they completed a questionnaire. In addition to the women's viewing preferences, the researchers also were able to gather information on exactly where the women were in their monthly menstrual cycles. Although this might seem like an odd piece of data to gather in a study of media preferences, there was actually a very good reason for getting this information. The chemistry of the menstrual cycle is well documented. When women experience a premenstrual syndrome, levels of progesterone and estrogen take a precipitous drop. These chemical changes typically trigger emotional changes as well—often leading to feelings of bad moods and even depression. In contrast, when women are in the middle of their cycles, progesterone and estrogen are high and typically accompanied by more positive mood states.

When the researchers examined their data, they discovered a systematic difference in the program preferences of the women in their sample. The women who were at the premenstrual point in their cycle and presumably experiencing lower moods were much more likely to report a preference for watching situation comedies. Women who were in the middle of their cycles, presumably having no bad moods to manage, tended to prefer dramas over situation comedies.[20] The findings of this study were essentially replicated by other researchers who studied women during and after pregnancy, when these same hormones vary in the body. Once again, women with low levels of the hormones who felt more depressed expressed a strong preference for watching comedies.[21]

Does Mediated Emotion Disrupt
and Confuse Our Emotional Well-Being?

So far, this chapter has outlined both negative and positive emotions that people experience from media exposure. Although some types of media can terrify viewers, other types can induce positive moods and even move people to experience euphoria. As we've seen, people seem to deliberately use the media to manage their emotional states. Nevertheless, some lines of analysis suggest that the most profound effects of electronic media on human emotion may be more disturbing than helpful. A woman who lives in my local community

(Dr. Sally Miller) is well known for her work with people who are grieving the loss of a loved one. One of the problems that she frequently confronts is the expectation that media messages often convey about how quickly people deal with the emotional trauma of a loss. She points out that just 24 hours after the attacks on September 11, 2001, some media commentators were already referring to people who had "started the recovery process." Miller found such phrases to be incredibly inappropriate—almost ludicrous. First, Miller points out that people who lose loved ones don't really ever "recover" from their loss. Instead, they find ways to deal with it. Second, she notes that people who lose someone have rarely even begun to comprehend the reality of their loss during the first 24 hours. They are still in a state of shock. They haven't even had time to begin grieving.

I find Miller's observations very interesting in the light of speculations from Dolf Zillmann about what modern media may be doing to our emotions. Consider the following provocative comments from an essay that Zillmann wrote in 1991:

> ... [T]he pace that characterizes contemporary audiovisual storytelling and reporting is likely to produce affective confusion and shallowness in both children and adults. ... The rapid pacing of affect-inducing effects in modern media presentations, then, appears to minimize affective and, especially, empathetic reactions (a) by preventing the complete unfolding of the response because distracting, competing information is provided too soon after the elicitation of affect; and (b) by creating affective confusions through the intensification (by excitation-transfer) of subsequent, potentially non-empathetic affect. Empathetic reactions, in short, are often deprived of their inherent intensity, while other reactions are often artificially intensified.[22]

Zillmann seems to be suggesting that by depicting a wide range of human emotional reactions over such a fast-paced medium like TV, new technology may disrupt and confuse the human tendency to experience emotions more slowly in a process that gradually unfolds over a longer period of time. When excitation transfer processes are also considered, things can really get quite confusing. A viewer may find that a more minor emotional reaction to a depicted event is intensified by arousal left over from a preceding emotional reaction just a few minutes earlier. The emerging picture of our emotions when we are subjected to a stream of TV images is that we run through different affective states at highly artificial speeds and often get confused about which emotions we initially reacted to with greatest intensity. Moreover, this mediated world of emotions may be increasingly the one we're turning to as a source for learning how we ought to respond emotionally to the events all around us. Is it possible that the media may be conditioning us not to linger too long in any one emotional state? Could this be one reason why Dr. Sally Miller observes such a preoccupation in our culture with "getting over" the loss of a loved one? These sorts of questions about media impact may ultimately be difficult to test. Nevertheless, they may be extremely important ones for researchers to address in future studies.

SUMMARY

In this chapter, you have seen some facets of the research on frightening media and on media that induce other emotional reactions. One thing that emerges clearly is that paranormal themes are often front and center when fear reactions occur. Although the emotional effects of this type of media are not nearly as sensational as the effects of media violence, these effects may be far more common. For children, the research shows that there is a wide range of material capable of inducing emotional upset at various points in the child's development. For young children 2 to 5 years old, animated features hold the potential to terrify. For older children and even for adults, fictional violence represented in a realistic fashion or themes of the paranormal may be emotionally disturbing. News reports of war, famine, and other disasters may be distressing as well. By focusing on the research in this area, you should be a little better prepared to manage these emotional reactions in children entrusted to your care.

It would be too simplistic, though, to dismiss frightening films by focusing only on their capacity to induce negative emotions. As Zillmann's research shows, these films may be popular for good reason. They help to reinforce important patterns of socialization. It is also possible that, in some cases, a person experiences a frightening film therapeutically. The viewer is able to compare real-life circumstances favorably with the dread and horror in the lives of the film characters. Although there is less research to substantiate this point, this possibility certainly seems reasonable.

In concluding these thoughts about frightening media, I would call attention to the fact that the MPAA movie ratings and the new system for TV ratings are terribly vague when it comes to warning parents about frightening content. The wise consumer realizes that a movie like *The Sixth Sense* is going to be potentially frightening to children. But fewer people may realize that Walt Disney's *101 Dalmatians* may also be upsetting to preschoolers. One reason to call attention to the research studies on children is to let Hollywood know that it is time for the industry to create program and movie labeling that draws directly from the academic research. The vast majority of parents want a more specific labeling system that gives information about the specific content. Researchers agree that this seems like the best approach. Now the message has to get through to those people in Hollywood who can do something about it.

Finally, this chapter encourages you to think about emotional reactions other than fear. The media present a rich, fast-paced tapestry of characters who experience a wide range of emotional reactions and, through empathy processes, induce various emotions in viewers. This sort of entertainment is unprecedented in the history of the human race. Perhaps the ways in which we are expected to respond emotionally are being shaped daily by our media experiences.

KEY TERMS AND CONCEPTS

Paranormal media content 128

Developmental theory 129

Perceptual thought versus conceptual or abstract thought 129

Reality and fantasy 137

The meaning of "real" from a child's perspective 137

Cognitive and non-cognitive strategies 138, 139

Theory of excitation transfer 139

Gender role socialization 140

Empathy 142

Theory of mood management 143

To learn more about the topics in this chapter, enter the Key Terms and Concepts found in this chapter as subject and keyword searches on your InfoTrac® College Edition.

NOTES

1. The term *paranormal* has been defined in many ways in the scholarly literature. I use it here to refer to events that clearly violate the known laws of nature. Such events might include extrasensory perception (ESP), astrological forecasts, prophetic dreams, psychic detectives, space aliens, UFOs from outer space, palm reading, astral projection, psychokinesis (moving objects just by thinking about them), and so forth.

2. Bozzuto, J. C. (1975). Cinematic neurosis following "The Exorcist." *Journal of Nervous and Mental Disease, 161,* 43–48.

3. Blumer, H. (1933). *Movies and conduct.* New York: Macmillan.

4. Himmelweit, H. T., Oppenheim, A. N., & Vince, P. (1958). *Television and the child.* London: Oxford University Press.

5. Cantor, J. (1994). Fright reactions to mass media. In J. Bryant & D. Zillmann (Eds.), *Media effects: Advances in theory and research* (pp. 213–245). Hillsdale, NJ: Erlbaum.

6. Palmer, E. L., Hockett, A. B., & Dean, W. W. (1983). The television family and children's fright reactions. *Journal of Family Issues, 4,* 279–292.

7. Cantor, J., & Sparks, G. G. (1984). Children's fear responses to mass media: Testing some Piagetian predictions. *Journal of Communication, 34*(2), 90–103.

8. Flavell, J. (1963). *The developmental psychology of Jean Piaget.* New York: Van Nostrand.

9. Sparks, G. G., & Cantor, J. (1986). Developmental differences in fright responses to a television program depicting a character transformation. *Journal of Broadcasting and Electronic Media, 30,* 309–323.

10. Cantor, J. (1998). *"Mommy, I'm scared": How TV and movies frighten children and what we can do to protect them.* San Diego, CA: Harcourt Brace.

11. Sparks, G. G. (1997). Unpublished raw data.

12. Sparks, G. G., Nelson, C. L., & Campbell, R. G. (1997). The relationship between exposure to televised messages about paranormal phenomena and paranormal beliefs. *Journal of Broadcasting & Electronic Media, 41,* 345–359.

13. For years, the Committee for the Scientific Investigation of Claims of the

Paranormal (CSICOP) has published *Skeptical Inquirer,* a journal devoted to scientific skepticism concerning paranormal claims. CSICOP often takes the media to task for exploiting paranormal themes in order to make a profit. Rarely, however, has the committee considered the fright potential of paranormal depictions.

14. Cantor, J., & Wilson, B. J. (1984). Modifying fear responses to mass media in preschool and elementary school children. *Journal of Broadcasting, 28,* 431–443.

15. Wilson, B. J., & Cantor, J. (1987). Reducing children's fear reactions to mass media: Effects of visual exposure and verbal explanation. In M. L. McLaughlin (Ed.), *Communication yearbook 10* (pp. 553–573). Newbury Park, CA: Sage.

16. Sparks, G. G. (1986). Developmental differences in children's reports of fear induced by the mass media. *Child Study Journal, 16,* 55–66.

17. Zillmann, D. (1980). Anatomy of suspense. In P. H. Tannenbaum (Ed.), *The entertainment functions of television* (pp. 133–163). Hillsdale, NJ: Erlbaum.

18. Sparks, G. G. (1991). The relationship between distress and delight in males' and females' reactions to frightening films. *Human Communication Research, 17,* 625–637.

19. Zillmann, D. (1988). Mood management: Using entertainment to full advantage. In L. Donohew, H. E. Sypher, & E. T. Higgins (Eds.), *Communication, social cognition, and affect* (pp. 147–171). Hillsdale, NJ: Erlbaum.

20. Meadowcroft, J., & Zillmann, D. (1984, August). *The influence of hormonal fluctuations on women's selection and enjoyment of television programs.* Paper presented at the meeting of the Association for Education in Journalism and Mass Communication, Gainesville, Florida.

21. Helregel, B. K., & Weaver, J. B. (1989). Mood-management during pregnancy through selective exposure to television. *Journal of Broadcasting & Electronic Media, 33,* 15–33.

22. Zillmann, D. (1991). Empathy: Affect from bearing witness to the emotions of others. In J. Bryant & D. Zillmann (Eds.), *Responding to the screen: Reception and reaction processes* (pp. 135–167). Hillsdale, NJ: Erlbaum.

8

■

Persuasive Effects
of the Media

WHAT IS PERSUASION?

What does it mean to say that the media have persuasive power? Scholars have identified at least three dimensions of **persuasion** that help to answer this question. First, when you are persuaded, there is a change in your **attitude.** You feel differently about something as a result of being exposed to some message. I can remember a conversation with my older brother several years ago in which he told me that he had changed his attitude about smoking cigarettes. He no longer felt very good about his smoking habit and had resolved to change it. When I checked back with him a few months later, I discovered that he was still expressing this new attitude. Unfortunately, he was still smoking just as much as he did before he adopted his new attitude. This helps to illustrate the fact that a change in attitude is only part of what is involved in persuasion.

In addition to attitude change, significant persuasion also results in changes of **behavior.** It wasn't until my brother actually started to alter his smoking behavior that I became convinced that he had been persuaded by antismoking messages. A few weeks after he started smoking less, he found the new behavior to be very difficult to maintain. Nicotine has addictive properties, and, as almost any smoker will testify, the habit is not easily broken. After battling the urge to smoke for months, my brother finally kicked the habit. He hasn't smoked in over a decade. Truly significant persuasion results in behavior that **persists over time.** Together, these three features (attitude change, behavior change, and **persistent change**) help to define what we mean by persuasion.

As you read in chapter 3, the history of media effects research revolves around the idea that media messages exert persuasive influence on people. In this chapter, we will explore the basis for this assumption in more detail. Are the media really persuasive?

HOW MEDIA MESSAGES
PERSUADE WITHOUT EVEN TRYING

Although we usually think of persuasion as an intentional action on the part of a "persuader," it is quite possible to persuade someone to change an attitude or behavior without even consciously trying to do so. In fact, numerous examples seem to show that people are often persuaded by media messages that weren't even designed explicitly to change attitudes or behavior. A high proportion of media messages are designed to entertain. Over the years, scholars have learned that these entertainment messages can exert a powerful influence on attitude and behavior. Let's take a brief look at some of these examples.

One well-documented example of media influence that was purely unintended occurred when "the Fonz" applied for a library card in an episode of the popular sitcom *Happy Days*. In the weeks following this episode, libraries around the country reported a 500% increase in library card applications.[1] Apparently, children and young adolescents who admired the Fonz were motivated to copy his behavior and get a library card for themselves. There was no persuasive ploy featured in the *Happy Days* episode; the producers of the program had no idea that this scene would trigger a surge in library card applications.

Another example of unintended media influence involved the controversial 1983 broadcast by the ABC-TV network, *The Day After*. This movie depicted the aftermath of a nuclear war in the United States. Once again, the movie was designed primarily for entertainment purposes, not persuasion. But two researchers discovered that exposure to the movie was sufficient to change attitudes about the seriousness of nuclear war. People who watched the movie were especially likely to change their attitudes and express the view that nuclear war was a critical concern. They also expressed their intent to take some action to help prevent nuclear war.[2]

More recently, during the summer of 2004, researchers in England decided to investigate the impact of the movie *The Day After Tomorrow* while it was playing commercially in movie theaters. The film depicts a scenario in which global warming ultimately produces another ice age over just a few days. The film shows such disasters as a major tidal wave plowing into New York City. Interviews were conducted with movie patrons either before or after seeing the movie and their responses compared. The researchers reported that those questioned after seeing the film were willing to give 50% more money toward efforts to mitigate changes in climate. At the same time that exposure to the film sensitized people to the importance of the climate issue, it also produced less realistic expectations about the climatic effects that scientists had actually predicted for England. The researchers wondered whether this type of movie portrayal could be made more accurate while simultaneously maintaining its appeal with audiences seeking suspenseful and dramatic entertainment.[3]

The persuasive impact of *Happy Days* and *The Day After* was not very controversial. Few people could get upset about children wanting library cards or people wanting to do something to curb the risk of nuclear war. Occasionally, however, the impact of entertainment media is not so positive. Consider the well-known case of the CBS movie *Cry Rape*. As social psychologist Elliot Aronson describes the situation, this movie depicted a rape victim who discovered that pressing charges against her rapist could result in an ugly ordeal that only prolonged a rape victim's suffering.[4] In the weeks following the broadcast of the movie, actual rape reports to law enforcement authorities decreased significantly. Apparently, viewers were persuaded by the nature of the rape victim's experience in the film and learned the lesson of the high cost of pressing charges.

What can we learn from these examples of persuasion that occurred in the context of entertainment programs? Think about the last time you went to a movie or watched your favorite TV program. The chances are good that, as you sat back in your seat to relax, you were not preparing to process a persuasive message. As psychologists have studied the persuasion process, they have discovered that ordinarily people approach a persuasive situation with their defenses up. Richard Petty and John Cacioppo describe this situation in their **elaboration likelihood model** of persuasion. According to them, there are two main routes by which people might be persuaded. One of these is called the **central route to persuasion.** The central route is a highly rational or cognitive route to persuasion. People scrutinize the message carefully and tend to think up many counterarguments that the persuader must defeat in order to be successful.[5] This route to persuasion is especially likely if people know that the message they will hear is **counter-attitudinal** (i.e., different from the position they hold themselves). Persuasion through the central route is more difficult for the would-be persuader to achieve. Whenever a salesperson calls me on the telephone, I find that I am ready to resist the message no matter how good it sounds. I am motivated to think up one counterargument after another. If the salesperson is persistent, I may just decide to say goodbye and hang up the phone. But when I sit down to watch a movie or TV show, I am not planning on having to do a careful analysis of a persuasive message. In the entertainment context, all sorts of messages can get through my normally strong defense system and exert their influence. Persuasion that takes place with less careful scrutiny of the message is referred to by Petty and Cacioppo as **peripheral-route persuasion.** In persuasion by the peripheral route, certain cues in the message lead people to accept the persuasive proposition with little cognitive thought or scrutiny. When people are persuaded while watching movies and programs that are designed to entertain, any influence that occurs is likely to be peripheral-route influence. From the perspective of advertisers who attempt to use the media to sell their products, the biggest obstacle to success is the fact that people recognize a TV commercial or a magazine ad as an attempt to influence attitude or behavior. This recognition can trigger central-route processing, which is a more difficult path to influence.

This may be one reason that many advertisers use creative ways to entertain their audience rather than using a strong persuasive appeal. If people process an ad as another entertaining bit of media, they may be more willing to change their attitudes or behaviors with little thought or scrutiny instead of carefully weighing the relative advantages of a particular product. Perhaps this helps to explain why advertisers were willing to pay over $75,000 per *second* for an ad in the 2001 Super Bowl game. Over the years, people have become accustomed to processing the ads during this game as entertainment instead of persuasion. Advertisers may realize that this state of affairs is very favorable for their purposes—which, ultimately, are persuasive.

The Theory of Media Cultivation:
Cultivating Attitudes Is Attitude Change

The idea that consumption of entertainment media can change people's attitudes is an idea that has been formalized in one of the major theoretical perspectives of mass communication. George Gerbner's **theory of media cultivation** does not use the term *persuade* to describe the impact of media, and his theory is often treated in the context of discussions of media violence or media stereotypes. Nevertheless, the theory is all about the cultivation of attitudes, which is, after all, another way of talking about attitude change. According to Gerbner, the cultivation process is gradual and cumulative. Many people tend to think of persuasion in terms of a direct response to a single message. This is one reason that Gerbner's theory is not typically presented in the context of persuasion. In reality, Gerbner's perspective actually fits very well into a discussion about the media and persuasion. According to Gerbner, the world of media entertainment presents a particular view of **social reality.** For example, content analyses of prime-time TV programs reveal that about 12% of the male characters who hold jobs work in law enforcement. This proportion is a gross exaggeration; in reality, only about 1% of employed males hold jobs in the general area of law enforcement.[6]

What happens to the person who makes a steady habit of watching prime-time TV? According to Gerbner, this person gradually becomes "cultivated" into the television view of social reality. Even though there is no particular intent on the part of the creators of the media messages to change attitudes or beliefs, over time, the heavy viewer will begin to believe that the real world resembles the world presented in the media. According to Gerbner, the heavy TV viewer tends to believe that the world is a more violent place than it really is. Accordingly, heavy TV viewers are more likely to express **fear of criminal victimization** and to overestimate their own chances of being involved in violence. While the theory of media cultivation emphasizes gradual changes in beliefs and attitudes, some of Gerbner's studies show behavior changes as well. According to some of the results, heavy TV viewers are more likely to purchase home security devices because of their beliefs in the high probability of criminal victimization. Gerbner summarizes his view in the following way:

> The repetitive "lessons" we learn from television, beginning with infancy, are likely to become the basis for a broader world view, making television a significant source of general values, ideologies, and perspectives as well as

specific assumptions, beliefs, and images. . . . One example of this is what we have called the "mean world" syndrome. . . . [W]e have found that long-term exposure to television, in which frequent violence is virtually inescapable, tends to cultivate the image of a relatively mean and danger-ous world. Responses of heavier compared to matching groups of lighter viewers suggest the conception of reality in which greater protection is needed, most people "cannot be trusted," and most people are "just look-ing out for themselves."[7]

Gerbner and his colleagues believe that they have uncovered evidence in several studies for two processes that show evidence of media cultivation. The first process, **mainstreaming,** refers to what happens when people of differ-ent groups are exposed to the same media. Over time, Gerbner believes that the differences that might be expected on the basis of group membership become less pronounced because everyone is being similarly cultivated by media messages. The second process, **resonance,** refers to what happens when a person's real-life environment strongly resembles the environment depicted in the media. Such a person receives a "double dose" of the same message, making the impact of media cultivation particularly likely. For example, a per-son who lives in a high-crime neighborhood might naturally fear criminal vic-timization. If that person also consumes heavy doses of the violent world of TV, the cultivating effect of the media would be particularly powerful because the message is already consistent with the person's real-world experience.

Gerbner's theory of cultivation has certainly had its critics over the years. One of the major constraints that causes reservation among media scholars is that the theory describes processes that seem to defy conclusive testing. Gerbner maintains that the process of media cultivation occurs gradually over time. Consequently, laboratory experiments, which by their very nature observe changes over short time intervals, are not able to shed any light on the process. Unfortunately, this leaves the survey method as the only major methodological tool for testing the theory. As you know from chapter 2, the survey method is limited in its ability to document causal relationships with certainty. Typically, evidence for media cultivation is presented with positive correlation coefficients between TV exposure and some particular belief about the world. As you will see in the following example, such correlations are difficult to interpret unequivocally as evidence of a causal process.

In an effort to explore the evidence in favor of media cultivation, two researchers, Anthony Doob and Glenn Macdonald, conducted a survey in the city of Toronto.[8] When they examined their data, they found the same basic relationship between TV exposure and fear of criminal victimization that Gerbner had found in many of his studies. The relationship was positive and statistically significant, showing that heavy TV viewers were more likely to fear being the victim of a crime. Whereas Gerbner tends to interpret such a relationship as evidence for media cultivation (viewing TV causes fear of vic-timization), Doob and Macdonald wondered whether the relationship wasn't due to a variable that Gerbner had ignored in previous studies: level of crime in a person's neighborhood. They reasoned that people who live in high-crime neighborhoods might naturally fear criminal victimization because crime is indeed a high risk. Moreover, they thought that such people might also tend to stay inside their homes more than people who live in safer places. As a result, the people in high-crime neighborhoods might naturally tend to watch more TV. According to this scenario, the correlation observed by Gerbner between TV viewing and fear of victimization might not be the result of a cultivation effect. Instead, it might result from the fact that both of these variables are simultaneously affected by the level of crime in one's neighborhood. When Doob and Macdonald divided the city of Toronto into four areas (high- versus low-crime areas in both the city and its suburbs), they found that the relationship between TV viewing and fear of victimization was no longer present in three of the four areas. They interpreted this result as evidence in favor of the role of the neighborhood variable and against the media cultivation hypothesis. Gerbner might interpret the same result as evidence for the resonance hypothesis. As it turned out, in the high-crime area of the city, there was still a significant relationship between TV viewing and fear of victimization. This is exactly where Gerbner would expect the strongest relationship to exist between the two variables, as a result of the double dose of the message received by residents of this type of neighborhood.

Over the past few decades, Gerbner and his colleagues have produced enough data to keep the theory of media cultivation alive and well. Most researchers do give some credence to the idea that media messages unintentionally exert an influence on the attitudes and beliefs that people hold about the real world.

Do Media Messages About the
Paranormal Influence Paranormal Beliefs?

In the previous chapter, you read about the research on frightening mass media and the intense emotional effects that scary films have on children and adults. I was personally involved in conducting many of these studies. After a number of years, I started paying more attention to the actual content of the movies that people reported as scary. One of the themes noted in the chapter 7 discussion was that many scary movies have paranormal content. Depictions of the paranormal might include ghosts, witches, devils, psychics, extrasensory perception (ESP), UFOs and space aliens, and people who claim they can talk to the dead. I became interested in the question of whether or not these depictions, quite apart from their capacity to scare people, could change people's beliefs. Are you more inclined to believe in the existence of space aliens after watching a movie like *Close Encounters of the Third Kind*? Just as Gerbner was concerned about the possibility that media messages might cultivate beliefs about the level of crime in the real world, I became concerned about the possibility that media depictions of the paranormal might cultivate beliefs about the existence of a paranormal world. Once again, just as in the case of media cultivation, this type of persuasion is not necessarily intentional on the part of the media source—but the persuasive effect might be a very important one to understand.

In order to study this possibility, I began with a very simple experiment.[9] College students were randomly assigned to watch a 30-minute episode of the program *Beyond Reality*. This episode depicted people who could "astral-project" themselves to different locations. What is astral projection? According to those who practice it, it is the ability to leave one's body through deep meditation or a drug-induced state and transport one's spiritual essence to some other location in the universe. The city of Indianapolis has an institute where one can pay hundreds of dollars to learn how to master this incredible skill. (My personal advice would be to save your money.) I was interested in whether or not seeing such behavior depicted in a fictional, entertainment program would affect what people believe about the reality of astral projection.

When the USA network aired this episode, they started it off with an announcer's voice and a brief tag that said, "The following incidents are based on actual reports." In my experiment, I decided to assign the students to watch the program in one of four conditions. In the first condition, the "reality" condition, I included a tag that emphasized the fact that the actors and actresses in the show were fictitious, but that the events shown were based on actual reports and were real. In the second condition, the "fiction" condition, the preliminary tag emphasized that the events were completely fictitious. In the third condition, the "impossible" condition, the tag emphasized that the events were completely fictitious and also impossible from a scientific perspective. It included a statement that events like this had never actually happened and that if they had happened, it would violate the known laws of nature. In a fourth condition, the "no tag" condition, the students watched the program without any tag at all. Finally, in a control group condition, some students watched an episode of the situation comedy *Perfect Strangers,* which had no references to any paranormal phenomenon.

A few weeks before the students watched the program, I measured the extent to which they believed in astral projection and other paranormal activities. After the program was over, I once again measured these beliefs to see if there was any change. Of course, in order to be careful about tipping the students off to what I was studying, I took steps to draw their attention to the fact that I was not very interested in their reactions to the program. Instead, students were led to believe that I was really interested in what they thought about the commercials in the program. At the very end of the study, I asked the students what they thought the study was about. The nearly unanimous verdict was that the study was concerned with reactions to advertising. Most students expressed surprise to learn later about the true purpose of the experiment.

What did the results of the study reveal? The major results concerned the students who watched the program with no tag at all and those who watched the program with either the fiction tag or the impossible tag. The students who saw no tag *increased* their beliefs in astral projection over their pre-viewing levels; the students in both of the other two conditions *decreased* their beliefs in astral projection. The difference between the groups was statistically significant ($p < .05$; see chapter 2 for a review of this concept). You might expect that the students who were told that the program was real would have increased their beliefs the most. That's not what happened. In fact, there was a slight decrease in belief in astral projection among these students, although the decrease was not statistically significant. It could be that telling these students that the events were real caused them to wonder about why they had been told this. As they thought about it, they ended up doubting the veracity of the events more than if they had been told nothing at all. This experiment demonstrated that, depending on the information included in a program, viewers' beliefs about a paranormal phenomenon could be affected. I have now completed several studies that investigate the relationship between media depictions of the paranormal and paranormal beliefs.[10] Taken together, these studies show that media messages do exert an influence on what people believe. Depending on the message, people may be persuaded to change their beliefs.

INTENTIONAL PERSUASION IN THE MEDIA

So far in this chapter, we have defined persuasion and seen how it might occur as a result of media exposure to entertainment messages that are not particularly designed to change attitudes and behaviors. One implication of the fact that entertainment messages can persuade unintentionally is that media practitioners could study these instances and learn to master the principles of persuasion so that they could be applied in an intentional way. Clearly, many messages that appear in the media are designed explicitly with persuasion in mind. How well do these messages work? If they do work, what are the theoretical principles behind their success? Let's consider these two questions.

Using Entertainment to Improve Public Health

If a single episode of *Happy Days* can increase library card applications, can entertainment programs be used deliberately to persuade people to adopt behaviors that contribute to their overall health? The answer, based on recent attempts to try this strategy, seems to be "yes." According to Jane Brown and Kim Walsh-Childers, when the entertainment program *Felicity* decided to treat the topic of date rape in a special two-part episode, the producers of the program advertised a telephone number at the end of the show that would connect callers with the rape hotline. Over 1,000 calls were received. Viewer reactions to the program *ER* were also studied after that program showed a victim of date rape being treated with the morning-after pill. Viewer knowledge of this type of contraceptive treatment increased 17% after the show—even though a follow-up study showed that this knowledge may not have persisted for very long.[11]

One problem with using entertainment in a deliberate way to persuade the audience is that these techniques may not always be met with enthusiasm on the part of the creators or the producers. They may tend to view such efforts as interfering with their creative license and ultimately turning entertainment into more advertising. Although these "embedded health messages" will undoubtedly continue to appear in various forms, most future persuasion efforts probably will still be more direct. An advantage of studying embedded messages is that it provides a chance to see persuasion happen in the natural environment. The next section describes an important study that attempted to look at persuasion outside of the typical laboratory setting that most researchers use to study persuasion.

The Great American Values Test

One of the major weaknesses of academic research on media effects is that too many of the studies are conducted in the carefully controlled confines of the laboratory. Although much is learned from this approach about whether certain message features can cause specific effects, there is the inevitable limitation in generalizing the effects to what happens in a more natural environment (see chapter 2). For this reason, three researchers, Sandra Ball-Rokeach, Milton Rokeach, and Joel Grube, decided to break away from the confines of the laboratory to test the persuasive impact of TV in the real-world setting. The findings of their study, the "great American values test," are among some of the most important findings on the persuasive impact of the media.[12] Let's look briefly at what these researchers managed to do.

Back in 1979, the research team was able to produce a 30-minute program designed solely for the purpose of their experiment. The program was cohosted by Ed Asner of the old *Lou Grant* show and Sandy Hill of ABC's *Good Morning America*. The program was structured such that the cohosts presented viewers with national survey results showing that Americans ranked "freedom" very high as a value priority but ranked "equality" quite a bit lower. The first part of the program was designed to encourage viewers to think about both of these values and to consider renewing their commitment to each one. The second part of the program was designed to convince viewers to likewise place high value on the importance of the environment and living in a "world of beauty."

The real master stroke that the researchers were able to pull off in this study came with the broadcast of the program. It aired on the evening of February 27, 1979, at 7:30 P.M. Somehow, the researchers were able to get all three commercial channels in Richland, Pasco, and Kennewick (the Tri-Cities area in eastern Washington State) to air the program at the same time. This essentially guaranteed that if anyone in those cities watched TV during the 7:30–8:00 P.M. time slot, they would be exposed to the persuasive message. At the same time that the program was on in the Tri-Cities, the authors managed to arrange for the show to be totally blacked out in the city of Yakima, a comparable city about 80 miles away. In advance of the program's broadcast, they were also able to promote the show in *TV Guide* and commercial spots that appeared on the stations.

Through a combination of phone calls to randomly selected households in the four cities, follow-up opinion surveys, and mail solicitations from organizations that promoted the values of freedom, equality, and a world of beauty, the researchers were able to determine whether their program had any persuasive impact. The results were nothing short of impressive. On the mail solicitations that were sent out to random recipients in the four cities, significantly more people from the Tri-Cities area donated to the causes than did the people from Yakima, the city where the program was not shown. Of particular interest in the study was a comparison between those people who reported that they watched the program without interruption versus those who never saw the program and those who were interrupted during the program by such events as phone calls or an unexpected visitor. The uninterrupted viewers responded to the mail solicitations with anywhere from four to six times the amount of money contributed by the non-viewers. They gave about nine times as much money as the interrupted viewers. In general, the uninterrupted viewers also changed their value structure so that freedom, equality, and a world of beauty were all elevated as a result of exposure to the program.

Just as laboratory experiments have limitations in terms of generalizing results beyond the experimenter's carefully controlled research situation, natural experiments such as the one conducted by Ball-Rokeach, Rokeach, and Grube are also limited in terms of reaching conclusions about the exact reasons for the results. Perhaps the differences in the amount of money given by the various groups had little to do with the fact that some people were interrupted during the program and others were not. Maybe there was something different about the people who reported interruptions in viewing (for example, living in a busier household) that made it less likely that they would give money to *any* solicitation. Nevertheless, despite the study's limitations, it is clear that the broadcast did exert a powerful influence on the audience. Advertisers probably were not surprised by the results.

How Does an Advertiser Determine Success?

As we attempt to address the question of persuasive effectiveness of the media, it is important to keep in mind that "effectiveness" is a relative term. If you were an advertiser who paid for a 30-second ad on TV, how would you decide if the ad was worth the cost? One criterion that advertisers use is the cost-per-person statistic. Because national TV ads reach millions of people, the cost per person for the ad is often extremely low (just pennies per person), even though the total cost of the ad might be over $1 million. Of course, even if the cost per person is extremely low, the investment would not be worthwhile if no one responded to the ad by purchasing the product. How many purchases need to result from one ad to make the advertising venture worthwhile? When millions of people are in the audience, a very small response rate might still make the ad cost-effective. The point here is that, from the advertising perspective, a relatively small effect can transfer into profits. An ad is often deemed to be an effective example of persuasion when 99% of the audience fails to respond. The 1% who do respond are more than enough to offset the cost of the ad.

Some Evidence for the Effectiveness of Advertising

Having recognized the important point that advertising effectiveness may not always be impressive in terms of the percentage of people who respond to the message, it is still instructive to contemplate some of the impressive results that have been achieved with persuasive campaigns in the media. Years ago, when I taught an advertising class, I invited an executive from an ad agency to be a guest speaker, and he told me that a single-page ad in a large metropolitan newspaper is expected to yield a minimum revenue equal to 10 times the cost of the ad. Thus, if the ad costs $15,000, the department store that runs the ad expects revenues to increase $150,000 over the amount that would have been received if the ad had not appeared. If you're in the advertising business, these figures translate into the realization that newspaper advertising is a powerful persuasive technique.

Many other companies have also realized that media advertising is a powerful choice. A few years ago, the executives of the Northwest Mutual Life Insurance Company discovered that their company had very poor name recognition. In fact, people tended to have better recognition of 33 other insurance company names than of theirs. But after two weeks of advertising on TV, they improved their name recognition so that only two company names were recognized ahead of theirs. It cost the company $1 million to accomplish this feat, but the effort was considered to be cost-efficient.[13]

Advertisers discovered the power of television to increase sales back in the 1950s. That's when the Mattel toy company decided to pour money into a TV ad campaign. The results of that campaign are now legendary. The company increased its value by a factor of about 25![14]

The effectiveness of campaigns like Mattel's raised a number of issues related to children. For the most part, Mattel was advertising to the children in the TV audience. Studies by Charles Atkin reveal that children who are heavy viewers of TV ads are more likely to consume the products in those ads and more likely to ask their parents to buy the products that they see advertised.[15] A political action organization, Action for Children's Television (ACT), actively lobbied Congress for years to prohibit advertising directed to children. Even though the data point clearly to the conclusion that children are heavily influenced by advertising, lawmakers found the proposals from ACT to be unworkable. The Saturday-morning time slot is still an advertising bonanza directed to children. The fact that advertisers continue to pay huge sums of money for their messages should be instructive. Advertising works. It is persuasive. This point was reiterated recently by a team of scholars from the fields of psychology and communication in a report of the American Psychological Association's task force on advertising and children.[16]

SOME KEY PRINCIPLES
OF MEDIA PERSUASION

If media messages are persuasive, what are the key ingredients that contribute to their power? Psychologists have studied the persuasion process scientifically for more than 50 years. As a result of their study, much has been learned about the dynamics of persuasion. Study Box 8-1 on pages 160–161 details some of the common principles of persuasion identified by Robert Cialdini in his classic text on the subject. Let's take a brief look at what the research has discovered about how people change their attitudes and behavior.

The Power of the Source

Back in the 1950s, Carl Hovland and Walter Weiss reported a groundbreaking experiment that is now famous in the annals of persuasion research.[17] In a simple experiment, they exposed people to a persuasive message that argued that atomic-powered submarines were perfectly feasible for future development. At the time they ran the experiment, such submarines were nonexistent and little more than a fanciful dream. It might be similar to arguing today for the feasibility of establishing a city on Mars or for the feasibility of traveling back in time. Hovland and Weiss set up the experiment so that some of the participants received the message from the official newspaper of the Communist Party, *Pravda*. The rest of the participants received the message from J. Robert Oppenheimer, a well-known and well-respected atomic physicist. Prior to the experiment, the participants indicated their opinions on this topic. After they read the message, they indicated their opinions once again. You can probably guess which group of participants was more persuaded about the feasibility of atomic-powered subs. The participants who heard the message from Oppenheimer were much more likely to change their view. Why? As it turns out, the key reason has to do with the **credibility** of the source. Oppenheimer was a much more credible source than *Pravda*.

What makes a source more or less credible? Two of the chief components of source credibility are *expertise* and *trustworthiness*. **Expertise** has to do with the extent to which people perceive that the source of the message is a real expert on the topic that he or she is speaking about. **Trustworthiness** has to do with the extent to which people find the source of the message to be reliable or truthful. If advertisers can find sources who have both of these ingredients, they stand a good chance of putting together a persuasive ad. One practitioner of persuasion, Tony Schwartz, was able to design a brief antismoking commercial for the Foundation for a Smoke-Free Indoor Environment. The brief spot simply featured a single man talking to the camera. The spot worked because the man was not just any man. He was a source who had maximum expertise and trustworthiness. I have included the text of this ad so you can see a vivid example of source credibility in action:

> My name is Patrick Reynolds. My grandfather, R. J. Reynolds, founded the tobacco company which now manufactures Camels, Winstons, and Salems. We've all heard the tobacco industry say that there are no ill effects caused by smoking. Well, we have plenty of cigarette-caused disease and death right here in the R. J. Reynolds family itself. My grandfather, R. J. Reynolds Jr., smoked heavily and died of emphysema. My mother smoked and had emphysema and heart disease. And two of my aunts, also heavy smokers, died of emphysema and cancer. Three of my older brothers who smoke have emphysema. I smoked for 10 years and have small airways lung disease. Now tell me, do you think the cigarette companies are truthful when they tell you that smoking isn't harmful? What do you think?[18]

This brief spot managed to combine expertise and trustworthiness in a single source. Who would be perceived as more of an expert on the effects of

---

STUDY BOX 8-1   Weapons of Influence

In his analysis of persuasion, Robert Cialdini has identified at least six principles that he claims are ubiquitous in daily life. By learning to recognize these principles, you may be able to guard against the bombardment of persuasive attempts from the mass media. After you read about the principles, see if you can identify how they are used in the media. The principles are as follows:

1. **Reciprocity:** If someone does something for you, you usually feel that you need to reciprocate and do something in return. This principle can be used to persuade you. When some charity group sends you free address labels with its logo and slogan to place on your mailing envelopes, you may be more vulnerable to the charity's persuasive pitch. Because the group has given you something, your automatic response may be that you need to give it something. The danger, of course, is that you end up giving much more than you received.

2. **Commitment and Consistency:** People strive for consistency in their behavior. Sometimes, your determination to appear consistent can be used against you. Suppose you resist the reciprocity rule and decide to use your address labels without sending any money to the charity. You might not be off the hook just yet. As you continue to attach the address labels to your envelopes, you realize that every piece of mail you send out is an expression of support for the charity. A few months later, when the charity solicits you for a donation, you may feel more inclined to give in order to maintain consistency with your prior commitment.

3. **Social Proof:** When we are not sure how to behave, we look to others around us for guidance. Producers of TV sitcoms know that their programs will be perceived as funnier if they include laugh tracks. Apparently, people are persuaded that the content of the show is more humorous if they

---

smoking than a member of a family who owned a tobacco company? As for trustworthiness, by appearing to speak against the financial interests of his own family, the message delivered by Patrick Reynolds seemed particularly reliable. When the audience perceives that the source of the message has little to gain by delivering a particular message, then the source is likely to be perceived as particularly trustworthy.

Message Features: Simplicity and Repetition

Bill Moyers, an award-winning journalist who has made a series of videos for the Public Broadcasting Company, conducted an interview in one of his documentaries with Fritz Hippler, the mastermind of most of the German propaganda films made during Adolf Hitler's reign of terror.[19] When asked what made propaganda so effective, Hippler didn't hesitate. The two principles he identified were **simplicity** and **repetition.** These were essentially the same principles noted in another interview that Bill Moyers did, this one with Rosser Reeves, the advertising man who developed campaigns for Dwight Eisenhower, M&M candies, Bic pens, and Anacin pain reliever, to mention just

hear other people laughing at the one-liners.

4. **Liking:** If we like someone, we are more susceptible to being influenced by that person. One car salesman attributes his great success to the cards he sends his customers that simply say "I like you." The power of this strategy may reside in the fact that few people want to believe that such an expression of affection could be disingenuous. After all, you are a very likeable person, aren't you?

5. **Authority:** We tend to respond more readily to messages delivered by people whom we regard as authority figures. Which would you tend to believe more about the virtues of spending money to travel to Mars—the author of this textbook, or Leonard Nimoy, who played Spock in the *Star Trek* episodes? You may have found yourself instantly wanting to go with Leonard Nimoy. But does playing a part in a TV show really make one an authority? Persuasive practitioners often try to capitalize on our urge to go with an authority figure by presenting us with messages from people who only appear to be authorities. Appearances can often be deceiving.

6. **Scarcity:** We tend to go after things that appear to be in high demand. If everyone wants it, it must be good. How many advertisers use the scarcity appeal by telling us that their offers are good "only while supplies last." This phrase gives the impression that people are going to be beatingdown the door to obtain the product. If the product is in such high demand and will soon be gone, it must be worth whatever price is being charged. Right? Well, maybe. The danger of relying exclusively on the scarcity of a product to determine its worth is that you might soon discover that the true merits of the product weren't worth the price you paid.

SOURCE: Cialdini, R. (1985). *Influence: Science and practice*. Glenview, IL: Scott Foresman.

a few. Reeves stated that too many advertising people "get tangled up in their own underwear" instead of communicating messages that are simple and to the point.[20] Both Hippler and Reeves had discovered something that researchers have documented in laboratory experiments. John Cacioppo and Richard Petty showed that a repeated message was more persuasive than one that was heard only once. But repetition does have its limits. After about three exposures, Cacioppo and Petty found, people started to become bored by the same message, and persuasive impact started to decrease.[21] Commercial advertisers who use radio and TV often fail to appreciate how quickly a commercial message "burns out" with the audience. The research suggests that campaigns need regular infusions of new life in order to prevent consumer boredom.

More Message Features: Fear, Guilt, and Humor

If you think about some of the commercials that you have seen or heard over the years, you will probably have little trouble identifying messages that used one of the three appeals just listed: fear, guilt, or humor. Let's look briefly at each of these message features from the perspective of persuasion research. How effective are they?

Fear appeals have been a standard part of the persuader's arsenal for as long as persuasion has been practiced. Not long ago, I saw a commercial for a children's fever-reducing remedy. The commercial seemed designed to induce a mild level of fear about what might happen if my child's fever went too high. Of course, use of the advertised pain reliever was presented as the remedy. Do such appeals work? In their exhaustive review of the theory and research results pertaining to fear appeals in persuasion, psychologists Alice Eagly and Shelly Chaiken answer the question:

> What is the effect of fear or threat on persuasion? . . . For the applied health professional, then, the most important question about public health communications is whether scare tactics enhance or inhibit their efficacy. On this bottom line issue, the research findings are fairly clear: The vast majority of experiments have found that higher levels of threat lead to greater persuasion than lower levels.[22]

Fear appeals do tend to increase persuasion. Although this research conclusion seems simple enough, the theory and research behind the conclusion are anything but simple. Over the years, researchers have had to wade through many studies appearing to contain inconsistent findings. The theories in the area are quite diverse, yet no particular theory seems to enjoy clear support. One example of the complexity involved in predicting the success of fear appeals is the **protection motivation theory.**[23] According to this view, to the extent that fear appeals convince an audience of the severity of a threat, their vulnerability to the threat, and their ability to respond effectively to the threat, they will be persuasive. On the other hand, to the extent that the audience perceives that yielding to the persuasive message will be costly in some way, even high-fear appeals might not be effective.

Sometimes, media messages bypass the strategy of inducing fear in favor of trying to make you feel *guilty* for not responding to a persuasive appeal. One reason for the prevalence of guilt appeals is that it is relatively easy to make people feel guilty. Parents who have their children's welfare at heart are easy prey for the persuader who wants to induce guilt. As a parent, how can I live with myself if I don't have the very best tires on my car to keep my child as safe as possible? Or how about the very best computer for my child's pursuit of education? Advertisers are well aware that it is relatively easy to play on feelings of guilt. Does it work? According to communication researcher, Em Griffin, guilt appeals are certainly persuasive—at least in the context of interpersonal communication.[24] If you feel guilty and I am standing in your face asking you to comply with a request, the chances are good that you will comply. People can be motivated to do many things because they feel guilty. But Griffin warns about some side effects of the guilt appeal that persuaders would do well to consider carefully. He maintains that most people tend to avoid and devalue those who make us feel guilty. This would seem to hold important implications for using guilt in a mass media campaign. Because there is no individual person who has to be confronted directly, media campaigns that are based on guilt may tend to backfire. Indeed, there is evidence that consumers respond with anger when a media advertisement makes them feel guilty.[25]

The final message ingredient examined briefly in this chapter is humor. If you've ever had the chance to see the annual Clio Awards given for outstanding achievement in advertising, then you know that many of the award winners are commercials that feature some type of humorous appeal. Practitioners of persuasion have long believed that being funny makes them more persuasive. The idea is based on the notion that humor tends to attract attention to the message, creates a more favorable attitude toward the source of the message and the product, and may produce a general orientation toward the message that is less critical. In other words, if people are laughing, they can't be thinking too hard about the arguments against your message.

Perhaps the really funny thing in all of this is that researchers have had a difficult time documenting the superiority of humorous messages in persuasive campaigns. There may be good reason for the difficulty. Although humor may attract attention, it may attract attention to itself instead of to the persuasive message. People may remember the joke—but not what product they're supposed to buy. It may also be the case that humor tends to discourage the consumer from taking the product very seriously. It may be true that people who are laughing are not thinking up reasons for why they shouldn't buy the product. On the other hand, they may not be thinking seriously about buying the product at all. They are simply too busy laughing. Still, advertisers continue to use humor in campaign after campaign. Why? One reason may be that humor is tolerated much easier on repetition. It wears well. Another reason may be that advertisers are convinced that people feel positive sentiment toward the source that makes them laugh. In today's competitive media market, positive sentiment is a precious commodity. Regardless of the research findings, it is a relative certainty that advertisers will continue to pack their ads with humorous appeals.

The Health Campaign

It is one thing to use the media to persuade people to buy products. It is another thing to use the media to persuade them to adopt healthy behaviors. Earlier in the chapter, you read about how entertainment media can sometimes be used to promote healthy behaviors. But what about more deliberate advertising that attempts to persuade people to change their behaviors for their own health? Over the years, advertising messages have often brought consumers conflicting messages about appropriate health-related behaviors. Up until 1971, when cigarette ads were banned from the public airwaves, TV and radio saturated the culture with commercial messages designed to encourage smoking behavior. More recently, the airwaves have been used to deliver a very different message about smoking. At the same time that the government wants to invest in persuasive messages to reduce drug use, the commercial messages during sporting events sell young people on the virtues of alcohol consumption. Is there any evidence that media messages can be used to change public health behavior for the good? As it turns out, persuasive principles are persuasive principles. The same principles that persuade people to engage in unhealthy behavior can also be used to persuade them to engage in healthy behavior.

Some of the most impressive data sets that argue in favor of using the media to address public health problems come from other countries. Working in Bolivia, researchers Thomas Valente and Walter Saba reported the results of two surveys taken a year apart and involving over 3,000 respondents. The goal of these surveys was to evaluate the effectiveness of a major campaign to encourage reproductive health practices (the use of safe contraception, etc.). The campaign included 11 different TV and radio spots, and the researchers measured how the campaign affected both information and behavior. The results indicated that people who were exposed to the mass media campaign were more likely to adopt contraception into their sexual practices. There was also some evidence that the media campaign was likeliest to have an effect on those who did not have a rich interpersonal network. It is worth noting here that the effect of exposure to the campaign was not particularly large in statistical terms, but it was statistically significant (see chapter 2 for a review of these concepts).[26]

Similar to the findings in Bolivia, another survey of over 1,200 mothers in the Philippines found evidence that exposure to a media campaign about preventing the measles had a significant impact on increasing specific knowledge about the disease. Once again, the media—and not interpersonal networks—seemed to be the source of the information gains.[27] A study of nearly 1,700 smokers and ex-smokers by researchers working on the Finnish North Karelia Project also found that for the men in the study, weekly exposure to mass media health messages was significantly correlated with attempts to stop smoking. Unlike the studies in Bolivia and the Philippines, interpersonal communication also had an impact on efforts to quit. The respondents who received both media and interpersonal communication were the most resistant to the temptation to begin smoking.[28]

Health communication is an emerging area of study. To this point, much of the research has been correlational. You know from the preceding chapters that we must be careful about assuming that the media exert a causal force if we don't have the data needed to make that conclusion. Still, the evidence does seem to be mounting that persuasive health campaigns using the mass media can have an effect on individual behavior. Researchers at the University of Kentucky have done a number of investigations that look at how individuals differ in their response to media health messages. They have found that sensation seekers are more likely to use drugs and are more likely to respond well to media messages that are high in novelty and action.[29] Another researcher, Richard Perloff, has recently summarized research on media campaigns designed to convince people to have safer sex.[30] The implication that this research holds for addressing the AIDS crisis and other sexually transmitted disease is obvious. We shouldn't be surprised to find that research on media health campaigns is turning up evidence that persuasive tactics work. If the media are able to persuade people to buy products, laugh, adopt attitudes of

---

**STUDY BOX 8-2   Questions About Media Campaigns
                   for Future Research**

1. How much message-exposure is needed to get behavior change?
2. Exactly when does message "burn-out" occur? How much message exposure is too much?
3. What is the optimum mix of persuasive strategies? What sort of balance should messages contain between positive incentives and negative appeals like fear?
4. What is the best balance of channels for a campaign? To what extent should a campaign rely on paid ads or public service announcements? To what extent

should the campaign rely on TV, radio, print, or websites?
5. What is the latest research on new communication technologies and health campaigns? Given that technologies are evolving so quickly, how are we to understand these changes in terms of their effects on campaign strategies?

SOURCE: Salmon, C. T., & Atkin, C. (2003). Using media campaigns for health promotion. In T. L. Thompson, A. M. Dorsey, K. I. Miller, & R. Parrott (Eds.), *Handbook of health communication* (pp. 449–472). Mahwah, NJ: Erlbaum.

---

fear toward their environment, and even take their own lives, they should be able to influence people to change their health habits.

As much as researchers have learned about health campaigns, a recent overview of the research by Charles Salmon and Charles Atkin reveals that we still have quite a bit of progress to make in this area.[31] In a major meta-analysis that was conducted on this research over nearly 50 different campaigns, media effects were discovered to be quite modest.[32] Compared to the control conditions where people didn't receive the health messages, the conditions that received the health messages resulted in behavior changes in only about 7% to 10% more of the people. Another important finding from this literature is that it seems a bit easier to persuade people to *adopt a new behavior* such as beginning an exercise routine or changing dental care practices than it is to persuade them to *stop an unhealthy practice* such as smoking or engaging in risky sex. To highlight some of the unknowns about health campaigns and to help set the agenda for future research, Salmon and Atkin raised several critical questions that future researchers need to attempt to answer (see Study Box 8-2).

SUBLIMINAL PERSUASION:

THE MAGIC KEY?

Before concluding the discussion on the persuasive effects of media, there is one topic that we dare not ignore because it is one of the most interesting to think about and it holds a special place in the history of advertising. Shortly after I earned my master's degree in communication (1976), I took a part-time teaching job that required me to teach a course on persuasion. One of the questions that arose in the class at the very outset was about the effectiveness of something called **subliminal persuasion.** I knew a little about the topic from my graduate studies but not enough to feel competent teaching a class of curious undergraduates who wanted the truth about this persuasive technique. My students' curiosity was fueled by two books published in the 1970s by Wilson Bryan Key.[33] Key argued that media advertising contained hidden or subliminal appeals that penetrated into the unconscious mind of the consumer. Because these messages presumably bypassed the conventional process of rational scrutiny that people typically give to persuasive messages, they were supposedly particularly effective in motivating human behavior. According to Key, advertisers were so committed to the technique that occasionally, they even put subliminal messages on the product itself.

After reading about the contention that a popular brand of cracker had the word *sex* hidden on the surface of the product, I became suspicious. I purchased a box of the crackers and proceeded to spread them out over the kitchen table at the home of my mother-in-law. With a magnifying glass in hand, I examined each cracker carefully to see if I could find evidence of the subliminal technique. As I was deeply engaged in my search, my mother-in-law came into the room and asked me what I was doing. Without batting an eye, I replied, "I'm looking for sex." Only after I uttered these words did I realize that I had a lot of explaining to do. At that point in my study, I was prepared to explain much more than I had been ready to explain to my persuasion class.

As it turns out, the academic study of subliminal persuasion is a fascinating one. Let's take a brief look at some of the highlights.

Early History

Subliminal messages are messages that presumably enter the unconscious mind without being detected. The primary example of such a message was outlined in 1957 by an advertising expert, James Vicary. Mr. Vicary claimed that in extensive tests he designed for movie audiences watching the film *Picnic,* he had clearly established that subliminal messages were persuasive. He claimed that by splicing into the film the phrases "Eat Popcorn" and "Drink Coke," he dramatically increased the sales of these products at the concession counter. Even though the phrases were on the screen for only one-third of one millisecond (too brief to be perceived consciously), they registered in the brain and stirred the urge to eat and drink. According to Vicary, after people were exposed to the subliminal messages, Coke sales increased 18% and popcorn sales increased 58%.[34] As you might imagine, this revelation caused quite a controversy. Articles appeared in popular magazines that scorned this technique as highly unethical. In an article that appeared in the *Saturday Review,* Norman Cousins wrote that subliminal persuasion was so insidious that we should "take this invention and everything connected to it and attach it to the center of the next nuclear explosive scheduled for testing."[35]

Even before any supporting data could be examined on the effect that Vicary announced, the Federal Communications Commission threatened that any use of the technique by broadcasters would result in loss of their broadcasting license. The National Association of Broadcasters also prohibited the practice of subliminal persuasion for any of its members, which included nearly every broadcast facility in the United States. The advertising community wanted to see the supporting data from Vicary's study before it rendered a final opinion about subliminal persuasion. The little-known truth about the history of this topic is that James Vicary confessed in 1962 that the study reported in 1957 was, in fact, a fabricated account that was intended to increase the number of customers for his marketing business.[36] But the confession appeared in an advertising trade journal and the word never seemed to circulate very widely. The notion of subliminal persuasion had taken on a life of its own. Despite Vicary's confession, the idea was so intriguing that it just wouldn't go away.

The Presumed Mechanism

How is subliminal persuasion supposed to work? When Key popularized the notion of subliminal persuasion in the 1970s, he argued that many of the subliminal messages in advertising revolved around two themes: sex and death. Any casual reader of Sigmund Freud would recognize these two themes instantly. According to Freud, the death wish and thoughts about the sexual appetite are repressed in the unconscious mind because there are few socially acceptable outlets for their expression. Subliminal messages, which directly enter the unconscious mind, unlock these repressed urges and motivate a person to purchase the particular product that the unconscious has linked with those urges. It is no accident that many of the supporters of the notion of subliminal influence in the psychological community are those who take a **psychoanalytic** or **Freudian perspective** in their general outlook on human behavior.

Two Important Questions

Two important questions need to be answered regarding subliminal persuasion. First, to what extent are subliminal messages actually present in today's mass media? Second, if they are present, are they persuasive? The first question is difficult to answer. The advertising community is not particularly interested in confessing to the use of subliminal messages, and there appears to be no good source to document their prevalence. Back in the 1980s, I asked an advertising executive at Wyse Advertising if he had any insights into the use of subliminal messages in advertising. His answer was only an estimate, but it was more concrete than anything I had encountered up to that point or have encountered since. He estimated that about 10% of all ads use some form of subliminal technique. Of course, there are also various audiotapes and videotapes marketed to the public that supposedly encourage weight loss, relaxation, avoidance of tobacco use, and similar behaviors. So, even though we can't be certain about the exact prevalence of subliminal messages, we can be confident that at least some messages attempt to employ the subliminal strategy.

Are subliminal messages effective? In order to answer this question, two psychologists, Anthony Pratkanis and Anthony Greenwald, decided to run an experiment that tested the power of subliminal tapes marketed to the public to increase self-esteem and memory.[37] The tapes that they used contained classical music that was clearly audible or **supraliminal.** The manufacturer had altered the tapes to include subliminal audio that could not be perceived consciously. Some of the tapes contained messages designed to enhance the listener's self-esteem (e.g., "I have high self-worth and high self-esteem"); others contained messages designed to improve memory (e.g., "My ability to remember and recall is increasing daily"). After testing volunteers on measures of self-esteem and memory, the experimenters randomly assigned them to listen to the tapes daily for 5 weeks. There were four experimental conditions. Each of the four groups received tapes that contained labels indicating the type of subliminal content that they would hear. For two of the groups, the labels were correct and indicated either the memory or self-esteem message. For the other two groups, the labels were incorrect. For one group, the tapes labeled "self-esteem" actually had subliminal messages about memory. Likewise, for the final group, the tapes labeled "memory" actually had subliminal messages about self-esteem.

The results of the study were very clear. First, the authors found absolutely no evidence that the subliminal messages were effective in changing self-esteem or memory. Second, the study revealed what the authors dubbed as an **illusory placebo effect.** The volunteers who listened to the tapes labeled as self-esteem tapes thought that the tapes had increased their levels of self-esteem. The volunteers who listened to the memory tapes thought that the tapes had increased their memory ability. This happened regardless of the actual subliminal content of the tapes. Thus, the effect that emerged here was a placebo effect because the volunteers expressed opinions that were based on the labels on the tapes. The effect was illusory because, in fact, actual levels of self-esteem and memory were unaffected by any of the tapes.

The study by Pratkanis and Greenwald is typical of many that scholars have published over the last 40 years. Although psychologists have documented the fact that some subliminal messages can affect human behavior, these effects do not last for more than just a few seconds after the message is perceived. Moreover, there is virtually no evidence that subliminal messages are capable of influencing the kinds of large changes in attitude and behavior that marketers of products attempt to bring about in consumers. As Pratkanis concluded in a recent article on this topic, "Perhaps now is the time to lay the myth of subliminal sorcery to rest and direct our attention to other, more scientifically documented ways of understanding the causes of human behavior and improving our condition."[38] It is worth noting that there are still some cognitive psychologists who believe that subliminal persuasion is a possibility that may be documented in future research.[39] Until more confirming data appear in the literature, however, the consensus of scholars is probably best summarized in the statement by Pratkanis. From the perspective of a consumer who might wonder about whether to buy a subliminal tape to facilitate weight loss, relaxation, or some other desirable result, it is important to realize the inherent inconsistency in such marketing strategies. The effectiveness of subliminal messages is predicated on the notion that the messages enter the mind undetected. When a consumer buys a tape that promises to deliver subliminal messages of a certain type, then the process is no longer under cover. Once the nature of the subliminal message is known, the entire presumption of the message's effectiveness is undone. It is no longer subliminal. Any positive benefits that listening to such tapes might produce cannot be attributed to the subliminal nature of the messages. Following the study by Pratkanis, these effects are more plausibly due to the power of prior expectations or to the placebo effect.

A final warning about claims for the effectiveness of subliminal persuasion is in order. As I have taught classes in persuasion over the years, I occasionally have heard or read about fantastic claims that seem to support the notion that subliminal appeals are effective. For example, a TV program on the PBS network reported that some department stores incorporate subliminal messages about honesty into their music systems as a way of reducing shoplifting. One store supposedly reported that the move had saved them hundreds of thousands of dollars. The problem with such claims is that the data do not come from carefully controlled laboratory experiments. We have no way of knowing whether the department stores in question took other security measures at the same time that they implemented subliminal messages. Perhaps the reduction in shoplifting was due to changes in the economy or the time of year. In the end, these kinds of anecdotal reports simply fail to meet the strict rigors of scientific testing. For that reason, you should be very careful about attaching too much significance to them.

The Third-Person Effect

As you've read through this chapter, you may have thought a bit about the extent to which the people you know have actually been persuaded to change their attitudes or their behaviors as a result of exposure to media messages. Suppose someone asked you if you thought that the mass media persuaded people to change their attitudes and behavior. What would you say? Suppose someone asked you if you thought that the mass media persuaded *you* to change your attitudes and behavior. If you are like many people, you will agree that the media influence others. When the question turns in a personal direction, however, you will resist admitting that you are personally affected. This tendency to think that media influence is stronger for other people than it is for oneself is a phenomenon that media researchers have documented in several studies.[40]

Years ago, a psychologist named Phillip Zimbardo noticed the same tendency when he studied persuasion in the context of cult groups that employ brainwashing. He referred to this tendency as the **"illusion of personal invulnerability."** He discovered that students of persuasion tended to think of themselves as people who would never succumb to the pressures of brainwashing. At the same time, they found it easy to assume that the same brainwashing techniques would work on others. Zimbardo noted that this attitude was not particularly healthy. In order to maximize resistance to persuasion, it is best to have a proper understanding of one's own vulnerability.[41]

In concluding this chapter, it is important to note that persuasion in the media is a topic that goes well beyond a single chapter in a text like this one. About all we can do here is touch on some of the highlights. The next chapter explores some other dimensions of this topic when it takes up research on politics in the media. In politics, persuasion is the name of the game, and we will take a closer look at how that game is played.

SUMMARY

Significant persuasion involves attitude and behavior changes that persist over time. In the 1950s, James Vicary made claims about the effectiveness of subliminal advertising in the media. Although such advertising is practiced today, research studies have generally failed to find evidence that it works effectively. There is no doubt that media messages persuade, however. Much of this persuasion is unintentional. Gerbner's theory of media cultivation claims that media messages cultivate particular views of social reality. The theory is somewhat controversial but does enjoy some empirical support. Of course, the media are full of persuasive messages that are deliberately designed to influence. Researchers have studied the influence process and have identified many important variables and developed theoretical ideas to explain how persuasion works. Much of the research has concentrated on understanding how the source of a message affects persuasion and how particular message factors contribute to the process. Recent research in the field of health communication shows promise for documenting how media messages are capable of improving people's health habits.

KEY TERMS AND CONCEPTS

Persuasion 148

Attitude 148

Behavior 148

Persistence 148

Elaboration likelihood model 150

Central route to persuasion 150

Counter-attitudinal message 150

Peripheral-route persuasion 150

Theory of media cultivation 151

Social reality 151

Fear of criminal victimization 151

Mainstreaming 152

To learn more about the topics in this chapter, enter the Key Terms and Concepts found in this chapter as subject and keyword searches on your InfoTrac® College Edition.

NOTES

1. Public Broadcasting System. (1984). *On Television: The Violence Factor.*

2. Schofield, J. W., & Pavelchak, M. A. (1989). Fallout from "The Day After": The impact of a TV film on attitudes related to nuclear war. *Journal of Applied Social Psychology, 19,* 433–448.

3. Balmford, A., Manica, A., Airey, L., Birkin, L., Oliver, A., & Schleicher, J. (2004). Hollywood, climate change and the public. *Science, 305,* 1713.

4. Aronson, E. (1995). *The social animal.* New York: W. H. Freeman.

5. Petty, R. E., & Cacioppo, J. T. (1986). The elaboration likelihood model of persuasion. In L. Berkowitz (Ed.), *Advances in Experimental Social Psychology* (pp. 123–205). Hillsdale, NJ: Erlbaum.

6. Dominick, J. R. (1999). *The dynamics of mass communication.* Boston: McGraw-Hill.

7. Gerbner, G., Gross, L., Morgan, M., & Signorielli, N. (1994). Growing up with television: The cultivation perspective. In J. Bryant & D. Zillmann (Eds.), *Media effects: Advances in theory and research* (pp. 17–41). Hillsdale, NJ: Erlbaum.

8. Doob, A. N., & Macdonald, G. E. (1979). Television viewing and fear of victimization: Is the relationship causal? *Journal of Personality & Social Psychology, 37,* 170–179.

9. Sparks, G. G., Hansen, T., & Shah, R. (1994). Do televised depictions of paranormal events influence viewers' paranormal beliefs? *Skeptical Inquirer, 18,* 386–395.

10. The main studies that I have conducted on this topic include the following:

Sparks, G. G., Nelson, C. L., & Campbell, R. G. (1997). The relationship between exposure to televised messages about paranormal phenomena and paranormal beliefs. *Journal of Broadcasting & Electronic Media, 41,* 345–359.

Sparks, G. G., & Pellechia, M. (1997). The effect of news stories about UFOs on readers' UFO beliefs: The role of confirming or disconfirming testimony from a scientist. *Communication Reports, 10,* 165–172.

Sparks, G. G., Pellechia, M., & Irvine, C. (1998). Does television news about UFOs affect viewers' UFO beliefs?: An experimental investigation. *Communication Quarterly, 46,* 284–294.

Sparks, G. G., Sparks, C. W., & Gray, K. (1995). Media impact on fright reactions and belief in UFOs: The potential role of mental imagery. *Communication Research, 22,* 3–23.

Sparks, G. G., & Miller, W. (2001). Investigating the relationship between exposure to television programs that depict paranormal phenomena and beliefs in the paranormal. *Communication Monographs, 68,* 98–113.

11. Brown, J. D., & Walsh-Childers, K. (2002). Effects of media on personal and public health. In J. Bryant & D. Zillmann (Eds.), Media effects: Advances in theory and research (pp. 453–488). Mahwah, NJ: Erlbaum.

12. Ball-Rokeach, S. J., Rokeach, M., & Grube, J. W. (1984, November). The great American values test: Can television alter basic beliefs? *Psychology Today*, 34–41.

13. Aronson, E. (1995). *The social animal.* New York: W. H. Freeman.

14. Liebert, R. M., & Sprafkin, J. (1988). *The early window: Effects of television on children and youth.* New York: Pergamon Press.

15. Atkin, C. K. (1978). Observation of parent–child interaction in supermarket decision making. *Journal of Marketing, 42,* 41–45.

16. Kunkel, D., Wilcox, B. L., Cantor, J., Palmer, E., Linn, S., & Dowrick, P. (2004). *Report of the APA task force on advertising and children,* pp. 1–35.

17. Hovland, C., & Weiss, W. (1951). The influence of source credibility on communication effectiveness. *Public Opinion Quarterly, 15,* 635–650.

18. Hoffman, D., & Duggan, W. (Producers). (1989). *Guerrilla media: A citizen's guide to using electronic media for social change. The inside story from Tony Schwartz* [Video recording]. Princeton, NJ: Films for the Humanities.

19. Moyers, B. D. (Producer). (1988). *World War II: The propaganda battle* [Video recording]. Washington, DC: PBS Films.

20. CEL. (1984). The 30-second president. In *A walk through the twentieth century with Bill Moyers.* Washington, DC: Public Broadcasting Service.

21. Cacioppo, J. T., & Petty, R. E. (1979). Effects of message repetition and position on cognitive response, recall, and persuasion. *Journal of Personality and Social Psychology, 37,* 97–109.

22. Eagly, A. H., & Chaiken, S. (1993). *The psychology of attitudes.* Fort Worth, TX: Harcourt Brace Jovanovich.

23. Rogers, R. W. (1975). A protection motivation theory of fear appeals and attitude change. *Journal of Psychology, 91,* 93–114.

24. Griffin, E. (1976). *The mindchangers: The art of Christian persuasion.* Wheaton, IL: Tyndale.

25. Pinto, M. B., & Priest, S. (1991). Guilt appeals in advertising: An exploratory study. *Psychological Reports, 69,* 375–385.

26. Valente, T. W., & Saba, W. P. (1998). Mass media and interpersonal influence in a reproductive health communication campaign in Bolivia. *Communication Research, 25*(1), 96–124.

27. McDivitt, J., Zimicki, S., & Hornick, R. C. (1997). Explaining the impact of a communication campaign to change vaccination knowledge and coverage in the Philippines. *Health Communication, 9*(2), 95–118.

28. Korhonen, T., Uutela, A., Korhonen, H. J., & Puska, P. (1998). Impact of mass media and interpersonal health communication on smoking cessation attempts: A study in North Karelia, 1989–1996. *Journal of Health Communication, 3*(2), 105–118.

29. Donohew, L., Palmgreen, P., & Lorch, E. P. (1994). Attention, need for sensation, and health communication campaigns. *American Behavioral Scientist, 38*(2), 310–322.

30. Perloff, R. M. (2001). *Persuading people to have safer sex: Applications of social science to the AIDS crisis.* Mahwah, NJ: Erlbaum.

31. Salmon, C. T., & Atkin, C. (2003). Using media campaigns for health promotion. In T. L. Thompson, A. M. Dorsey, K. I. Miller, & R. Parrott (Eds.), *Handbook of health communication* (pp. 449-472). Mahwah, NJ: Erlbaum.

32. Snyder, L. (2001). How effective are mediated health campaigns? In R. E. Rice & C. K. Atkin (Eds.), *Public communication campaigns,* 3rd ed. (pp. 181–190). Thousand Oaks, CA: Sage.

33. Key, W. B. (1973). *Subliminal seduction.* Englewood Cliffs, NJ: Signet. Key, W. B. (1976). *Media Sexploitation.* Englewood Cliffs, NJ: Signet.

34. Pratkanis, A. R. (1992). The cargo-cult science of subliminal persuasion. *Skeptical Inquirer, 16,* 260–272.

35. Cousins, N. (1957, October 5). Smudging the subconscious. *Saturday Review.*

36. Danzig, F. (1962, September 17). Subliminal advertising—Today it's just

historic flashback for researcher Vicary. *Advertising Age.*

37. Pratkanis, A. R., & Greenwald, A. G. (1988). Recent perspectives on unconscious processing: Still no marketing applications. *Psychology & Marketing, 5,* 339–355.

38. Pratkanis, A. R. (1992). The cargo-cult science of subliminal persuasion. *Skeptical Inquirer, 16,* 260–272.

39. Epley, N., Savitsky, K., & Kachelski, R. A. (1999). What every skeptic should know about subliminal persuasion. *Skeptical Inquirer, 23,* 40–45.

40. Shah, D. V., Faber, R. J., & Youn, S. (1999). Susceptibility and severity: Perceptual dimensions underlying the third-person effect. *Communication Research, 26,* 240–267.

41. Zimbardo, P. G., Ebbesen, E. B., & Maslach, C. (1977). *Influencing attitudes and changing behavior.* Reading, MA: Addison-Wesley.

9

■

The Effects of News and Political Content

THINKING ABOUT THE NEWS

During the 2004 presidential campaign, you might recall, CBS News broke a story about George Bush's past service record in the National Guard. Within several weeks after the story was first broadcast, the origin and authenticity of the documents that formed the core of the story were challenged. Soon after that, as the nation prepared for the first presidential debate, the story seemed to have faded into the background—at least for most people. In my own household, the story had not faded much at all. Each day, my wife, Cheri, would give me the latest speculations and analysis from various web sources on the Internet. Over dinner, we discussed the possibilities and amused ourselves by making up plausible scenarios about Bush's wartime history and how the documents that were supposedly from his superior officer might have surfaced.

By this time, my own interest in the story had certainly faded a bit since it first broke on the airwaves, but Cheri seemed just as motivated to think about all the possible angles to the story as she was on the day it first broke. It isn't a secret in our house that Cheri would win any prize given for analytical thinking. It often seems to me that she can generate more lines of analysis on a given topic in five minutes than I can do in five days. Clearly, some people are more highly motivated than others to think about the stories they hear in the news. Perhaps this is because of a particular interest in the news—or perhaps it has something to do with more general individual differences that apply across a variety of different domains.

Need for Cognition

John Cacioppo and Richard Petty, in their research on attitude change, developed a concept that has proved helpful in some studies on media effects. These researchers introduced the idea that certain people have a high **need for cognition** compared to other people, who are said to have a low need for cognition.[1] That is, some people are simply motivated to think a lot. If there is an opportunity to think about a topic, people with a high need for cognition will be inclined to take it. One media scholar, Elizabeth Perse, thought that Cacioppo and Petty's concept might be useful for predicting who pays attention to local television news. In a survey of more than 300 people, she found a statistically significant correlation between need for cognition and attention paid to government news.[2] This general finding was replicated in 1992 by Mollie Condra, who found that people with a higher need for cognition were more likely to be interested in media dealing with politics.[3] Most recently, in a study of Flemish television viewers, additional evidence emerged for the notion that people with a high need for cognition prefer public television and news programming.[4]

The need for cognition concept suggests that some people may be more likely to think about a news report and ruminate on it after exposure. I'm sure that my wife, Cheri, has a high need for cognition. I also believe that this helps to explain how she is able to continue to sustain deep thought about a news story when most of the public has nearly forgotten that the story ever existed in the first place.

Political Sophistication

Another concept that seems related to the need for cognition was introduced into the communication literature recently by June Rhee and Joseph Cappella.[5] These authors were interested in trying to explain why some news viewers come away from a story having learned very little information while other viewers learned quite a bit. Working in the realm of politics, these authors developed the concept of **political sophistication.** One's level of political sophistication is a function of knowledge and political ideology. A person who knows very little and doesn't have a well-developed political ideology has a low level of sophistication. In contrast, a person who knows a great deal and has definite political views has a high level of sophistication. Rhee and Cappella found that after exposure to news stories about health care reform and a mayoral election campaign, those viewers who were politically sophisticated had learned more and had higher quality arguments about the issues when they were given a chance to write about their own views.

The studies that link need for cognition with a preference for viewing news seem to suggest that the news media may naturally tend to appeal to those with a disposition to think about ideas, concepts, or implications. The research on political sophistication seems to suggest the same kind of news effect on certain individuals. But is there any hard evidence that exposure to news in the media has a definite impact on what people are actually thinking?

For the answer to that question, we need to look no farther than the theory and research associated with the notion of agenda setting that was introduced years ago by two journalism professors, Maxwell McCombs and Donald Shaw.[6]

Agenda-Setting Theory: A Theory About Thinking

For years, the **agenda-setting theory** of the press has been summarized succinctly in a single quotation from the political scientist Bernard Cohen: "The press may not be successful much of the time in telling people *what to think,* but it is stunningly successful in telling its readers *what to think about.*"[7] The idea here is that the news media set the public agenda. Their coverage of issues helps to define for the public what they should be thinking about on a given day. As you read these words, the chances are very good that you haven't heard or used the word "impeachment" or the name "Monica Lewinsky" in the last few weeks. But if you think back to December 1998, the chances are much better that these words were often on your lips in your interactions with friends and family. The news media hardly stopped in their coverage and analysis of President Clinton's impeachment hearings. For weeks, the country was immersed in nothing else. During that time, the theory of agenda setting would have predicted that if a survey had been taken of public opinion, the crisis of the presidency would have been the No. 1 public concern. That is, according to the theory, public opinion about what should be on the public agenda is heavily influenced by the topics and issues that appear in the news. The coverage may not determine exactly what position people take on a given issue, but it helps to guarantee that the issue is considered to be an important one. Is there any evidence to suggest that this might be true?

The theory of agenda setting has by now spawned many individual research studies that support the basic idea of media influence. McCombs and Shaw first sought to test the theory in the context of the 1968 presidential campaign (Richard Nixon versus Hubert Humphrey). Their study included an exhaustive analysis of the media agenda that included four newspapers from North Carolina, *Time* and *Newsweek,* CBS and NBC television news, and the *New York Times.*[8] According to the results, the five issues given the most prominent coverage by the press were foreign policy, law and order, fiscal policy, public welfare, and civil rights. When McCombs and Shaw asked voters to identify the key issue of the campaign, quite apart from their perceptions of what the candidates had been saying, there was a remarkable convergence with the issues that emerged from the media analysis. Indeed, just as the theory predicted, the media agenda and the public agenda tended to correspond.

Of course, the mere fact that the media's agenda corresponded with the public's does not really provide the most powerful evidence in favor of agenda-setting theory. Recall from chapter 2 that in order to establish a causal relationship between two variables, it isn't sufficient simply to establish a relationship between them. It is also important to establish that the causal variable precedes the other in time. Researchers who study agenda setting are most interested in documenting that the media agenda actually precedes the public agenda. Is there any evidence that it does?

In one of the few experimental tests of the theory, Shanto Iyengar and Donald Kinder studied this question by exposing people to one of three different presentations of the news over a four-day period.[9] The presentations differed according to the topic of one of the stories placed in the newscast on each day. For one group, the topic focused on pollution. For the second group, it focused on national defense. For the third group, the story dealt with inflation. After the four days of exposure, the researchers found that the experimental groups expressed greater concern about the issue that had been featured in their respective newscast.

The research by Iyengar and Kinder should remind you of some of the research covered in chapter 8. Recall the "great American values test" in which the researchers used a TV program to heighten viewers' awareness of certain values. Not only did the program succeed in changing the priority that viewers assigned to those values, it also triggered a number of behavioral changes. Although the show wasn't a news program in the strict sense and clearly had a persuasive edge, you might wonder if a continued focus on particular issues in the news could do more than just set the agenda about what topics people think about. Couldn't the news also have an impact on what people actually think about those topics?

In a revision of the agenda-setting theory, McCombs and Shaw believe that the answer to this question is a distinct yes. How do the media do this if they are not intentionally trying to persuade consumers? The answer is to be found in a concept known as **framing.** As James Tankard defines this term, framing is "the central organizing idea for news content that supplies a context and suggests what the issue is through the use of *selection, emphasis, exclusion,* and *elaboration*" [emphasis in the original].[10]

One of my favorite parts of the local newspaper in the wintertime is the coverage of the aftermath of a big snowstorm. Consider how the media might frame such news coverage. In the wake of a huge snowfall, the news could concentrate on winter recreation and the fun that children in the area have playing with snowballs and sledding down steep hills. On the other hand, the media could focus on how slowly snow removal is progressing and attempt to track down local government officials to comment on the problem. Depending on which way the story of the snowstorm is framed, consumers may have very different thoughts as a result of reading the news. Traditionally, this effect might be described in the standard agenda-setting terminology: "The media don't tell us what to think, they tell us what to think about." But a closer inspection of what goes on here suggests that there is more to it. By framing the story in terms of poor snow removal instead of recreational activities, the media are doing more than just telling us *what to think about*. In a very real way, they are telling us *what to think* by focusing attention on one particular angle of the story instead of another one. I can remember years ago when I lived in the Chicago area, the city changed mayors because of what many perceived as the failure of the administration to set up adequate snow removal. The press helped to frame the poor snow removal as a major failure in planning, and the public apparently accepted the frame. As Em Griffin concludes in his discussion of these theoretical concepts: "McCombs and Shaw have established a plausible case that some people look to print and broadcast news for guidance on which issues are really important. Agenda-setting theory also provides a needed reminder that news stories are just that—stories. The message always requires interpretation."[11] In the end, the way a story is framed by the media can have great impact on the interpretations that people carry away from the message.

The theory of agenda setting is currently recognized as one of the tried-and-true theoretical contributions to the literature in mass communication. It continues to spawn new research projects on a variety of different topics. Most recently, in a longitudinal study of agenda setting reported by Spiro Kiousis, news coverage of the Monica Lewinsky scandal was linked to changing interpretations of President Clinton. The news coverage tended to lead to increases in favorability toward Clinton while simultaneously leading to decreases in his job approval rating.[12] In another study, based on a random-digit-dialing telephone survey in Washington, D.C., Kimberly Gross and Sean Aday discovered that people who watched TV news were much more likely to have higher estimates than others of the importance of local crime. Apparently, the preoccupation with crime in local news reports helped to set a public agenda about this issue's overall importance.[13] The most recent research also tends to support an agenda-setting effect on the Internet. When researchers tracked discussions on electronic bulletin boards, the topics discussed corresponded with the topics that had appeared days earlier in the news.[14] Some researchers have argued that the new media environment is relatively free of the formal gatekeeping structures of the old media.[15] That is to say, political information is now available from a nearly limitless number of sources, when one considers the Internet. If this is true, perhaps strong agenda-setting effects might be more difficult to find. Although the data will tell the tale as to the validity of this hypothesis in future years, it certainly appears as if the theory of agenda-setting is alive and well in the first decade of the 21st century.

The Spiral of Silence

One media theorist, Elisabeth Noelle-Neumann, believes that the media's impact on the interpretations that people carry away from a story can have a dramatic effect on the entire course of public opinion in the culture.[16] Her **spiral of silence** theory is based on the idea that most of us don't feel very comfortable speaking out about our views if we perceive that we are in the minority. If we think that our view is really the minority view, we would rather keep quiet than risk being isolated or rejected by those to whom we wish to feel attached. This process can eventually gather steam and spiral into a relative silence when it comes to certain minority views. That is, the more often people who feel like they are in the minority decide not to speak their views, the less we hear those views and the more we tend to believe that most people agree with the majority viewpoint. According to Neumann, this process can lead to views that eventually die out and exert little influence, even though they are actually held by substantial numbers of people. Once those large numbers of people get the impression that their views are not widely shared, they stop talking. And this simply reinforces the notion that their views are *not* widely shared. And so on.

The role of the news media in this spiral of silence can be quite dramatic. To the extent that people tune in to TV news and perceive that most people hold a particular opinion or viewpoint on a given issue, the spiral of silence can be off and running. Media researchers William Eveland, Douglas McLeod, and Nancy Signorielli found evidence supporting the spiral of silence theory when they conducted a sample survey on attitudes toward the Gulf War back in 1991.[17] In contrast to the strong consensus in favor of the war that the news media reported, the survey revealed that very few people actually expressed strong support in their answers to the questions. In fact, whereas less than 7% of the respondents expressed strong support for the war, over half of the respondents expressed either neutrality, disagreement, or strong disagreement. When the researchers examined how the supporters differed from the nonsupporters, they found that their perception of public opinion was a key variable. Those who thought that public opinion was running strongly in favor of the war tended to be the ones who expressed strong support themselves. Those who thought that public opinion was mixed or not so strongly in favor of the war were more willing to express neutrality or disagreement. This close link between how people perceive public opinion and the attitudes they are willing to express is a fundamental prediction of the spiral of silence. The fact that media coverage of the war was decidedly distorted in favor of support may have contributed to the unwillingness of many to speak out publicly against the war effort. After people watched the news coverage, they carried away an interpretation of the events that suggested that public opinion was heavily in favor of what the United States was doing.

Most recent evidence on the spiral of silence suggests that evidence for the effect cuts across decades of research. Dan McDonald and his colleagues went back to an old, but infamous, set of data collected during the presidential campaign of 1948. When they analyzed that data, they found evidence for a spiral-of-silence effect.[18] Today, most researchers acknowledge that the spiral of silence is more than just a theoretical idea. It also has some empirical teeth.

How Much of the News Do We Remember?

With a story like the Iraq War or the Persian Gulf War that appears night after night, the public gradually comes up to speed on the basic facts and begins to comprehend and commit to memory certain details. When we speak of people "carrying away" an interpretation of a message that has been framed in a particular way, we are talking about memory. The question that is raised here has to do with how well people typically remember the information that they are exposed to in a newscast. As it turns out, the answer may be very different depending on the nature of the newscast and how many times a person hears the story. In most cases, unlike coverage relating to the Persian Gulf War, we are exposed to a story just a single time.

A few years ago, I was contacted by an attorney who wanted me to provide an expert opinion on a legal matter that arose out of a TV newscast. Her client, a TV station, had recently broadcast a story that clearly identified by name a young man who was in his late twenties. According to the report, which relied heavily on information provided by the local law enforcement authorities, the man had gone to a suburban home, knocked on the door, and promptly shot a young teenager in the stomach. A day or two later, law enforcement authorities discovered that the man had an airtight alibi and could not possibly have been at the boy's home at the time the crime occurred. The young teenager who had been shot also confessed that he had lied about the incident. As it turned out, he was a very disturbed young boy who had, in fact, turned a gun on himself! In the aftermath, the man who had been identified in the TV news story decided to file a lawsuit against the TV station, charging that they had libeled his good name. The case was settled out of court and never went to trial. But if it had, I might have been called upon to give an opinion about the extent to which the man who sued the TV station had really been injured by the news report. Two of the issues that would have entered into my analysis would have been the extent to which people comprehend the news they are exposed to in an average newscast and the extent to which they retain information or remember it after the newscast is over. What does the research reveal about these two issues?

Two researchers, John Robinson and Dennis Davis, provided some insights on these issues in their article "Comprehension of a Single Evening's News."[19] In tracking the responses of a group of people who watched the evening news on one particular night, the authors used an 8-point coding scheme to assess how well the news was recalled. If a viewer's recall was rated as a "0," it indicated recall of the wrong story or information that was not even contained in the newscast. A "1" indicated the inability to recall a story, no reply, or a "don't know" response. On the other end of the scale, a "7" indicated recall of the central point of the story plus two additional important details. An "8" indicated recall of the central point plus three or more additional details. After coding the data, the researchers noted that, on average, viewer response to stories fell between "2" and "3" on the 8-point scale. A "2" indicated that viewers could "recall something but then can give no details" from the specific news broadcast. A "3" indicated that viewers could provide only "vague, general responses related to the story."

If these results surprise you, think about the way most people probably watch the news. Only rarely do people sit down and glue their attention to the TV screen during a newscast. On many occasions, the news comes into the home amid a host of daily activities that might include meal preparation, conversations with family members, and other routine tasks. People are more likely to monitor the news audio and engage in the well-documented practice of **selective exposure** to news material. The principle of selective exposure emphasizes that people come to any communication message with their own attitudes, interests, beliefs, and values (see chapter 3). These attitudes and interests help to guide attention to particular messages. If a person is especially interested in the news story, attention will be high. But if a story is perceived as uninteresting, a person will be more inclined to tune out. During an average newscast, a person's attention may fluctuate from low to high and back to low many times as the stories change. Many news stories are simply not attended to very well because viewers find them to be irrelevant, uninteresting, or too demanding in terms of the effort required to fully comprehend the major points. Consistent with this point of view, Hans Kepplinger and Gregor Daschmann recently presented a model for how people process news content. In summarizing their understanding on this topic, they stated the following: "To put it more generally, much information is avoided, much is misunderstood, and only some is adequately retained."[20]

If I had been called on to give testimony about the man who was concerned about his reputation after the TV news broadcast his name as a potential gunman, I might have pointed out that, in light of what we know from research on news, the chances are very high that most of the viewers probably didn't even remember the alleged gunman's name. If this was the case, his reputation might not have been damaged to nearly the extent that he thought it was. On the other hand, a news story about a shooting incident might be a story of greater than average interest. It also might have an unusual emotional impact on local viewers. In this type of situation, sorting out the effects of the messages on comprehension can be pretty difficult. Researchers have only begun to discover how emotions, vivid images, and standard news content might mix together to produce different results in terms of overall comprehension.

John Newhagen and Byron Reeves attempted to study how vivid or intense images might affect what people remember from a news story. Their findings were intriguing. When they asked people to recall news topics and facts from the news stories six weeks after exposure to a newscast, the researchers found that people were able to recall the facts and topics better if they had been presented without a vivid visual. However, when vivid visuals were included, people definitely remembered the visuals.[21] These results support a type of **dual-coding theory** of news content. Images might be processed differently than verbal information. When a vivid image is presented alongside verbal information, it might actually tend to distract people from processing the verbal information efficiently. On the other hand, the vivid images themselves prove to be highly memorable and might even enhance memory for the information that comes right after the images appear.

There is probably some practical wisdom that news directors can glean from these results. If, for example, a station wants to give verbal instructions about how to avoid the calamity of being killed in a tornado, it probably wouldn't be a good idea to show dramatic video footage of a tornado destroying buildings at the same time the instructions are being given. Newhagen and Reeves's results indicate that tornado footage offered at the same time as instructions might actually prevent effective processing of the instructions. However, it might be a good idea to catch viewers' attention with the tornado footage and then, after it was over, immediately follow up with the verbal instructions for safety. Recent research with children conducted by Barrie Gunter and his associates also found evidence for dual coding of news. Children learned more information from television news than they did from print or audio versions of the same material. However, this advantage was only found when the pictures on TV were completely redundant with the verbal information in the news story.[22]

THE ROLE OF EMOTION

One reason why vivid images may tend to be memorable is that they evoke more intense emotional reactions than spoken words or plain written text. Of course, there may be exceptions to this rule. If you were highly involved with a particular issue, mere words in the newspaper or words spoken by a newscaster might be more than enough to set your emotions stirring. Generally speaking, however, vivid images have a more direct pathway to the emotions. John Newhagen recently reported some new research from his program of studies on emotional media images. Using news images, he found that the ones that provoked anger in viewers were the most memorable, followed by images that induced fear. Finally, people had the worst memory for images that they had found to be disgusting. Newhagen pointed out that these findings may have practical implications for the way news stories are put together. As he stated, "[P]roducers can use such images to first draw attention to a story, and then insert information they think viewers will want to remember right after them. Images that elicit disgust, on the other hand, inhibit memory late in the stories" (pp. 274–275).[23]

The research on emotional news images and memory is becoming a well-developed literature. Newhagen's research findings are not the only ones that point to the memory-enhancing effects of some types of negative news stories. In a study reported by Annie Lang, John Newhagen, and Byron Reeves, negative news stories increased memory for news items.[24] Lang and her coauthors speculated that the primary function of negative news video may be to heighten the overall emotional impact of a story. The greater impact of the story shows up in a person as increased physiological arousal. That arousal results in increased memory. As I write this brief summary of Lang's research, the news media all across the state of Indiana as well as the CNN Headline news have been replaying the last lap of the 2001 Daytona 500 NASCAR race. You don't have to be a race fan to know what happened in this fateful contest. Racing star Dale Earnhardt Sr. was killed instantly when he crashed into the wall at 180 mph. The news footage of this crash was dramatic and highly emotional. I am certain that if I had been wired to sensors monitoring my physiological state, I would have shown clear signs of arousal upon watching the tragic crash footage. Thanks to new video technology, viewers were actually able to see what the crash looked like from Earnhardt's perspective from inside his car. According to the research findings, my heightened physiological response was probably typical. People who watched this coverage were probably very likely to remember the news material that was reported during the video footage and directly following it.

Nowhere is the role of emotion in news more important than in politics. One of the first demonstrations of the potential role of emotion from TV images in politics came from the first presidential debates between the Republican candidate, Richard Nixon, and the Democratic candidate, John Kennedy, in the 1960 election. Even though 90% of Americans had a TV set in 1960, radio was still a popular medium for political news. Many people decided to listen to the debates on the radio instead of watching them on TV. According to Sid Kraus, who may be the only communication researcher who has been in attendance at every presidential debate since they began in 1960, the people who listened to the debates on radio were more inclined to perceive Nixon as the winner. In contrast, those who watched the debates on TV thought that Kennedy had the upper hand. Although the integrity of the supporting data for this conclusion has been debated through the past few decades, Kraus concludes after his exhaustive review of the data that, "[M]y own observation on the night of the debate in 1960, and my consultations with scholars conducting debate research at that time convinced me that the finding was a credible one."[25] In support of Kraus's conclusion, the following excerpt from *Broadcasting* magazine, a leading trade journal in the broadcasting industry, states the finding clearly: "In answer to the question who won the debates, 48.7% of the radio audience named Mr. Nixon and only 21% picked Mr. Kennedy. Among those who watched the debates on TV, 30.2% named Mr. Kennedy the winner and 28.6% picked Mr. Nixon."[26] Since the TV audience was so much larger than the radio audience, the advantage that Kennedy had on TV presumably meant a narrow victory. There is also another very recent source of support for Kraus's conclusion on this debate. In an experiment reported by James Druckman, subjects in the UK, who knew nothing of the history of the Kennedy–Nixon debates, were randomly assigned to either watch the debate on TV or listen to an audio version.[27] Druckman's conclusions about the impact of the television images is completely consistent with Kraus's conclusions that viewers who watched the debate were more likely to conclude that Kennedy won, whereas viewers who heard the debate were more likely to conclude that Nixon won.

The fact that TV images of political debaters may exert greater influence on voters than the actual words spoken has been reinforced by more recent research by Michael Pfau and Jong Kang. These authors emphasized that on TV, political candidates with a "softer, warmer communication, similar to communication in an interpersonal context" will be more influential among the voters.[28] One of the first political ads that demonstrated how images may be more powerful than words was the now infamous "Daisy Girl" commercial designed by advertising genius Tony Schwartz for Lyndon Johnson's 1964 presidential campaign against Barry Goldwater. The ad began by showing a young girl picking petals from a daisy and counting (incorrectly) from 1 to 10. When she reached the number 10, the camera slowly zoomed in on the child's eye and then farther into the pupil of the eye as a cold, military-sounding voice began a countdown from 10 to 1. The pupil of the girl's eye became transformed into a window where the viewer saw a nuclear explosion. As the screen went black, an announcer's voice said, "These are the stakes, to make a world in which all God's children can live, or to go into the darkness. Either we must love each other or we must die."[29] The ad aired only one time, but it caused a national discussion about political advertising techniques. Most political analysts agree that it virtually ended Barry Goldwater's campaign without even mentioning him by name. Schwartz believes that the ad used powerful images to connect to the deep-seated emotions that people had about nuclear war. By surfacing the fears associated with the possibility that Goldwater might actually be inclined to use nuclear weapons to settle global conflict, the ad drove people to vote for Johnson in packs. In a documentary on political advertising made for public television, the news commentator Bill Moyers complained that he found it troubling to note that Johnson was portrayed as the peacemaker in the 1964 election and Goldwater as the warmonger.[30] This image was effectively exploited with the "Daisy Girl" commercial. But, Moyers noted, it was Johnson who committed the country to the bloody conflict in Vietnam that we eventually lost. Not a single spot, according to Moyers's recollection, even touched on the Vietnam issue in 1964. The "Daisy Girl" ad may have been a triumph of image over issue, pictures over words, and emotions over deeper thinking. Study Box 9-1 focuses on the advertising philosophy of Tony Schwartz, considered by some to be a modern-day media guru.

Even though the "Daisy Girl" commercial never mentioned Goldwater's name, some analysts labeled it as an example of negative advertising because it implied that Goldwater was just fine with the possibility of blowing up little girls. Since this time, there have been a number of studies on the effects of negative campaign ads. One of the main questions surrounding this type of political advertising is whether they backfire and essentially turn the public off completely so that they don't even vote. Two recent studies suggest that although consumers often become disgusted with campaigns that feature negative ads, it is difficult to find evidence that the negative advertising actually leads to decreases in either voter apathy or voter turnout.[31]

In thinking about issues of news consumption, political campaigns, and voter participation as I was preparing my notes for this chapter, one of the things that struck me in the final analysis was how little attention research on news receives from the popular press relative to research on topics like violence, sex, and fright. It is important to note, however, that popular press coverage is a relatively poor barometer for determining the importance of a research topic. Media messages about news and politics potentially help people to understand the world and know how to respond to various social and political problems. Increasingly, media messages help shape the contours of leadership by determining who gets elected to public office. News content does not tend to be associated with the most dramatic and sensational effects. Because news is designed to inform readers, listeners, and viewers, its effects are generally taken to be functional rather than dysfunctional. This may predispose the press and even those of us who conduct research on media effects to deemphasize the topic.

Perhaps the very interesting trend in exposure to news that has been documented recently will serve to draw more attention to the study of news.

STUDY BOX 9-1   Who Is Tony Schwartz?

Tony Schwartz has been using electronic media to influence the political process for several decades. He has worked for countless candidates and has created public service campaigns for police departments, fire departments, the American Cancer Society, and many other organizations. He has also done numerous product campaigns. Schwartz believes that many people who use the media to influence others have a very poor understanding of how media work. Here, I have listed some of the key principles that Schwartz relies on when he works on a political campaign.

1. **Use PRE-search—not research.** Schwartz believes that most politicians create campaign material and then test the effects of that material before they decide to put it on the air. This, according to him, is totally backward. He does not test ad material. Instead, *before* he creates an ad, he conducts research to find out what people are thinking and feeling about the candidates in a campaign. Once he knows their feelings, he can design media that tap into those feelings easily. He feels no need to test his commercials. When his pre-search in the 1968 presidential campaign revealed that many people thought that the idea of Spiro Agnew as a vice presidential candidate was a joke, Schwartz made an ad that consisted of little more than a voice laughing in the background while viewing Agnew's name on a TV screen.

2. **Create "resonance" between the message and the audience.** Schwartz is a big believer in the notion that the audience has a lot to say about whether or not it is influenced by a message. The goal of a campaign message, he says, is to resonate with voters' inner feelings. A good campaign ad will take advantage of these feelings, stir them up, and then use them ever so gently to nudge the receiver in the desired direction. Schwartz is no fan of "hard-sell" advertising. He prefers the term "deep sell." The *Daisy Girl* ad discussed in this chapter is a good example.

3. **Use the audience as "workforce," not as a target.** Many practitioners of advertising treat the audience as a target. They just throw information at the receiver as if they were throwing darts at a dartboard. Schwartz rejects this practice. For him, the feelings and information that exist in the hearts and minds of the audience are the most powerful forces that he has at his disposal. If he can draw those feelings out, then the audience begins to work for his cause. They become his "workforce." In Schwartz's view, the goal of any commercial is not to put information inside of the audience. Instead, he tries to use commercials to draw information out of the audience. One way he knows what is inside of the audience is from news reports. If a jumbo jet crashes and kills hundreds of people, he might create a spot that asks people to think of that tragedy. Then he will follow by asking people to think about the fact that tobacco use annually kills the equivalent of three fully loaded jumbo jets going down each day.

As recently as the year 2000, survey results reported by the Pew Center for the People and the Press revealed that only 9% of people in the 18–29 age group relied on comedy shows for their news content—with 39% mentioning the more traditional network newscasts. However, just four years later, 21% of the respondents in this age range said that they relied on *The Daily Show* on Comedy Central as well as on *Saturday Night Live* for their news. This percentage is nearly equal to the percentage who reported reliance on the traditional networks (23%).[32] Will this trend continue? If it does, what will the impact be on the level of information that Americans have about their government and important social and civic affairs? One possibility is that the shrinking percentage of network news consumers is related to the fact that people are getting more and more of their serious news about public affairs from Internet sources. Although this certainly sounds plausible, the recent data would at least caution against this conclusion. David Tewksbury has studied the behavior of people who consume news online.[33] On the basis of a survey of more than 3,000 adults, he reports that "the chief conclusion one may take away from this research is that online news readers do not select public affairs content as often as they select other news content" (p.705). Future studies will probably help scholars determine whether these trends indicate that something very dysfunctional is occurring with respect to news consumption. After reading this chapter, you may come away with some sense of how important media effects in this area can be.

ANOTHER VIEW OF NEWS: DO CERTAIN NEWS REPORTS CAUSE MORE PEOPLE TO DIE?

Several years ago, soon after I had left a job at Cleveland State University for my current position at Purdue, I received a phone call from a news reporter who worked for the *Cleveland Plain Dealer*. Usually, phone calls from reporters mean that someone has read a press release from my university that gives details on one of my studies. In this case, however, the reporter was not interested in my research. Instead, he wanted to know my opinion about whether an article that he was about to submit for publication in the newspaper would bring about more death in the city of Cleveland. He believed that he was in an ethical dilemma. He wanted to report the news, but he also didn't want to bring about unnecessary harm to the city that he loved.

This reporter's concern was not typical. I had never before received a phone call quite like his and I have not received one since. Why did this reporter think that his article might cause an increase in deaths in the city of Cleveland? Was there any basis for his concern? As it turns out, there certainly was! The article he planned to submit was a news report that told about the death of a well-known city official who had committed suicide.

Imitative Suicides and the News

About 20 years ago, a sociologist, David Phillips, published an article that presented a provocative set of findings. Phillips took note of the dates on which suicide stories appeared in newspapers. Then he went to the statistical archives for the area served by the newspapers and discovered that, a few days after these stories appeared, the number of automobile fatalities in the area increased.[34] Phillips also noticed that the more publicity the suicide story received (front page versus succeeding pages), the greater the increase in automobile fatalities. Could it be that the publication of a suicide story in the newspaper actually served as a trigger for other people to commit suicide themselves? As incredible as it might seem, the more data that Phillips examined, the more convincing the case became. Phillips reasoned that if people were really using their cars to commit suicide, there should be more of an increase in single-car accidents than in other types of accidents after the suicide stories appeared. This is exactly what he found.

The increase in fatalities following newspaper suicide stories may not be limited to automobiles. In another study, Phillips discovered the same kind of effect for fatal crashes involving private, business, and corporate-executive airplane crashes.[35] Again, the more publicity given to the suicide, the greater the number of plane crashes that occurred. The increase in crashes was limited to the states in which the suicide story was most heavily publicized.

A prominent social psychologist, Robert Cialdini, is convinced that Phillips has unveiled an important media effect. He summarized his views in his own popular book on the subject of influence:

> The influence of suicide stories on car and plane crashes, then, is fantastically specific. Stories of pure suicides, in which only one person dies, generate wrecks in which only one person dies; stories of suicide–murder combinations, in which there are multiple deaths, generate wrecks in which there are multiple deaths. . . . I am left wholly convinced and, simultaneously, wholly amazed by it . . . Phillips' findings illustrate a distressing tendency for suicide publicity to motivate certain people who are similar to the victim to kill themselves—because they now find the idea of suicide more legitimate.[36]

Phillips reasoned that if the statistics he examined really indicated that news stories about suicide were causing an increase in suicides, the same effect might be observed with other types of media messages. He turned to the world of soap operas and found the same effect. Documented suicides and automobile accidents both increased immediately after soap opera story lines included plots that involved a suicide.[37] The sort of media effect that Phillips's data seem to support has turned up before in the context of books. In 1774, when Johann Wolfgang von Goethe published his book *The Sorrows of Young Werther*—in which the major character takes his own life—suicides increased in Europe to such a degree that the book was banned in several countries. Apparently, some empathetic readers decided to imitate the fictional character. Media effects scholars sometimes commemorated the European experience with this novel by referring to the imitative-suicide effect documented by Phillips and others as the **Werther effect.**

If you still are having a little trouble believing that news reports of suicides can trigger an increase in the suicide rate, consider the recent evidence documented by Elmar Etzersdorfer and Gernot Sonneck on the Vienna experience.[38] In the late 1970s, it apparently became quite common for people to use the new subway system in Vienna as a way to commit suicide. The news media organizations adopted the practice of reporting on these suicides in a very dramatic way. Consistent with Phillips's data, suicide rates spiraled upward. In order to address this situation, the Austrian Association for Suicide Prevention developed guidelines for media reporting of suicides that discouraged such dramatic reporting. The suicide rate promptly dropped more than 80% and has remained low ever since. A good portion of this drop was probably the result of a media campaign aimed at discouraging suicide, but some of the decrease was probably also related to the news media's change in reporting suicide stories with such sensation.

One important question that arises about the Werther effect is whether the effect is just a **repositioning** or **rescheduling effect** as opposed to an **additive effect.** That is, think about the situation where suicides increase after a well-publicized suicide story. Would the people who committed suicide after the news story decide to commit suicide anyway at some later point in time? If so, then over the long haul, we would expect to see some decrease in the normal rate of suicide such that the overall rate remained predictably stable. The media story in this case would simply cause a rescheduling of suicides. But when Phillips examined his data, he discovered that this was not what tended to happen. Instead, it appears that the sudden increases in suicide following a media story about a suicide result in a genuine addition to the number of suicides that would have occurred had the story never been published.

Given the research findings, you might be wondering what I told the conscientious reporter from the *Cleveland Plain Dealer.* I told him about Phillips's research and gave him some of the original study citations. Then I cautioned him about placing the story on the front page of the newspaper. Phillips's work definitely suggests that the imitative suicide effect decreases if the stories do not receive wide publicity by appearing on page one. I never received a copy of the reporter's story, but he told me that he would recommend to his editor that it appear somewhere other than the front page.

Phillips's studies on the impact of news stories about suicide do have a few important limitations in terms of documenting clear evidence for media effects. First, it isn't possible to know for sure that any of the people involved in the automobile or plane fatalities actually were exposed to the media suicide story. The only data Phillips presents are raw statistics. Some sociologists also note that the theoretical process behind this effect is not particularly clear. Why do some people commit suicide and not others? How can we understand the factors that bring about this effect? Although there is a need to develop in more detail the theory behind Phillips's data, one of the first things that happens after people process news reports is something relatively simple: thought or rumination. It seems clear that if a person reads a news story about suicide or hears a brief account on TV, the story may or may not trigger additional thoughts or ruminations. Some people may shake their heads and forget the story in an instant. Others may be struck about some feature of the story and begin to ruminate in a way that connects the story with their own personal experiences. What determines the amount of thought a person devotes to a news story?

SUMMARY

In this chapter, we have examined a number of effects of media news content. As we have seen, certain types of news content (suicide stories) actually may trigger imitative behavior in the population. This effect emerges because some people ruminate about the news stories they have read or seen. People who are high in their need for cognition are particularly likely to ruminate and think about the things they have processed in the news. Agenda-setting theory postulates that the media actually affect what people think about. Research on the theory is supportive. Through the process of framing, the media may not only affect what people think about; they may also affect what we think. What we think helps to determine public opinion. The spiral of silence theory details one way the media may affect public opinion by giving sanction to the expression of certain viewpoints. Still, one of the issues that emerges in the study of news content has to do with how much people actually remember from their news exposure. Emotion may be one key variable that helps to determine what we remember. In politics, emotional reactions to debates and short commercial messages can often play a pivotal role in election outcomes.

KEY TERMS AND CONCEPTS

Need for cognition 175	Framing 177	Werther effect 188
Political sophistication 175	Spiral of silence 178	Repositioning or rescheduling effect 188
Agenda-setting theory 176	Selective exposure 180	Additive effect 188
	Dual-coding theory 181	

To learn more about the topics in this chapter, enter the Key Terms and Concepts found in this chapter as subject and keyword searches on your InfoTrac® College Edition.

NOTES

1. Cacioppo, J. T., & Petty, R. E. (1982). The need for cognition. *Journal of Personality and Social Psychology, 42,* 116–131.

2. Perse, E. (1992). Predicting attention to local television news: Need for cognition and motives for viewing. *Communication Reports, 5,* 40–49.

3. Condra, M. B. (1992). The link between need for cognition and political interest, involvement, and media usage. *Psychology—A Quarterly Journal of Human Behavior, 29,* 13–18.

4. De Pelsmacker, P., & Geuens, M. (1998). Television viewing behaviour, program preference and individual differences: The role of affect intensity and need for cognition. *Communicatie, 27,* 2–19.

5. Rhee, J. W., & Cappella, J. N. (1997). The role of political sophistication in learning from news: Measuring schema development. *Communication Research, 24,* 197–233.

6. McCombs, M., & Shaw, D. (1973). The agenda-setting function of the mass media. *Public Opinion Quarterly, 37,* 62–75.

7. Cohen, B. (1963). *The press and foreign policy.* Princeton, NJ: Princeton University Press.

8. McCombs, M., & Shaw, D. (1973). The agenda-setting function of the mass media. *Public Opinion Quarterly, 37,* 62–75.

9. Iyengar, S., & Kinder, D. (1987). *News that matters.* Chicago: University of Chicago Press.

10. Tankard, cited in Griffin, E. (1999). *A first look at communication theory.* Boston: McGraw-Hill.

11. Griffin, E. (1999). *A first look at communication theory.* Boston: McGraw-Hill.

12. Kiousis, S. (2003). Job approval and favorability: The impact of media attention to the Monica Lewinsky scandal on public opinion of President Bill Clinton. *Mass Communication & Society, 6*(4), 435-451.

13. Gross, K., & Aday, S. (2003). The scary world in your living room and neighborhood: Using local broadcast news, neighborhood crime rates, and personal experience to test agenda setting and cultivation. *Journal of Communication, 53*(3), 411-426.

14. Marilyn, R., Wanta, W., & Dzwo, Tzong-Horng. (2002). Agenda setting and issue salience online. *Communication Research, 29*(4), 452-465.

15. Williams, B. A., & Carpini, M. X. (2004). Monica and Bill all the time and everywhere: The collapse of gatekeeping and agenda setting in the new media environment. *American Behavioral Scientist, 47*(9), 1208-1230.

16. Noelle-Neumann, E. (1991). The theory of public opinion: The concept of the spiral of silence. In J. A. Anderson (Ed.), *Communication Yearbook, 14* (pp. 256–287). Newbury Park, CA: Sage.

17. Eveland, W. P. Jr., McLeod, D. M., & Signorielli, N. (1995). Actual and perceived U.S. public opinion: The spiral of silence during the Persian Gulf War. *International Journal of Public Opinion Research, 7,* 91–109.

18. McDonald, D. G., Glynn, C. J., Kim, S., & Ostman, R. E. (2001). The spiral of silence in the 1948 presidential election. *Communication Research, 28*(2), 139-155.

19. Robinson, J., & Davis, D. (1986). Comprehension of a single evening's news. In J. P. Robinson & M. R. Levy (Eds.), *The main source: Learning from television news* (pp. 107–132). Beverly Hills: Sage.

20. Kepplinger, H., & Daschmann, G. (1997). Today's news—tomorrow's context: A dynamic model of news processing. *Journal of Broadcasting & Electronic Media, 41,* 548–565.

21. Newhagen, J. E., & Reeves, B. (1992). The evening's bad news: Effects of compelling negative television news images on memory. *Journal of Communication, 42,* 25–41.

22. Gunter, B., Furnham, A., & Griffiths, S. (2000). Children's memory for news: A comparison of three presentation media. *Media Psychology, 2,* 93–118.

23. Newhagen, J. E. (1998). TV news images that induce anger, fear, and disgust: Effects on approach-avoidance and memory. *Journal of Broadcasting & Electronic Media, 42,* 265–276.

24. Lang, A., Newhagen, J., & Reeves, B. (1996). Negative video as structure: Emotion,

attention, capacity, and memory. *Journal of Broadcasting & Electronic Media, 40,* 460–477.

25. Kraus, S. (1996). Winners of the first 1960 televised presidential debate between Kennedy and Nixon. *Journal of Communication, 46,* 78–96.

26. Debate score: Kennedy up, Nixon down. (1960, November 7). *Broadcasting,* 27–28.

27. Druckman, J. N. (2003). The power of televised images: The first Kennedy–Nixon debate revisited. *Journal of Politics, 65*(2), 559–571.

28. Pfau, M., & Kang, J. G. (1991). The impact of relational messages on candidate influence in televised political debates. *Communication Studies, 42,* 117.

29. Schwartz, T. (1973). *The responsive chord.* New York: Anchor Books.

30. CEL. (1984). The 30-second president. In *A walk through the 20th century with Bill Moyers.* Washington, DC: Public Broadcasting Service.

31. Clinton, J. D., & Lapinski, J. S. (2004). "Targeted" advertising and voter turnout: An experimental study of the 2000 presidential election. *Journal of Politics, 66*(1), 69–96. Pinkleton, B. E., Um, N., & Austin, E. W. (2002). An exploration of the effects of negative political advertising on political decision making. *Journal of Advertising, 31*(1), 13–25.

32. Associated Press. (2004). Young America's news source: Jon Stewart [Online]. Available: http://www.cnn.com/2004/SHOWBIZ/TV/03/02/apontv.stewarts.stature.ap/

33. Tewksbury, D. (2003). What do Americans really want to know? Tracking the behavior of news readers on the Internet. *Journal of Communication, 53*(4), 694–710.

34. Phillips, D. P. (1979). Suicide, motor vehicle fatalities, and the mass media: Evidence toward a theory of suggestion. *American Journal of Sociology, 84,* 1150–1174.

35. Phillips, D. P. (1978). Airplane accident fatalities increase just after newspaper stories about murder and suicide. *Science, 201,* 748–750.

36. Cialdini, R. B. (1988). Influence: Science and practice. Glenview, IL: Scott Foresman.

37. Phillips, D. P. (1982). The impact of fictional television stories on U.S. adult fatalities: New evidence on the effect of the mass media on violence. *American Journal of Sociology, 87,* 1340–1359.

38. Etzersdorfer, E. & Sonneck, G. (1998). Preventing suicide by influencing mass-media reporting: The Viennese experience 1980–1996. *Archives of Suicide Research, 4*(1), 67–74.

10

■

The Effects of Media Stereotypes

STEREOTYPICAL REPRESENTATIONS IN THE MEDIA

Perhaps you're familiar with the TV commercials run by Taco Bell that featured the dog named Dinky. Dinky was a Chihuahua, and the commercials were presumably successful at selling Taco Bell's products. They were also successful at stirring controversy about Latino stereotypes. Gabriel Cazares, the former mayor of Clearwater, Florida, and former president of the Tampa, Florida, chapter of the League for United Latin American Citizens (LULAC), complained about the content of some of the Dinky ads. Instead of using a talking dog to depict Mexicans as was done in some of the ads, Cazares pointed out, Taco Bell could have used any number of Mexican artists, singers, dancers, or other celebrities who would have had even greater selling impact when they uttered the famous lines given to Dinky—"*Yo quiero* Taco Bell." Apparently, part of the controversy had to do with the fact that the ads encouraged people to associate Mexicans with dogs. In addition, in some of the commercials, Dinky scampers around looking for food—an image that infuriated many Latinos who perceived that Dinky's actions were being taken as the actions of the entire race. On the other hand, in one ad, Dinky answered a question on *Jeopardy* correctly in order to get food. Some thought that this ad depicted Dinky as a clever dog and that this image was not offensive.

The controversy surrounding Dinky and how commercials might convey subtle messages about groups of people raises the issue of media stereotypes. When media representations tend to depict groups of people in particular ways, they may play an important part in determining how media consumers come to think about individuals who are members of those groups. Social psychologists do not necessarily agree on how to think about stereotypes, but Susan Fiske and Shelly Taylor offer an approach that seems clear and sensible. They say, "One can think about stereotypes as a particular kind of role schema that organizes people's expectations about other people who fall into certain social categories."[1] If, for example, you tended to think that a male was more likely than a female to be an attorney, we might say that you had a **role schema** that was part of your thought processes when it came to thinking about men and women. Schemas help to organize thoughts. In the case of a role schema, the thoughts and expectations you have for a specific person are guided by a general set of expectations that you might have for people who hold the same role as the specific person you're thinking about. If you think that females are not as likely as males to be attorneys, then your expectations for females are **stereotyped** in a particular way.

One's expectations about someone else's role may be based on accurate data. That is, it might be the case that males really are more likely to be attorneys than females. However, one negative consequence of holding a stereotype, even if it is accurate, is that it may function to reinforce the status quo and unfairly restrict the diversity of social roles that individuals might hold. Think about what might happen if most people held the stereotype that males were more likely to be attorneys than females. To the extent that people had such expectations, females might not be socialized into career paths that would lead them to law school. In this way, stereotypes, even if accurate at a given point in time, can serve to perpetuate the status quo and be unduly restrictive for various groups of people. Of course, if stereotypes are inaccurate rather than accurate, they produce false expectations about others.

The media may generally depict people in stereotypical ways such that consumers are encouraged to adopt expectations about the roles that those people occupy. Following the example of female attorneys, if the media depicted very few females in the role of attorney, then consumers of the media might come to think of males as much more likely to be attorneys. The media would be engaging in a stereotypical depiction that has an impact on media consumers.

If this is the case, then there are two fundamental issues to be addressed in any discussion of the media and stereotypes. First, one might ask about the particular role expectations that the media encourage. In other words, how do the media actually depict certain groups of people? Second, once we know the answer to the first question, we might ask whether these depictions actually affect the role expectations that media consumers have for those same people. As it turns out, there is much more data available for the first question than the second. Nevertheless, both questions are important to examine.

Sex Role Stereotypes

One of the most repeated findings from content analyses of TV programs is that men far outnumber women. Summarizing across a number of different studies, Tannis MacBeth Williams observed: "[T]here are more than twice as many male as female models on TV, and when women do appear, they are most frequently found on comedy and light entertainment programs. Furthermore, this situation has remained constant over time."[2] One of the few consistent exceptions to the strong tendency to employ males more than females in the world of TV is found in the content of afternoon soap operas. Research by Natan Katzman confirms that the proportion of male and female characters in the soap opera genre is roughly equal.[3] In a review of some of the more recent content analyses on the frequency with which males and females appear in the media,[4] Richard Jackson Harris pointed out that males are three times more likely to appear in children's cartoons,[5] twice as likely to appear in music videos, and four to five times more likely to be featured as voice-over announcers—even though they aren't any more persuasive than female voice-overs.[6] For many researchers, the fact that males outnumber females in the TV world is a troubling finding that may suggest to viewers that males, by virtue of their greater presence, should be considered more important or more significant. Of course, researchers must be extremely careful at this point. Remember that in previous chapters, the point was made that media content cannot be assumed to cause any particular effect. It is important to distinguish carefully between the two questions about content and effect. Media effects researchers cannot speak about the effects of any particular stereotype without having evidence of an effect. The mere presence of a stereotype does not constitute evidence for an effect.

In addition to documenting the fact that females don't appear on TV as frequently as males do, researchers have found a full range of other stereotypical depictions. Tannis MacBeth Williams reviews evidence showing that married females on TV are far less likely to be employed than females in the actual population. Moreover, when females do hold jobs on TV, they tend to be restricted to a more narrow range of occupations than males. George Gerbner has also contributed some interesting insights about sex role stereotyping from his research on media violence. He maintains that women are much more likely to be depicted as victims of crime and violence than males. Although males are depicted in violent scenarios more frequently as the perpetrators or the aggressors, females are depicted more frequently as the victims. To Gerbner, these sorts of systematic distortions communicate a strong message about who has power in the culture. According to him, the predominant message of TV is that males have power over females; males are relatively powerful, and females are relatively powerless.[7]

When all of the content studies are considered together, there seems to be little doubt about the appropriate conclusion when it comes to sex role stereotypes. Two researchers, Jennifer Herrett-Skjellum and Mike Allen, used a technique known as **meta-analysis** to examine this issue. A meta-analysis is a method designed to statistically summarize over a large number of studies so that researchers can reach a confident conclusion about what the literature actually reveals on a given question. They summarized the data in the following way: "Television programming generally portrays men and women in traditional gender stereotypical roles. . . . All content analyses illustrate the consistent finding that men are more often on TV, in higher status roles as characters, and are represented as having greater power than women."[8] The important question for our purposes is: So what? Why should stereotypical presentations of men and women be of concern? Are there any effects associated with these portrayals? That is, do the media stereotypes actually cause people's perceptions to change or cause them to act any differently? As it turns out, several researchers have attempted to answer the question of media impact with respect to gender role stereotypes. Let's take a look at some of the findings.

Effects of Sex Role Stereotypes

As I am writing this section, my daughter Jordan, a sophomore in high school, is preparing to attend a weeklong computer camp at Purdue University. Over the course of the week, she will learn various things about computers and actually compete in some computer projects with the other campers. One day last week, when we checked with the camp registration just to make sure things were in order, we discovered a shocking statistic. There were 19 girls signed up for the camp—along with 98 boys. Although Jordan and her female friends may have found this statistic to be quite exhilarating, the camp leaders would probably have preferred a better balance of girls to boys. But recruiting girls to computer camp is quite a challenge. Somehow, adolescent girls just don't seem to be that attracted to computers. Why might this be? One likely reason has to do with the way young girls construct their social reality. Many have adopted beliefs about the social world around them that do not leave much room for females being attracted to computer camps. Obviously, there are many things that might affect young people's view of their social world, but the media messages that are consumed might be one important factor. Two communication researchers who are concerned about how media messages influence the **construction of social reality** are Robert Hawkins and Suzanne Pingree. In one study that they reported with their coauthor, Ilya Adler, they surveyed more than 1,300 adolescents, most of whom were from Australia. The most important general finding from their investigation was that heavy TV viewers tended to have beliefs about the world that were consistent with the messages of TV.[9]

We might actually be able to get some insight into this question by looking at the natural experiment that Tannis MacBeth Williams conducted in Canada. You may recall reading about this study in chapter 4. Along with her colleague, Meredith Kimball, Williams examined what happened to boys' and girls' job expectations over a two-year period in a town that initially had no access to television (Notel) and then received access to one TV channel. The results were enlightening.

The researchers had two main hypotheses, both of which were confirmed. First, Kimball and Williams believed that children who lived in Notel would hold fewer stereotypical attitudes about the appropriateness of various behaviors than would the children who lived in towns that did have TV access. The researchers measured stereotypical attitudes by having children in the sixth and ninth grades fill out the Sex Role Differentiation Scale. As expected, the results showed that the children in the town with no access to TV (Notel) did not differentiate behaviors according to sex to the same extent as the children in the TV towns. Given that the towns were chosen to be similar in almost every other respect except TV access, the authors interpreted this as evidence in favor of the idea that children develop sex-stereotyped attitudes as a result of watching TV.

But the evidence is even more compelling when the second hypothesis is examined. Immediately after the first hypothesis was tested, the children who lived in the town with no TV gained access to TV reception. Two years later, when the researchers returned and administered the Sex Role Differentiation Scale once again to children in the same grades, they found that the pattern of the results had changed. In contrast to the scores two years earlier, now that the children in Notel had TV access, their scores on the Sex Role Differentiation Scale changed to show a dramatic increase in stereotyped attitudes. Given that the only major change over the two-year period was access to TV, the researchers felt comfortable interpreting this evidence as a clear media effect. In drawing implications about these findings, the researchers stated the following:

> Several studies, including this one, have documented links between TV viewing and stereotyped sex-role attitudes. The evidence for same-sex preferences in viewing television, greater recognition of same-sex characters and behaviors, and the role of gender schemata in processing sex-role information probably account for the effects of TV viewing. In light of this information, we recommend that more female characters be portrayed in more varied roles on television. This may be particularly important for young children.[10]

It wouldn't be good science to conclude that the great disparity between males and females who registered for the Purdue computer camp was due to the impact of media messages. But could media images have contributed, in part, to this enrollment pattern? Extending the conclusions from this research, it certainly seems like a plausible idea.

Media Images of Thin Bodies and Effects on Body Image

If sexual stereotypes in the media might have an impact on the socialization of young boys and girls that in turn might affect enrollment patterns at computer camps, then perhaps there are other important areas of media impact related to sexual stereotypes. One such area that has received a fair amount of research attention over the last decade is the way in which female bodies are represented and the impact of those representations.

In one of the most recent content analyses to address this topic, Gregory Fouts and Kimberley Burggraf studied 18 situation comedies from prime-time TV.[11] Their findings were striking. First, they discovered that the females in these programs were far more likely to be judged as being "below average" in weight as opposed to "average" or "above average." This finding is consistent with the results of other research that shows that media images of females tend to place a heavy emphasis on an idealized, overly thin standard compared to males.[12]

Second, and even more important, the higher the weight of the female character depicted, the more likely it was that negative comments were made by other characters about her or directly to her. Moreover, these negative comments were often followed by a laugh track that suggested to the audience that these negative comments were funny. The authors speculated that the combination of programming that presents a disproportionate emphasis on overly thin female bodies and creates a context that explicitly reinforces the value and attractiveness of this standard may amount to a huge social problem. If young girls internalize the idea that females should be thin, then the media might have some role in creating **body dissatisfaction** or **body-image disturbance** among females. That is, because of their natural tendency to engage in **social comparison,** young female viewers may compare their own bodies with the ones that are frequently depicted and reinforced in the media. To the extent that there is a perceived mismatch, young girls might start down a road that could lead to various eating disorders like bulimia or anorexia nervosa. Such a path might jeopardize the health, or even the life, of young girls.

Of course, these effects are largely speculative. Is there any research to suggest that overly thin females in the media actually have an impact on the way young girls think or behave? The answer to this question is yes. Let's take a brief look at some of the studies that have been reported.

In one of the few published experiments on this topic, two researchers, Eric Stice and Heather Shaw, randomly assigned 157 female college students to view pictures in magazines that contained either thin models, average models, or no models.[13] Immediately after viewing the pictures, the students responded to a number of items on a questionnaire. The results revealed that the students who had viewed the thin models were more likely to report a variety of negative emotions such as stress, shame, guilt, depression, and insecurity. They also indicated higher levels of body dissatisfaction. A second finding of the study was that, in general, students who reported high levels of body dissatisfaction, regardless of their experimental condition, were more likely also to report that they suffered from the symptoms associated with bulimia. More recently, Kristen Harrison and Joanne Cantor surveyed over 400 college students and asked questions about media consumption, body dissatisfaction, drive for thinness, and various symptoms related to eating disorders.[14] Their results, though not conclusive in terms of causality, were consistent with the experimental results reported by Stice and Shaw. For the female students, media consumption was related to higher body dissatisfaction, a drive for thinness, and reports of symptoms that suggest eating disorders. For the male students, media consumption was related to the tendency to endorse thinness and dieting for females. Harrison has reported the results of yet another study that replicates and extends these same findings.[15]

Some of the most recent investigations on this topic continue to point in the same direction as the earlier studies. One particularly interesting investigation was reported by Duane Hargreaves and Marika Tiggemann.[16] These authors attempted to explore the possibility of a cumulative effect of media exposure to ideal body types. They randomly assigned 80 adolescents, both boys and girls, to watch either 20 commercials that contained "female thin ideals" or 20 commercials that featured no physical appearance at all. As many studies have shown, exposure to the thin body ideals produced small changes in body dissatisfaction. The really interesting aspect of this study was that the authors came back to these adolescents two years later and again had them respond to measures on body dissatisfaction and drive for thinness. This type of longitudinal study is not so common, and the results can often be particularly illuminating. In this case, they found that the girls who were most affected by the commercials when they first viewed them were more likely to express body dissatisfaction and a drive for thinness than the group who had seen the neutral ads. This same effect was also observed for boys on the measure of a drive for thinness, but not on the measure of body dissatisfaction. The authors interpret these results as evidence for cumulative media effects. Apparently, the initial media effect continued to produce changes in body image that were detectable two years later.

The study by Hargreaves and Tiggemann is one of the few in the literature to include boys as well as girls. However, researchers appear to be more interested now than in years past in studying these sorts of body image effects on males. In a recent study reported by Daniel Agliata and Stacey Tantleff-Dunn, 158 males were randomly assigned to watch either neutral television commercials or ones that featured male ideal body images.[17] The authors reported that the group who watched the ideal body images reported significantly higher levels of depression and muscle dissatisfaction.

To summarize the research on this topic, it appears that a number of studies document that media images of females are stereotypical in that they tend to represent females with idealized, overly thin bodies. These depictions may be very important because a number of studies clearly point to the conclusion that they have negative effects on both males and females. Females are encouraged to internalize the ideal image and may strive to attain it even in the face of suffering from various eating disorders. Males are encouraged to reinforce the ideal image and thus may create additional social pressure on females to conform to this ultrathin body standard. There is still more research to be done on this topic. Some researchers are beginning to investigate the extent to which some program types may be more likely than others to produce these effects (see Study Box 10-1).

One question that has surely occurred to you by now is what one can do about a negative media effect such as this one. Researchers and scholars recommend teaching students to engage in **critical media consumption.** One of the hoped-for consequences of writing a textbook like this one is that college students will become more sensitive to media stereotypes and the possible effects of media exposure on attitudes and behavior. Many media scholars recommend that elementary and secondary schools explicitly teach children about these sorts of media stereotypes and their effects on viewers. Research on high school females strongly suggests that school curricula designed to expose sexual stereotypes in the media are effective in reducing the extent to which young girls embrace the idealized, overly thin body standard that consistently shows up in magazines, movies, advertisements, and TV shows.[18]

STUDY BOX 10-1   Do Sports Programs Promote Body Dissatisfaction?

In one of the most recent studies on the relationship between media exposure and body dissatisfaction, two communication researchers, Kimberly Bissell and Peiqin Zhou administered a questionnaire to 218 female college students. The students were asked to report the frequency of their exposure to 40 different TV programs that were on the air in 2001 when the study was conducted. Independent coders rated these programs on a scale designed to assess the "dominant body shape" seen in the program. A "1" on the scale indicated that the dominant body shape was "conspicuously thin"; a "5" on the scale indicated "conspicuously fat." Numbers between 1 and 5 were used to indicate varying levels from thin to fat. After each program was rated, the researchers examined the programs that were the most popular among the sample of respondents. Eight programs were identified: *Friends, Dawson's Creek, Will & Grace, 7th Heaven, Felicity, ER, Dharma & Greg,* and *Gilmore Girls.* For each of these programs, coders had rated the dominant body shape as conspicuously thin. Each respondent was assigned a total exposure score for these conspicuously thin programs based upon their reports of how frequently they watched the shows. The researchers also measured reports of body dissatisfaction and drive for thinness, as well as the experience of two eating disorders—anorexia and bulimia. They computed correlations between the measure of TV exposure and these four measures. In each case, the correlation was positive and statistically significant (see chapter 2 for a refresher on correlations and statistical significance). Higher levels of exposure to these programs were associated with the experience of anorexia ($r = .22$), bulimia ($r = .24$), a drive for thinness ($r = .21$), and body dissatisfaction ($r = .17$). Finally, the researchers computed correlations between the exposure that respondents reported to sports programs on TV and these same four measures. Unlike the results for the entertainment programs, none of these measures were significantly related to exposure to TV sports. Thus, the answer to the question posed in the title to this study box seems to be no.

SOURCE: Bissell, K., & Zhou, P. (2004). Must-see TV or ESPN: Entertainment and sports media exposure and body-image distortion in college women. *Journal of Communication, 54*(1), 5–21.

One organization that is dedicated to teaching students to consume media more critically is the Media Education Foundation. You can find its website by typing this name into a search engine. One aspect of the foundation's teaching mission is to produce videos that seek to reveal the way in which certain types of media depict stereotypes that are potentially harmful. For example, in a series of videos (*Dreamworlds*) on the way music television stereotypes both males and females, Sut Jhally has presented brief clips that encourage the viewer to see these videos in a new light.[19] Similarly, Jean Kilbourne's *Killing Us Softly* series examines how women are depicted in advertising in ways that are demeaning and stereotypical.[20] Although these videos are valuable instructional aids, their focus, like much of the research on stereotypes, is on the nature of media content—not on the scientific investigation of the effects of that content. Consequently, some social scientists find these videos to be long on claims and short on supporting evidence.

Racial Stereotypes

As the chapter's opening example about Dinky the Chihuahua illustrated, sex stereotypes are not the only area of research that concerns the student and scholar of media effects. Several years ago, the Frito-Lay company introduced a cartoon character in its advertising that was supposed to convey the message that Fritos corn chips are delicious. The character was dubbed the "Frito-bandito," and his role was to run around stealing bags of Fritos because he couldn't resist the taste. He wore a big yellow hat, and a gun on either side of his waist. His long mustache and Mexican accent clearly identified him as a Mexican. The company thought that it had come up with a smashing advertising campaign until the Mexican community began to protest. Their argument was very simple and reduced to two points: (1) The frequency of media depictions of Mexicans is so low that *any* depiction is crucially important in terms of the overall image it represents to the masses of media consumers, and (2) the image of the Frito-bandito, as one of the very few media representations of Mexicans, was an image that encouraged consumers to adopt a very undesirable stereotype, associating this ethnic group with crime and thievery. The storm of controversy surrounding the cartoon icon reached such a fever pitch that the Frito-Lay company decided to put the Frito-bandito in his grave. They abandoned the use of the bandito in all of their advertising.

Although the Frito-bandito certainly stirred controversy, perhaps the greatest concern over the years about stereotypes in U.S. media has been about the representation of African Americans. In his brief discussion of the history of how African Americans have been portrayed over the years, Richard Jackson Harris noted, "Until the 1960s, there were almost no African Americans as models in mainstream U.S. advertising . . . and the only African Americans in prime-time TV programming were limited to a few stereotyped and demeaning roles."[21] Although the situation has certainly changed over the last three decades, and the presence of African Americans is now much more commonplace in advertising and serious dramatic roles, a recent content analysis, discussed in the next section, reveals that negative media stereotyping of African Americans is still taking place in a surprising and dramatic way.

Overrepresentation of African Americans as Lawbreakers

In a fascinating study of TV news, two media researchers, Travis Dixon and Daniel Linz, carried out a major content study designed to reveal information about how TV newscasts in a major U.S. city represented African Americans and Latinos in stories about crime.[22] Using random-sampling procedures, these authors sampled news programs from TV stations in the Los Angeles area over a period of 20 weeks, extending from October 1995 to June 1996. Their final sample contained 116 news broadcasts and included examples from virtually every news program broadcast in the Los Angeles area during the selected time period. A team of coders viewed these newscasts and coded all stories that reported crimes. The race of the people who were shown as perpetrators of each crime was coded, along with the race of the people who were shown as law defenders (police, judges, lawyers, etc.).

In reporting their results, Dixon and Linz relied on three types of comparisons. First, they used the **intergroup comparison.** This is a very simple comparison of the percentage of one group to the percentage of another group. Intergroup comparisons have been used regularly in content analyses of racial representations. Dixon and Linz found that the news coverage across all the programs in their sample included 129 perpetrators of criminal offenses. Of those 129, 69 were Black perpetrators and 40 were White perpetrators. Stated in ratio form, for every White perpetrator shown on the news, there were 1.72 Black perpetrators. When the analysis was restricted to felony crimes, the ratio was even higher. For every White perpetrator, there were 2.46 Black perpetrators. The intergroup comparison is a convenient way to report and compare data for different groups. In this case, the data show that Blacks were more likely to be shown as perpetrators of crime than Whites. Dixon and Linz also reported similar data showing that Latinos were also more likely to be shown as crime perpetrators than Whites—but not as likely as Blacks.

A second type of comparison used by Dixon and Linz was the **interrole comparison.** It is used to compare the distribution of the same group of people according to particular roles. For example, in their study, Dixon and Linz coded the race of the police officers depicted in the news stories as well as that of the perpetrators. There were 87 Blacks depicted in their sample of news stories. Of those 87, 69 appeared as perpetrators of crime, whereas only 18 appeared as officers. In ratio terms, for every Black officer, there were 3.83 crime perpetrators. When the same analysis was conducted for Whites, a very different picture emerged. Of the 133 Whites who appeared in the crime stories, 93 appeared as officers and 40 appeared as perpetrators. In ratio terms, for every White officer, there were only .43 perpetrators. From this analysis, it seems clear that Blacks were more likely to be shown as perpetrators of crime than as officers; Whites were more likely to be shown as officers than as perpetrators.

Finally, Dixon and Linz used a comparison known as the **interreality comparison.** In this case, the authors were interested in comparing the percentages of Blacks, Whites, and Latinos who appeared in the TV crime stories with the percentages that showed up in actual crime statistics catalogued in the Los Angeles area. The interreality comparison is, perhaps, the most revealing of these three comparisons because it shows how media depictions may distort reality. When the authors went to the actual crime data, the records showed that Blacks accounted for 21% of all of the criminal arrests in Los Angeles. Whites accounted for 28%, Latinos for 47%. But when these percentages were compared to the percentages shown on TV newscasts, quite a difference emerged. Whereas Blacks actually accounted for the *lowest* percentage of arrests in the real crime statistics, they made up the *highest* percentage of perpetrators represented on TV news. Whereas their actual arrest rate was 21%, a full 37% of TV news perpetrators were Black. In contrast, compared to the actual arrest rate for Whites (28%), only 21% of the perpetrators shown on TV news were White. Just as Blacks were overrepresented as criminals on the news, Latinos appeared to be underrepresented. Compared to their actual arrest rate (47% of all arrests), only 29% of the criminal perpetrators on TV news were Latino.

In addition to providing a replication of some earlier studies on the depiction of Blacks and Whites as criminals on TV news, the study by Dixon and Linz is important because it is one of the first to report data on Latinos. It is also important in terms of the explanations that the authors advanced to explain their findings. Why might Blacks be overrepresented as criminals compared to Whites? The authors argued that TV news may be drawn to report blue-collar crime instead of white-collar crime. Blue-collar crimes such as assault and robbery are more visually dramatic and attractive to TV reporters. They may also be more likely to be committed by Blacks. Whites, who have access to more economic resources and positions of power, may be more likely to commit white-collar crime. In comparison with the highly visual drama of a violent arrest or car chase, white-collar crimes such as embezzlement don't offer very exciting news footage. This may partially account for the representational distortions that Dixon and Linz uncovered.

What about the effects of these representations? You have already been reminded several times in this text of the caution that media content does not equal media effect. Dixon and Linz studied the media content—not the way that content had an impact on viewers. Nevertheless, they did underscore the need for some systematic research on the impact of these depictions. At the end of their research report, they stated the following:

> We suggest that immediate work must be undertaken with regard to how these portrayals might encourage or discourage stereotyping and increase fear of African Americans. Cultivation theory as well as the mechanisms explicated in the social cognition literature suggest that these representations may have a powerful impact on viewers. (p. 151)[23]

You may want to review cultivation theory in chapter 8 and see if you can determine what Dixon and Linz are concerned about. Recall that the theory basically states that heavy consumers of media will tend to be cultivated in terms of their attitudes and values toward the view of reality depicted by the media. One of the "mechanisms explicated in the social cognition literature" that the authors may have in mind could be **priming,** a concept discussed in chapter 5. If the media continue to associate Blacks with the perpetration of crime and Whites with law enforcement, these associations may become so strong in a person's mind that merely thinking about one could prime thoughts of the other. Clearly, as Dixon and Linz suggest, future research efforts need to examine how these representational distortions may affect media consumers.

THE IMBALANCE IN MEDIA
RESEARCH ON STEREOTYPES

Countless content studies document representational distortions of various types. Such studies are so easy to conceive that if one of my graduate students seems lost in terms of a research idea for a seminar, as a last resort I will sometimes suggest a content analysis on the prevalence of some group or behavior that might be of interest in media messages. To give you a sense of what I mean here, consider just a sampling of the studies reported in the literature that use content analysis to study different media stereotypes.

In terms of different groups of people, the studies go far beyond the depictions of Blacks, Whites, and Latinos as studied by Dixon and Linz. As we have already seen, many studies have examined how women are represented in prime-time TV or in advertising. Other studies have examined the depictions of men and the types of behaviors that are deemed acceptable for men to perform. Harris documents studies on other groups as well, including Native Americans, Arabs, homosexuals, persons with disabilities, police officers, lawyers, farmers, and college students. Often, specific behaviors, rather than groups of people, are the main focus of content studies. Content studies of media have examined cigarette smoking, alcohol use and abuse, seat belt use, a variety of aggressive behaviors, helping and prosocial behaviors, and so forth (see Study Box 10-2 for a focus on how some of these behaviors are depicted in movies). All of these studies have helped to contribute to our understanding of how the media may communicate subtle and not-so-subtle stereotypes. But as I reviewed the literature in preparation for writing this chapter, one thing was very apparent: There are far more studies on the *presence* of media stereotypes than there are on the *effects* of those stereotypes on media consumers.

There are some good reasons that the media literature reflects an imbalance between content studies and effects studies. First, although content studies are often more time-consuming and tedious than studies of media impact, they also permit the researcher to avoid a number of obstacles that inevitably appear whenever people, instead of media messages, are the units of analysis in a study. Researchers who need human subjects must worry about securing approval from a human-subjects committee about the procedures that are planned. And once approval is granted, people don't always show up for the study. Sometimes, they show up and then decide not to participate. Researchers must also be concerned about the ethics of subjecting subjects to potentially harmful media messages. In short, research with human subjects can be considerably messier than research with media messages. Often, beginning researchers will get their feet wet with a content study and never move on to research with human subjects, which is where we learn about media effects.

Another factor contributing to the imbalance may be the obligation to document the presence or absence of content *before* doing a study on media impact. For example, before I started to investigate how depictions of paranormal messages affected people's paranormal beliefs, I was concerned about the

---

**STUDY BOX 10-2   Depictions of Unhealthy
Behaviors in the Movies**

Using data provided by *Variety's* annual reports of the top-grossing movies, Terre, Drabman, and Speer conducted a major content analysis of 200 movies (the top-20 films of each year over the 10-year period from 1977 to 1988). They coded a number of unhealthy behaviors, using each five-minute segment of the film as the unit of analysis. For each segment of each film, they coded whether characters were shown *possessing* cigarettes, drugs, junk food, or sports equipment. They also coded the *suggested use* of the things that were possessed. For example, if a cigarette was only being held but not actually smoked, its use was only suggested. *Overt action* was also coded. Taking drugs or drinking an alcoholic beverage counted as actual use. Finally, the *behavioral outcomes* of engaging in these actions were coded. The results of the content analysis revealed several significant trends over the decade, but there were two very important findings. First, the frequency of depictions of smoking and

illegal drug use increased significantly. Second, none of the risky behaviors that were coded (smoking, drug use, alcohol use) were consistently associated with either positive or negative outcomes. The authors concluded: "These results present a disturbing picture of the health-relevant social norms being portrayed in recent, popular films. . . . Of particular concern is the trend toward increasing portrayals of health-detrimental behaviors" (p. 1316). The authors explicitly noted that their report did not permit them to assume that the depictions had any effects on consumers. However, they do speculate on the basis of media effects already documented and existing theory about media impact that depictions of risky behaviors in movies may very well have negative social consequences.

SOURCE: Terre, L., Drabman, R. S., & Speer, P. (1991). Health-relevant behaviors in media. *Journal of Applied Social Psychology, 21,* 1303–1319.

---

prevalence of paranormal messages in the media. It took a content study to determine that the messages were prevalent enough to warrant concern. Sometimes content studies are produced that don't end up leading to studies of media effects.

Another reason for the imbalance between studies of content and studies of effects is probably the main one: Documenting media effects is considerably more difficult than documenting the presence or absence of media content. Even in the most carefully designed sample survey, evidence for a clear causal effect remains elusive. And the most carefully designed laboratory experiment still has significant limitations in what it can reveal about media impact. Most lab experiments reveal short–term effects but tell us little about media impact over the long term. Added to these inherent design limitations, there are a host of thorny procedural details that can easily confound the best-laid plans of a would-be media effects researcher.

I don't want to be overly negative at this point. I have spent my career studying media effects, and I remain just as enthusiastic about doing effects research today as I was when I started more than 20 years ago. But the point remains that solid conclusions about the content of the media are much easier to generate than solid conclusions about the impact of the media.

AN INTRIGUING AND UNDER-STUDIED MEDIA DEPICTION: FACES

Before concluding our coverage of media stereotypes, there is one final phenomenon in which I became personally interested starting about 20 years ago. I hope you'll find this phenomenon interesting as well. In the fall of 1984, I was busy conducting research on people's emotional reactions to frightening mass media when I ran across an article that referred to a concept I hadn't heard of before. A researcher named Dane Archer, along with his colleagues, had published an article in the *Journal of Personality and Social Psychology* that was called "Face-ism: Five Studies of Sex Differences in Facial Prominence."[24] The title piqued my curiosity. What exactly was "face-ism"? The more I read in Archer's article, the more fascinated I became. As it turns out, **face-ism** refers to the tendency to represent people in terms of their face or head as opposed to their body. The face-ism index is a very simple computation that Archer and his colleagues describe as

> . . . the ratio of two linear measurements. The numerator of this index is the distance (in millimeters or any other unit) in a depiction from the top of the head to the lowest point of the chin. The denominator of the index is the distance from the top of the head to the lowest visible part of the subject's body.

Figure 10-1 shows the ratio visually and computes the face-ism index for two figures. Once I understood how the face-ism index was computed, the research findings uncovered by Archer and his colleagues seemed almost incredible.

For starters, the researchers examined more than 1,700 published photographs in the news and advertising sections of five major U.S. periodicals. They computed the average face-ism index for the males depicted in the photos and compared it to the average face-ism index computed for the females. The results were startling. For males, the average index was .65. But for females it was over 30% less—about .45. Think about what these numbers mean. In photos of males, the head or face was depicted as about 65% of the entire male figure. But for females, the head or face was depicted as only about 45% of the entire female figure. Males were more likely to be represented in terms of their heads or faces, whereas females were more likely to be represented in terms of their bodies. It was unlikely that the difference in the face-ism ratio was due to chance. The probability of getting a difference by chance that was as large as the one documented in Archer's research was less than 1 in 1,000 ($p < .001$).

As I started to think about what differences in face-ism might mean (the authors refer to these differences as the "face-ism effect"), Archer and his colleagues

FIGURE 10-1 Face-ism Ratios

The face-ism ratio is computed by taking the distance from the top of the head to the bottom of the chin and dividing it by the distance from the top of the head to the bottom of the body. In the top picture, the ratio is 14 mm/67 mm, or 0.21. In the bottom picture, the ratio is 33 mm/64 mm, or 0.51. In general, media depictions of males are more likely to resemble the bottom picture. Media depictions of females are more likely to be like the top picture.

hit me with even more provocative findings. The face-ism effect is not limited to U.S. media. It was documented in publications from nearly a dozen countries across the globe. In addition to generalizing across countries, the effect apparently generalizes across centuries as well. The authors noted that in a study of nearly 1,000 portraits and self-portraits of art over a span of six centuries, the same face-ism effect emerged again and again. There was even some evidence that the size of the difference between male and female representations was increasing over time.

The authors also reported research that investigated the extent to which face-ism might be present in private representations as well as public ones. In drawings of college students that were requested from both males and females, the male images were repeatedly drawn with higher face-ism ratios than the images of females. I was intrigued by the factors that might lie behind this systematic difference in male and female representations. Of course, one obvious hypothesis is that the images simply reflect a real biological difference—that male heads are larger than those of females. However, this hypothesis turns out not to be true. As I searched for a less obvious explanation, Archer and his colleagues threw in the real kicker. In an experiment that manipulated face-ism ratios for photos of the same individual, naïve judges rated the people who were high on facial prominence in the photos as more intelligent, more ambitious, and better looking.

Frankly, when I read about this research, I thought the potential effects of face-ism in the media were nothing short of staggering. If high facial prominence was associated with intelligence, ambition, and attractiveness, then what was the impact of media depictions of females (who were characteristically low in facial prominence) on the general way females were perceived in the culture at large: Were females perceived as less intelligent? Less ambitious? Less attractive? These were potential effects that, as far as I knew, had never been explored by media effects researchers.

My fascination with the face-ism effect might have taken a back seat to my other research had it not been for a graduate student, Christine Fehlner, who occupied an office nearby and happened to be working on a project that tracked news coverage of the presidential campaign of 1984. Just after I finished reading about face-ism, I came out of my office and saw a stack of newspapers that Fehlner had been collecting for stories of campaign coverage. There on the front page was a picture of Walter Mondale, the Democratic nominee for president, along with his vice presidential running mate, the first female ever to occupy this role, Geraldine Ferraro. At that instant, the idea to begin investigating the face-ism effect in the 1984 political campaign was born. Fehlner and I went on to conduct a study on this topic that was published two years later in the *Journal of Communication*.[25] We looked at the face-ism ratios of the two male Republican candidates, Ronald Reagan and George Bush, as well as those of Mondale and Ferraro. We looked at these ratios for all photos that appeared in *Time* and *Newsweek* during the months of the campaign. Our findings diverged a bit from Archer's. The face-ism ratios of the four candidates were essentially equivalent. But when we went back and looked at other males and females pictured in the same magazines, we found evidence of the same face-ism effect that had been reported in past research. Males were more likely to be depicted with higher levels of facial prominence than females.

We can't be certain exactly why we found no face-ism effect in how Geraldine Ferraro was represented compared to the male candidates. Perhaps the results of our study are best explained by a norm of equivalent representation for all candidates in a presidential campaign. We noted that in many of the pictorial layouts in magazines, the presidential candidates were presented in photos that were framed identically and appeared as offsetting, competing representations. It may be that in politics at the national level, the press is constrained to represent candidates in a photographically similar manner, regardless of gender.

In the end, the most interesting aspect of the face-ism effect is the fact that people's perceptions of those with higher facial prominence are more positive. Some scholars have suggested that this has to do with the fact that the head is where the brain is and that people think of the head or face as the center of an individual's intelligence. Whatever the reason, if the media represent males with higher facial prominence than females, the experimental data would suggest that this practice has negative implications for the evaluation of women. I would like to conduct a study in which people are asked to report their exposure to mass media and also asked to provide their own drawings of males and females. One hypothesis based on the current literature would be that heavy media consumers who spend more time processing faces that are systematically different according to the sex-biased face-ism effect might be more likely to show this effect in their own drawings. This is a study waiting to be done.

I am certainly not alone in expressing interest in the face-ism effect after reading the work of Archer and his colleagues. The face-ism effect has attracted some recent attention from two other researchers, Miron Zuckerman and Suzanne Kieffer. They examined pictures of Whites and Blacks that have appeared in paintings, in periodicals, and on the face of postage stamps. Reasoning from the past literature that higher facial prominence was associated with impressions of power, they predicted that images of Blacks would have lower facial prominence than images of Whites. This is exactly what they found. Moreover, they also found concrete evidence that people represented in photos with higher facial prominence were perceived as being more dominant.[26]

So, where does all this leave us? The research reviewed in this chapter leaves little doubt that media stereotypes do affect people. Nevertheless, the challenge for the research community is to begin taking some of the well-documented stereotypical depictions (e.g., sex and race stereotypes) and showing precisely how they affect people's attitudes and behaviors. It is one thing to speculate on the importance of media stereotypes; it is quite another thing to actually document the importance with a carefully executed study that shows evidence of media impact.

SUMMARY

This chapter reviewed research on various stereotypes in the mass media that have been documented by content analyses. Sexual stereotypes and racial stereotypes are two areas of research that have received the most attention. Although some studies on the effects of stereotypes have been undertaken, it was noted that content studies are far more prevalent than studies of impact. One area of effects is in the study of female body images and their possible impact on body dissatisfaction and eating disorders. The reasons for the existence of fewer studies on effects and more on content were discussed, and the important distinction between content and effect was again emphasized. The chapter concluded with an examination of a very intriguing phenomenon involving the depiction of male and female faces and bodies in the media. In comparison to males, females tend to be shown in terms of their bodies instead of their heads or faces. The implications of this phenomenon in terms of people's perceptions of males and females was highlighted.

KEY TERMS AND CONCEPTS

Role schema 193

Stereotype 193

Meta-analysis 194

Construction of social reality 195

Body dissatisfaction 197

Body-image disturbance 197

Social comparison 197

Critical media consumption 198

Intergroup comparison 201

Interrole comparison 201

Interreality comparison 201

Priming 202

Face-ism 205

To learn more about the topics in this chapter, enter the Key Terms and Concepts found in this chapter as subject and keyword searches on your InfoTrac® College Edition.

NOTES

1. Fiske, S. T., & Taylor, S. E. (1991). *Social cognition.* New York: McGraw-Hill.

2. Williams, T. M. (1986). *The impact of television: A natural experiment in three communities.* Orlando, FL: Academic Press.

3. Katzman, N. (1972). Television soap operas: What's been going on anyway? *Public Opinion Quarterly, 36,* 200–212.

4. Harris, R. J. (1999). *A cognitive psychology of mass communication.* Mahwah, NJ: Erlbaum.

5. Dobrow, J. R., & Gidney, C. L. (1998). The good, the bad, and the foreign: The use of dialect in children's animated television. *The Annals of the American Academy of Political and Social Science, 557,* 105–119.

6. Bretl, D. J., & Cantor, J. (1988). The portrayal of men and women on U.S.

television commercials: A recent content analysis and trends over 15 years. *Sex Roles, 18,* 595–609.

7. Jhally, S. (1994). *The killing screens: Media and the culture of violence* [Video]. Northampton, MA: Media Education Foundation.

8. Herrett-Skjellum, J., & Allen, M. (1996). Television programming and sex stereotyping: A meta-analysis. In B. R. Burleson (Ed.), *Communication yearbook* (pp. 157–185). Thousand Oaks, CA.: Sage.

9. Hawkins, R. P., Pingree, S., & Adler, I. (1987). Searching for cognitive processes in the cultivation effect: Adult and adolescent samples in the United States and Australia. *Human Communication Research, 13,* 553–577.

10. Kimball, M. A. (1986). Television and sex-role attitudes. In T. M. Williams (Ed.), *The impact of television: A natural experiment in three communities* (pp. 265–301). Orlando, FL: Academic Press.

11. Fouts, G., & Burggraf, K. (2000). Television situation comedies: Female weight, male negative comments, and audience reactions. *Sex Roles, 42,* 925–932.

12. Malkin, A. R., Wornian, K., & Chrisler, J. C. (1999). Women and weight: Gendered messages on magazine covers. *Sex Roles, 40,* 647–655.

13. Stice, E., & Shaw, H. E. (1994). Adverse effects of the media portrayed thin-ideal on women and linkages to bulimic symptomatology. *Journal of Social & Clinical Psychology, 13,* 288–308.

14. Harrison, K., & Cantor, J. (1997). The relationship between media consumption and eating disorders. *Journal of Communication, 47,* 40–67.

15. Harrison, K. (2000). The body electric: Thin-ideal media and eating disorders in adolescents. *Journal of Communication, 50,* 119–143.

16. Hargreaves, D., & Tiggemann, M. (2003). Longer-term implications of responsiveness to "thin-ideal" television: Support for a cumulative hypothesis of body image disturbance? *European Eating Disorders Review, 11*(6), 465–477.

17. Agliata, D., & Tantleff-Dunn, S. (2004). The impact of media exposure on males' body image. *Journal of Social & Clinical Psychology, 23*(1), 7–22.

18. Irving, L. M., DuPen, J., & Berel, S. (1998). A media literacy program for high school females. *Eating Disorders: The Journal of Treatment & Prevention, 6,* 119–132.

19. Jhally, S. (1990). *Dreamworlds: Gender/sex/power in rock video.* Northampton, MA: Media Education Foundation.

20. Jhally, S., & Kilbourne J. (2000). Killing us softly 3: Advertising's image of women. Northampton, MA: Media Education Foundation.

21. Harris, R. J. (1999). *A cognitive psychology of mass communication.* Mahwah, NJ: Erlbaum.

22. Dixon, T. L., & Linz, D. (2000). Overrepresentation and underrepresentation of African Americans and Latinos as lawbreakers on television news. *Journal of Communication, 50*(2), 131–154.

23. Ibid.

24. Archer, D., Iritani, B., Kimes, D. D., & Barrios, M. (1983). Face-ism: Five studies of sex differences in facial prominence. *Journal of Personality and Social Psychology, 45,* 725–735.

25. Sparks, G. G., & Fehlner, C. L. (1986). Faces in the news: Gender comparisons of magazine photographs. *Journal of Communication, 36,* 70–79.

26. Zuckerman, M., & Kieffer, S. C. (1994). Race differences in face-ism: Does facial prominence imply dominance? *Journal of Personality & Social Psychology, 66,* 86–92.

11

■

The Impact of New
Media Technologies

THE REVOLUTION IN
NEW MEDIA TECHNOLOGY

Over the last 75 years, media effects researchers have usually lagged behind in
studying the impact of the very latest media. As late as 1960, when TV had
exploded on the scene, the prevailing wisdom among researchers was that electronic media had limited effects. You might recall from chapter 3 that this "wisdom" was mainly the consequence of a single study—a large survey conducted
during the 1940 presidential campaign, before the days of television. It wasn't
until the mid–1960s, almost 25 years after the survey that ushered in the era
of limited media effects, that researchers began systematically studying the
effects of TV.

Of course, it makes some sense that research on a given medium would lag
a bit behind. Any new technology has to be in place and in use by a reasonable
proportion of the population before the research community deems it worthwhile to focus on the impact of that new technology. Consequently, when we
ask questions about the effects of new technology, it makes sense that the number of studies at our disposal is not nearly as great as when we ask questions
about the effects of a well-established medium such as TV or movies.

As I write these words, the students on my campus have already down-
loaded several hundred thousand songs from a new subscription downloading
service that contracted with the university. Many universities around the country have entered into such contracts in order to provide students with a legal

way to get their music. Just a few years ago, the music industry dominated the headlines with articles about the problem of the Napster website. If you are a typical student consumer, you may not have regarded Napster as a problem. Upon arriving at the site, you could make music files available to anyone else on the site—files that you had copied from a CD onto your computer hard drive. You could also search through hundreds of thousands of other music files that were available from others on the site and copy whatever you wished. The problem, of course, is that the music industry was not very happy about what it regarded as a violation of copyright law. Anyone could potentially download an entire album and avoid paying the purchase price. A judge tried to shut down the site until some legal solution can be found, but her action was overturned. However, an appeals court upheld the basic judgment to shut Napster down if the language was changed in the initial injunction. As of this writing, the downloading of free music is still taking place on various Internet sites—but things are changing rapidly. The pace of change of new media technologies nearly guarantees that by the time you read these words, the situation will be different than it is at the moment these words are written.

When we talk about the impact or effects of new media technology, there are a host of effects that we might potentially contemplate. Computers and the World Wide Web have certainly changed the way we behave in many domains. People shop online, trade stocks online, get their news online, initiate friendships online, and so forth. Children spend time playing the latest computer games. The potential effects that we could discuss might easily turn into a separate, book-length volume.

What is all of this new technology doing to us? One thing that it is doing is encouraging traditional media effects scholars to ask new questions and design new research paradigms. One of the old labels used in media curricula at various universities is "mass communication." If you think about some of the new technologies that are emerging today, it seems clear that they challenge the traditional concept of mass communication. According to the old definition, the source of a mass communication message was a large organization. The message was sent out to large, heterogeneous, scattered audiences.[1] Today, single individuals use the Internet to set up websites that millions can view. Some sites get huge amounts of traffic, but other sites may get none. All of this seems to blur the lines between the traditional notion of mass communication and the new communication environment. Consequently, scholars who were trained under the assumptions of the old environment are having to make some adjustments in their thinking about what counts as a legitimate phenomenon to examine. In the confusion, however, there is also much excitement about conducting research on media that are brand new and may be affecting us in different and undiscovered ways.

Two media scholars, Jane Brown and Joanne Cantor, recently outlined a series of crucial questions surrounding new technology that researchers need to study in future years. They framed these questions in terms of the concept of **perpetual linkage,** the new tendency for youth to be constantly connected with each other through some type of technology. The authors asked the following questions:

> What is the impact of the connectedness that the newer media promote, i.e., the almost constant technological links that youth have with each other, using their cell phones, beepers, E-mail, and other devices soon to be developed? What about the relationships young people have with others they have met only via technological links? Do youth, for example, have stronger social ties to their peers because they are in virtual contact for so much more of the time? Or are they more alienated because this techno-logical contact comes at the expense of potentially richer face-to-face interaction?[2]

These questions are ones that are just beginning to appear in the research literature, and there are no clear answers at the present time.

Another area of research that has caught the attention of researchers and public health officials in the past few years is the impact of video games on youth. You will recall from chapter 5 that there has been a modest amount of research on games that involve graphic violence and permit the player to take the role of a "first-person shooter." In these games, the player handles a gun and fires directly at characters on the screen in an attempt to "kill" them. But violence in video games is not the only issue. Like the questions raised by Brown and Cantor, the questions that arise about the general impact of video games still demand more research before a consensus emerges among scholars. Even though questions about computer use and video games have not yet yielded clear answers in the research literature, there have been studies published in the last few years that begin to address some of the issues. This chapter introduces you to some of the studies that have been done in each of these areas and outlines some of the current controversies and issues that remain for future studies.

COMPUTERS AND THE INTERNET: CONNECTION OR ALIENATION?

Media Metrix, an organization that monitors Internet use, released a report in August 2000 that surprised many analysts and media researchers. For the first time in its brief history, the Internet was being used by more women than men. In addition, every day more women than men go online for the first time. According to a more recent report based on data from the Census Bureau, well over half of the U.S. population (54%) uses the Internet, and each month sees approximately 2 million new users. Amazingly, 90% of the children between 5 and 17 years old now use a computer.[3] Broadband connections are now in over a third of the homes that are connected to the Internet. Clearly, the late 1990s and early years of the new millennium will go down in media history as the years when the Internet exploded onto the scene, much as TV did between 1950 and 1960.

With such tremendous growth at such a rapid pace, the question of the effects of this new technology is obviously one that people are curious about. But because the technology is so new, the media effects community is unable at this point to provide definitive answers. Nevertheless, there have been a few major studies that took aim at Internet technology to try to figure out what was going on.

The Carnegie Mellon Study

In September 1998, a research team at Carnegie Mellon University, led by Robert Kraut of the Human Computer Interaction Institute, published one of the first major studies on the impact of Internet use. The researchers titled their study with a provocative question: "Internet Paradox: A Social Technology That Reduces Social Involvement and Psychological Well-Being?"[4]

The question gives a strong clue to the answer that their research provided. One thing that emerges quite quickly upon reading the original research report is that studying the impact of the Internet is not an easy proposition. The researchers had to put in a lot of effort to set up their study in a way that would yield meaningful results. As you will see, even after all of this effort, the study has been severely criticized.

One of the positive features of the Carnegie Mellon study (sometimes referred to as the HomeNet study) was the fact that the researchers employed a longitudinal design. Recall from chapter 2 that a longitudinal study is one in which data are collected at several points in time. In this case, the study involved 256 people in 93 different households during their first two years of being online. Each family actually received a computer, a free telephone line, and a free Internet connection. The families who participated had a high school student in the household or belonged to at least one community group in the Pittsburgh area. In return for the freebies, the families agreed that the researchers could track their Internet use with special software and periodically ask them survey questions during the time of the study.

Despite the fact that the researchers found that the people in the study used the Internet to engage in communication with others, they also found evidence of a rather alarming state of affairs. Use of the Internet was associated with a general decline in communication with family members who lived in the household. In addition, those who used the Internet more frequently tended to report that the number of people in their social circle declined over the years of the study. Finally, Internet users tended to report greater levels of depression and feelings of loneliness than they did before the study began.

If using the Internet is really associated with these negative psychological effects, what specifically is it about using the Net that causes them to occur? According to Kraut and his associates, there are two main possibilities. First, the data might reveal an **activity displacement effect.** This sort of effect was discussed in chapter 4 in connection with TV. People have a limited amount of time during any day to engage in their various activities. Once family members are hooked up to the Internet, perhaps they tend to spend more time in isolation from others, using the Internet for private entertainment and Web surfing. Second, perhaps the data reveal that the Internet **displaces strong social ties.** According to this explanation, when people go online, they often end up talking to people in chat rooms and even occasionally make new friends. But overall, the kinds of relationships that are formed online tend to be more superficial and are characterized by weaker ties than the relationships that people tend to have with family members and significant others who appear in one's life face-to-face on a daily basis. When people use the Internet, they may be depriving themselves of the richness of their deeper, strong ties with family and other significant friends in favor of relationships that simply are not nearly as deep or involving.

After considering these two alternatives, the authors clearly seemed to prefer the second option to the first. The main reason that they reject the activity displacement explanation is that their data showed that so many people in their sample used the Internet for social purposes. Clearly, if the reason for increasing isolation and loneliness was the fact that the Internet was displacing social contact, the data would have to show that social contact on the Internet was much lower than it was before use of the Internet began. But the data didn't show that at all. People used the Net for exchanging e-mail, going to chat rooms, and so forth. Moreover, the authors claimed that some of their data actually showed that those who used the Internet for social purposes were more likely to suffer the negative social effects than those who used the Net for less social purposes. If the negative effects were due only to social displacement, we probably wouldn't observe that particular pattern in the data.

The authors prefer to focus on the possibility that, rather than displacing social activity, Internet use tends to encourage a particular type of social relationship at the expense of another. They suggest that Internet users form more superficial relationships instead of connecting deeply to other human beings. If you take a moment to think about it, this view does make some sense. If the extent of your involvement with a person is through e-mail, there is much about that other person that you don't know. Online relationships also don't tend to encourage the kind of mutual help and service that characterize most close friendships. When I think of the people in my own life who are closest to me, they all tend to be people who would feel comfortable calling me on the phone and asking me to run an errand for them. And I would feel equally comfortable calling them for the same. It may be that the deep intimacy that comes with relationships is built on a kind of involvement and mutual service that online connections simply don't tend to produce. And if people spend time online in these more superficial relationships, they are using up time that they would otherwise have for relationships of the deeper variety.

You may be skeptical of the "weak ties" idea. We have all heard about people who met through using the Internet and eventually decided to get married. The popular 1998 movie *You've Got Mail* was based on this premise. But the stuff of Hollywood and media feature stories may not be the stuff of normal life. Although there are some people who may have discovered deep intimate friendships while using the Internet, Robert Kraut and his colleagues point out that the best data seem to refute this pattern as normative. They note that their own data appear to converge with data collected by two other researchers, James Katz and Philip Aspden. In a national survey conducted by these authors, they found that only "22% of the respondents who had been using the Internet for two or more years had ever made a new friend on the Internet."[5]

On the other hand, some new experimental work on Internet interaction suggests that even communicating with strangers can induce strong feelings. In one study, the amount of communication between participants in a chat room was positively correlated with the nature of the statements that people were making. The researchers examined both positive statements and negative statements made during chats. Positive statements were ones that complimented another person, expressed agreement with the other, expressed approval of some idea or behavior, expressed a positive emotion, and so forth. Negative statements were ones that criticized another person, expressed disagreement with the other, expressed disapproval, or expressed a negative emotion. Intuitively, you might think that the more positive the comments, the more communication took place. Actually, the correlation was in precisely the opposite direction. The more negative the comments, the more communication took place. At least in chat rooms, positive comments don't seem to get many takers. People seem more willing to argue and engage in various forms of hostility.[6] Study Box 11-1 focuses on some new experimental work on Internet communication that confirms that people experience intense feelings in Internet interactions. Clearly, the research community is just beginning to scratch the surface in its attempts to discover the relational dynamics of Internet communication.

Applying the Lessons of History

You might recall from chapter 5 on media violence that one of the earliest theorists who conducted research on the impact of televised violence was Seymour Feshbach. His theory of symbolic catharsis actually received some initial support from a few studies, and in the early 1960s many researchers thought that this idea would become a dominant one in the literature. Alas, as often happens in science, some ideas that receive initial support turn out to be wrong. In interpreting the results from the Carnegie Mellon study, we should be careful. The study is not without its critics. Donna Hoffman, editor of the journal *Marketing Science,* was quoted shortly after the study's release as saying, "Speaking as an editor, if this had crossed my desk, I would have rejected it. . . . The mistakes are so bad that they render the results fairly close to meaningless."[7] What mistakes is Hoffman referring to? After all, the study was published in a major journal, *American Psychologist.* In the final analysis, the Carnegie Mellon study suffers from three key limitations that should lead us at least to be cautious in interpreting the study's results.

First, the sample of people used in the study was not chosen randomly. This is certainly an important limitation: It means that we can't be confident that the results pertain to any general population of people other than the specific

---

STUDY BOX 11-1   Virtual Relationships Can Induce Strong Emotions

Researchers are now using the Internet to set up various kinds of experiments. Although there are some limitations to this type of research, psychologists and communication researchers will undoubtedly use the Internet to collect valuable data in future years. In one recent experiment, three researchers set up an Internet study that had nearly 1,500 participants from 62 countries. When the participants arrived at the website, they were told that the purpose of the experiment was to see if computers could be used as a tool in mental visualization. They were asked to engage in a relatively simple exercise in which they would virtually toss a flying disk to one of two other players who they thought were playing the game online at the same time. Actually, the other two players were generated by the computer software and were controlled by the program. During the task, the players were asked to visualize themselves throwing the disk and catching it. No disk actually appeared on the screen. The computer program informed the players when the disk was tossed, who caught it, and who should throw it next. Each player was represented on the screen with a color. The participants had to push a button when they were in possession of the disk in order to throw it to one of the other players. They also could select which of the other players (colors) to throw it at.

After two throws, the computer program assigned each participant to one of four experimental conditions.

In two of the conditions, the participants were ostracized—they were almost never on the receiving end of a throw from the other two players. In one of these conditions, they were *never* thrown the disk. In the other condition, they were thrown the disk only 20% of the time. In the other two conditions, participants were either included in the game at a rate equal to the other two players, or they were overincluded—receiving the throws 67% of the time.

Following the game, participants reported their feelings. As levels of ostracism increased, so too did the respondents' reports of bad feelings, perceptions of less control, and feelings of a loss of belonging. Even though the supposed players could not be seen, were complete strangers, were unlikely ever to be engaged in future interaction, and were throwing a virtual disk that was only imaginary, the participants in the experiment felt a dampening of their mood when they were excluded from the game. The authors concluded, "As our global society moves closer to worldwide use of the Internet, opportunities for exacerbating these feelings through real or perceived ostracism clearly exist and demand our attention" (p. 760).

SOURCE: Williams, K. D., Cheung, C. K. T., & Choi, W. (2000). Cyberostracism: Effects of being ignored over the Internet. *Journal of Personality & Social Psychology, 79,* 748–762.

---

people who participated in the study. Kraut and his colleagues acknowledge the fact that the sample was not random, but they defend their technique. In choosing families who were involved in a community group or had a high school student living at home, they made sure that they included people in the study who already had some social connections with others in the community.

Starting with a group who had connections meant that they had the possibility of observing some changes. Consequently, they had to control who participated to a much greater extent than a random sample would have permitted. True random samples permit no control at all about who gets into the study. The selection process is strictly by chance.

Second, there was no control group in the Carnegie Mellon study. Critics argue that the data would have been much more valuable if the results for those using the Internet could have been compared to those for a control group of people who did not use the Internet. Perhaps, the critics argue, there was some change across the entire society during the two years of the study such that even those without Internet connections would have reported more depression and loneliness. Again, Kraut and his colleagues counter that the use of a control group was simply not possible. There was no acceptable incentive to offer people in a control group for their continued cooperation in answering questions over a two-year period.

Finally, critics have complained that Kraut and his colleagues went too far in suggesting that their data supported a **causal claim.** Recall from the earlier chapters on research methods and the chapters on specific effects that surveys suffer from an important limitation. In principle, they simply cannot be used to argue unequivocally for causal relationships. The experiment is the only method that really solves that problem. Because Kraut's data are based on the survey method, it is always possible that the relationships observed are due to some other unmeasured variable. So what's the bottom line?

Since Kraut conducted his initial study, his research team and unrelated teams of other researchers have published more data on the impact of Internet use. The amount of data that we now have is increasing, and a complicated picture appears to be emerging that isn't well understood at present. Kraut's first study after the one described here "revisited" the negative effects of the original study by following up on the participants after three years. The results of this follow-up suggested that "the negative effects dissipated over the total period." Specifically, the authors stated the following:

> The original HomeNet sample began using the Internet in 1995 or 1996. Our follow-up of participants remaining in the sample in 1998 showed that, overall, the previously-reported negative outcomes associated with more use of the Internet had all but disappeared, except for the association with increased stress.[8]

A visit to Kraut's website (http://www-2.cs.cmu.edu/~kraut/RKraut.site. files/pubs/articles.html) shows that he has remained interested in this topic and has continued to produce new research. In a new longitudinal study that he reports in June 2004, Kraut's conclusions again seem to point toward negative social effects for Internet use. He and his coauthors conclude:

> Longitudinal analyses from a large panel of Internet use suggest that using the Internet may lead to declines in visiting with friends and family and perhaps phoning as well. In addition, the data suggest that while visiting

a family member stimulates exchanging email with that person and phoning him or her stimulates visiting, emailing doesn't increase the likelihood of either visiting or phoning.[9]

Before concluding that social impact of using the Internet is primarily negative, it is important to realize that a number of other researchers would disagree and have produced theory and data to suggest positive effects. Some researchers have found evidence that using the Internet leads to the formation of a new social circle,[10] promotes the development of deep and significant new relationships,[11] and provides a new social space for existing communities to flourish.[12]

Although it may be frustrating to encounter good arguments about why we shouldn't accept the findings of a particular study, and even more frustrating to read that scholars have produced conflicting data on an important question, it is a good lesson to learn that science can often be frustrating. But the flip side of that frustration is excitement. As we stand on the frontier of new research on the impact of the Internet and other new technologies, there is an excitement about doing more research and homing in on the ultimate answers to the important questions. Does Internet use cause more social isolation, depression, and loneliness? Perhaps you or one of your fellow students will go on to do graduate work in communication and help us to answer these important questions with a greater sense of certainty.

Thinking About New Technology

When professors around the country who were using the first edition of this book were asked to provide an evaluation of its content, one reviewer commented that this chapter on new technologies ought to be eliminated. His point was that nearly all of the material in the chapter could be moved to other chapters in the text. He went on to suggest that the history of media effects shows that we tend to replay the same issues over and over again when any new technology is introduced—violence, sex, displacement effects, advertising, and so on. Why devote a separate chapter to new technology when the essential research that emerges can easily be placed under other, more traditional rubrics? As I pondered this reviewer's comment, I was nearly persuaded. In fact, I decided to move the material on violent video games, which formerly appeared in this chapter, to chapter 5 on media violence. In the final analysis, most of the research issues that emerge with new technology do lead us back over familiar ground. The main reason that I decided to keep a chapter on new technology was that it seems to reflect more accurately the way most scholars are currently thinking about the area of media effects. Nevertheless, a casual survey of other media effects texts for undergraduate students reveals that the chapter on new technology is usually the shortest chapter and contains the smallest amount of material on studies that actually seek to document media effects.

In thinking about what's really *new* about new technology, William Eveland recently contributed a helpful conceptual scheme that encourages scholars to integrate their thinking about traditional media with their thinking about media that are newer. He refers to this scheme as the **"mix of attributes" approach**

to the study of media effects.[13] Eveland contends that some researchers tend
to react to a new technology with the attitude that it "changes everything."
As he puts it:

> Virtual reality, these researchers might argue, requires new theories and
> new concepts, which then require all new research. Similarly, the Internet
> and its World Wide Web are somehow supposed to be fundamentally
> different from all that has come before, and thus research and theory must
> start from scratch.

In contrast to an approach that would emphasize that everything must change
with a new technology, Eveland likes to think of all media in terms of a common set of attributes. Differences between media can then be discussed in terms
of differences in these attributes. For example, he proposes that we might think
of some of the common attributes as **interactivity, structure, channel, textuality,** and **content.** *Interactivity* refers to the extent to which a person is
actually able to interact with the technology in a meaningful way. *Structure*
might refer to the extent to which a medium is linear or nonlinear. A newspaper article takes you from the beginning to the end in an uninterrupted, linear
fashion. But an article on the Web might have various hyperlinks that divert
you from the main text in order to explore other tangents. The Web article is
more nonlinear. The *channel* might refer to whether information is presented
visually, acoustically, or in both channels at once. *Textuality* refers to how much
of the information in a medium is communicated in text form. Finally, *content*
refers to the actual information conveyed by the medium, such as violence,
sex, persuasive messages, or information.

To illustrate Eveland's point, let's take interactivity and textuality as examples. When the Internet exploded on the scene, some scholars hailed this
new medium as a complete and total innovation, unrelated to anything that
had come before. One of the qualitatively different things about the Internet
was its interactivity. That is, on the Internet, people had nearly complete
control over what information they were exposed to and what information
they wanted to screen out. Unlike TV, which was thought of as a relatively
one-way, non-interactive medium, the Internet was something completely
different. But instead of thinking of these two media as qualitatively different, Eveland encourages us to simply think of them as occupying different
places on the continua of common attributes. Although it may be true that
the Internet typically has a higher level of interactivity than conventional
TV, by thinking of interactivity as something that theoretically characterizes
all media to some degree, we are now better prepared to talk about TV as
being more or less interactive. Depending on where you live, you may find
that you now have the capacity to order a movie "on demand" and control it
just as if you were watching a videotape. Consequently, your TV has become
more interactive than it once was. The traditional label of the Internet as
"interactive" and TV as "non-interactive" doesn't really apply. Each medium
has a certain level of interactivity. The Internet may have more, but TV has

changed over the last few years so that, at times, it has a higher level of inter-activity than it did in the past.

Similarly, a traditional approach might refer to newspapers as a "print medium" and TV as a "visual medium." A few years ago, however, the cable news channels introduced something new: They started to scroll text at the bottom of the screen that reported various stories that were not being discussed by the news commentator. By taking the position that *textuality* is one dimension of all media that can hold different values, scholars can talk about how certain programs have *increased* in textuality over what they were before. Likewise, if you pick up a magazine from the 1950s, you might be struck by the density of text on the page compared with today's typical news magazines. Perhaps magazines have decreased in textuality.

One consequence of the mix of attributes approach is that the advent of a new technology does not necessarily revolutionize the study of media effects. Instead of thinking about new technology as qualitatively different, we can think of it as simply having different values on the common set of attributes that all media share. This may result in a more sophisticated understanding of the differences between various media because we can precisely identify how media differ in terms of the core set of attributes.

In support of Eveland's contention that the so-called revolution of new technology seems to take us back over familiar ground, consider some of the various research topics that are being investigated as part of the revolution of new technology. As chapter 5 points out, one of the hot topics is the effects of violent video games. Although the technology is newer, concern about media violence has produced hundreds of studies over several decades. Similarly, concern about the effects of sexual material on the Internet, particularly when seen by children, echoes the concerns reviewed in chapter 6 about the impact of sexual content in the media. A recent review of the effects of new technology by Norbert Mundorf and Kenneth Laird reveals that with a few exceptions, the topics in the research are really not very "new" at all. See Study Box 11-2.

Speculation About New Technology Effects

As you will see in the last chapter of the book, some fairly provocative theoretical thinking is going on today about the impact of electronic media—thinking that doesn't have much to do with the actual content of the media itself. After studying the effects of media messages for about 25 years, I confess that I've been somewhat attracted to at least considering this line of thought myself. A few years ago, I teamed up with Dr. Will Miller, the former spokesperson for Nick at Nite. We wrote a book for the layperson called *Refrigerator Rights: Creating Connections and Restoring Relationships*. In that book, we engage in a kind of informed speculation about the effects of new technology. Consider how our social environments have changed today just in terms of the importance of looking at screens. If you're like me, your daily screens are very important.

**STUDY BOX 11-2   The Research Topics Associated
with New Technology**

The five areas mentioned in this box have been summarized recently as areas of current research on new technology. For each one, I illustrate the fact that although the technology is new, the area of research has been around for a quite a while.

1. **Uses and Gratifications of Internet Use:** Researchers study the ways people use the Internet and the gratifications they derive from such use. As discussed in chapter 4, the uses and gratifications perspective has been around for a long time and has been applied to conventional media such as newspapers and TV for years.

2. **Effects on Social Interactions:** Chapter 4 discusses how one of the early concerns about TV had to do with the possibility that TV use displaced other important social activities. With the advent of the Internet, this concern is appearing again as a major theme in the media effects literature.

3. **Internet Addiction:** Chapter 4 discusses the notion of addiction to TV and reviews some research on TV addicts. The idea of addiction to media has been around for several decades. The only difference is that scholars are now discussing it as a possible effect of the Internet.

4. **Individual Differences:** Just as past studies on media effects show that the impact of media may depend on the individual, so studies on new technology are tending to show the same thing.

5. **Effects of Age and Gender:** Most media effects studies undertaken in past years have investigated the effects of age and gender. Today, these variables are also used to study video games and Internet use.

SOURCE: Mundorf, N., & Laird, K. R. (2002). Social and psychological effects of information technologies and other interactive media. In J. Bryant & D. Zillmann (Eds.), *Media effects: Advances in theory and research* (pp. 583–602). Mahwah, NJ: Erlbaum.

I spend time looking at my TV screen at home, so I want that screen to be sufficiently large and as clear and vivid as possible. Today, many people want HDTV or plasma screens (I have neither). At the office and at home, I also spend lots of time staring at my computer screen, as I'm doing right now. Sitting beside my computer monitor is a much smaller PDA screen that I'll drop into my pocket and take with me tonight when I leave campus. The chances are good that on the way home, I'll spend some time staring at my cell phone screen in an attempt to send or receive a message or phone call. The newest automobiles feature built-in DVD and video screens, either for entertainment or for monitoring one's global position while on the road.

What is the collective impact of all of this screen time? This is not an easy question to answer, but it may be an important question to ask. As our society spends increasing amounts of time looking at virtual images on screens, are we spending less time looking at human faces in the context of a face-to-face, in-person encounter? If so, what are the implications of this shift in how we spend our time? Are children who grow up in the electronic environment being socialized away from cultivating the social skills that we emphasized 50 or 60 years ago? Does this mean that people growing up today may be more inclined to be rude to others or lack the civility that used to characterize polite social interactions? Are professors treated with less respect in the classroom today because students are so accustomed to being in the mode of processing "entertainment," where laughter, ridicule, and boredom are responses that need not be inhibited?

I don't know the answers to these questions. Perhaps your class can explore them in a discussion. Although these questions may hold provocative and important implications, gaining answers through the traditional methods of media effects research will probably be quite difficult. These questions do not lend themselves to carefully controlled experiments in laboratory settings. Nevertheless, the inability to study an effect doesn't mean the effect isn't taking place. Perhaps in future years the scholarly community will find some creative ways to begin to provide insights on these sorts of questions.

SUMMARY

This chapter has examined some of the newest research on the impact of the Internet. One of the central questions being explored concerning the Internet is whether this technology increases social alienation, depression, and loneliness. The Carnegie Mellon study suggested that this was the case. But the study has its critics. Research studies seem to offer mixed results with respect to whether the Internet is affecting social relationships. In the coming years, we can expect to see more research that will help to provide insight into this question and clarify the impact of the Internet on individual relationships. In considering the impact of new technology, it may be more helpful not to think in terms of qualitatively different media. Instead, it may be better to think of all media in terms of a "mix of attributes." Regardless of how we think about it, there are still provocative questions for researchers to address in future research.

KEY TERMS AND CONCEPTS

Perpetual linkage 212

Activity displacement
    effect 214

Displacement of strong
    social ties 215

Causal claim 218

Mix of attributes
    approach 219

Interactivity 220

Structure 220

Channel 220

Textuality 220

Content 220

To learn more about the topics in this chapter, enter the Key Terms and Concepts found in this chapter as subject and keyword searches on your InfoTrac® College Edition.

NOTES

1. Dominick, J. (2005). *The dynamics of mass communication,* 8th ed. New York: McGraw-Hill.

2. Brown, J. D., & Cantor, J. (2000). An agenda for research on youth and the media. *Journal of Adolescent Health, 27*(2) (Supp.), 2–7.

3. NTIA & ESA. (February, 2002). Americans on-line: How Americans are expanding their use of the Internet [Online]. Available: http://www.ntia.doc.gov/ntiahome/dn/

4. Kraut, R., Patterson, M., Lundmark, V., Kiesler, S., Mukhopadhyay, T., & Scherlis, W. (1998). Internet paradox: A social technology that reduces social involvement and psychological well-being? *American Psychologist, 53,* 1017–1031.

5. Katz, J. E., & Aspden, P. (1997). A nation of strangers? *Communications of the ACM, 40,* 81–86.

6. Rollman, J. B., Krug, K., & Parente, F. (2000). The chat room phenomenon: Reciprocal communication in Cyberspace. *Cyberpsychology & Behavior, 3,* 161–166.

7. Caruso, D. (1998, October 28). Critics pick apart study on Internet and depression. *America Online: Poptatari.*

8. Kraut, R., Kiesler, S., Boneva, B., Cummings, J., Helgeson, V., & Crawford, A. (2002). Internet paradox revisited. *Journal of Social Issues, 58*(1), 49–74.

9. Shlovski, I., & Kraut, R. (2004). The Internet and social participation: Contrasting cross-sectional and longitudinal analyses [Online]. Available at: http://www-2.cs.cmu.edu/~kraut/RKraut.site.files/articles/shklovski-pew-change-v4-4.pdf

10. Kraut, R., Kiesler, S., Boneva, B., Cummings, J., Helgeson, V., & Crawford, A. (2002). Internet paradox revisited. *Journal of Social Issues, 58*(1), 49–74.

11. McKenna, K. Y. A., Green, A. S., & Gleason, M. E. J. (2002). Relationship formation on the Internet: What's the big attraction? *Journal of Social Issues, 58*(1), 9–31.

12. Wellman, B., Quan Haase, A., Witte, J., & Hampton, K. (2001). Does the Internet increase, decrease, or supplement social capital? Social networks, participation, and community commitment. *American Behavioral Scientist, 45*(3), 436–455.

13. Eveland, W. P. Jr. (2003). A "mix of attributes" approach to the study of media effects and new communication technologies. *Journal of Communication, 53*(3), 395–410.

12

■

Meet Marshall McLuhan

A Less Scientific Approach
to Media Impact

IS THERE ANY VALUE TO
CONSIDERING MARSHALL MCLUHAN?

Some researchers who study media effects may raise an eyebrow of curiosity or feel some confusion about finding a chapter on **Marshall McLuhan** at the end of this text. From the very beginning, this book has taken great pains to introduce you to the scientific perspective of studying media impact. Each of the preceding chapters has emphasized empirical evidence collected in a systematic fashion as the most reliable way to learn about how media affect us. In contrast to the many other researchers mentioned in the earlier chapters, Marshall McLuhan didn't collect any research data. He never did content analyses, surveys, or experiments to test his ideas. Instead, he simply proclaimed what he thought about the effects of the mass media. To make matters worse, from the scientific perspective, most of his ideas seem to be unfalsifiable (see chapter 1) and beyond scientific scrutiny. Why should his ideas be presented in a text of this sort?

I believe there are three good reasons for including a chapter on McLuhan's ideas about the media. First, whatever approach one might take to the study of media effects, McLuhan's ideas about media influence have stirred discussion and analysis from media scholars for nearly 40 years. Some would argue that his ideas are enjoying a resurgence as we enter the digital age of communication. Students of media effects, regardless of their commitment to the scientific approach, should at least be familiar with McLuhan's analysis. Second, his ideas are so provocative and far reaching in their implications that students of media effects ought to at least consider what he has to say. Finally, McLuhan's "theory" provides a great contrast to scientific thinking. In the end, although you may find his ideas fun to think about, you should also be able to see the frustration that comes with a body of theory that defies testing by recourse to empirical procedures. Ultimately, we simply can't test very much of what McLuhan said. You may recall from chapter 1 that when an idea can't be tested and shown to be false, it can't be shown to be true, either. Such ideas have limited value to the scientific community. Rather than inventing such an idea for illustrative purposes, why not consider a very provocative one that already exists?

MEET MARSHALL MCLUHAN

One way to begin to understand what Marshall McLuhan was referring to when he talked about the impact of electronic communication is to stop reading this book and pick up your pencil. Draw a horizontal line across the width of an 8-1/2-by-11-inch piece of paper. Imagine that the line represents all of human history (roughly 40,000 years). The far left side of the line represents the beginning of that period of time, and the far right represents this exact moment. If we wanted to locate the point in human history where electronic communication really started, we would have to move to the far right and go nearly to the end of the line. Electronic communication is new. One communication scholar, Don Pember, expressed the historical record of communication in this way:

> Imagine those 40,000 years of modern human history as a single calendar year. And right now it is midnight on December 31st, the last day of that year. Mechanical printing first occurred on December 27th, not quite five days ago. Newsbooks, the precursors of newspapers, first appeared in 1610, or about three-and-a-half days ago. Radio and motion pictures emerged as viable media in the early 1900's, about 9 o'clock this morning. And television first appeared in the United States at the end of the 1930's, or about 3:00 P.M. today. Despite its short existence, mass communications has come to truly dominate our lives today.[1]

It is difficult for people to comprehend a world without electronic media, and yet most of human history has been without it. Most people can't imagine what life would be like without newspapers, radio, or TV. Consequently, there aren't many people who would feel comfortable issuing proclamations about how the electronic media have changed the very fundamentals of the human experience. Proving such claims would be next to impossible. And how could anyone really be sure of these changes unless they had actually lived in the past?

Marshall McLuhan didn't seem to mind the fact that he couldn't *prove* any of his claims. He thought of himself as a **prober** or an explorer and found that there was a certain luxury in thinking about things that eluded clear-cut **proofs.** True, he might never be able to prove that his analysis was right, but others could never prove that he was wrong, either. McLuhan found this state of affairs to his liking. The genius of McLuhan (if any) was in his ability to stimulate thought about the exact nature of those changes that the move to electronic media had triggered. Even though he had never lived in the past, that didn't stop him from talking as if he knew exactly what the media were doing to us.

Marshall McLuhan was a Canadian scholar, born in Edmonton in 1911. After earning bachelor's and master's degrees at the University of Manitoba, he won a scholarship to Cambridge, where he earned a second bachelor's degree, a second master's degree, and a doctorate. He taught English literature at St. Michael's College of the University of Toronto. He died in 1980 after suffering a series of strokes. In the early 1960s, his reputation as a provocative new thinker about mass media started to grow (it was McLuhan who coined the term "the media"). Harold Innis and Walter Ong influenced him, but it was McLuhan who wrote books like *The Gutenberg Galaxy* and *Understanding Media,* books that propelled him into the limelight.

It was not so much that his books prompted rave reviews. In fact, reviewers often complained that McLuhan's writings were dense, complex, and difficult to digest. Teachers, likewise, may be reluctant to suggest that their students begin their quest to understand Marshall McLuhan by reading his books. A popular anecdote about McLuhan illustrates this point well. Upon arriving at campus one morning, McLuhan expressed irritation when he discovered that a student had parked her car in his parking space. Before finding another space for his car, McLuhan dashed off a note and placed it on the student's windshield: "Please do not park in my space in the future." He signed the note "Professor McLuhan." At the end of the day, when McLuhan returned to his car to leave campus, he noticed that a note was attached to *his* windshield. It read, "Dear Professor McLuhan, the note that you left me on my windshield this morning was the first thing you've written that I've been able to understand." There is no doubt that some of McLuhan's ideas are difficult to understand. Nevertheless, many sensed something deeply provocative about much of what he had to say.

The best way to begin to grasp the importance of McLuhan's ideas is to consider his view of human history. In a way, his major thesis is historical in nature. If McLuhan was right about human history, then we are all currently living in one of the most amazing times to ever come upon the earth.

THE ERAS OF COMMUNICATION HISTORY

The Tribal Age

McLuhan saw the history of the human race in terms of **eras of communication.** When he looked at the dawn of human history, he saw people who lived in a **tribal state.** They communicated with each other orally, and they didn't have a well-developed alphabet or system of writing. In this period of history, there was a heavy reliance on acoustics, or sound. Because most communication took place through speech and other vocal sounds, the sense of hearing was very important. McLuhan liked to point out that the ear did not need to process information in any particular order to make sense out of it. That is, sounds from the environment come to one's ears in an "all-at-once" fashion, and it usually doesn't matter which ones we process first. It is true that the order of spoken words does matter in most languages. But McLuhan believed that in the tribal age, the order of spoken words was only a very small part of the meaning that people derived in the communication process.

If you are not in a totally quiet environment as you read these words, take a minute to close your eyes and see how many different sounds you can hear. How many were you able to identify? In order to appreciate McLuhan's point about the all-at-onceness of processing sound, ask yourself this question: "What difference would it have made if the sounds you identified had occurred in a different order?" The answer to this question is quite likely "not much difference at all." In fact, some of the sounds that you heard were probably happening simultaneously. As you will see in the rest of the chapter, McLuhan believed that this quality of acoustical information was very important.

McLuhan also believed that processing of information went beyond acoustics, with people relying heavily on the other senses as well. Sight, smell, touch, and even taste were all important sources of information to tribal peoples, who lived, as McLuhan pointed out, in a state of **sensory balance;** the five senses were all important sources of information.

Moving from the Tribal Age to the Print Age

In terms of human history, the tribal age was the longest. Speech and the oral tradition persisted over thousands of years as the most important form of communication. Around 1500 B.C., however, the beginning of the end of the tribal age became evident when the phonetic alphabet emerged. This emergence, according to McLuhan, signaled the beginning of a major transition period to a new medium of communication and a new age of human history. The invention of the printing press allowed documents to be mass produced. This invention ushered in the formal **print age.**

McLuhan noted several things about the transition to the print age. First, he pointed out that the move to print was one that altered the sensory balance of the tribal age. McLuhan argued that, in the print age, the sense of *sight* became completely dominant in terms of processing important information. It was now possible to detach oneself from the tribe and still have access to the important information of human culture. One could read books in a private place. One could process important information without being in the physical presence of other people. The senses of hearing, touch, smell, and taste became less necessary in the age of print. The print age disrupted the sensory balance of the tribal state as the eye became the central mechanism for processing information.

A second important consequence of the move to the print age, according to McLuhan, was that human beings started to think differently. Unlike the

all-at-onceness of the old acoustical processing, the age of print forced people to process information in a *linear* fashion.

To see what McLuhan meant by the linear nature of print, try this simple exercise: Close your eyes and drop your finger at random onto this page. Write down the word that your finger lands on. Now do it again; then do it five more times. Look at the string of seven words that you have written. The chances are good that they don't form a coherent sentence. In the age of print, we must process our information in a particular order. If something scrambles that order, the message is lost. Even the essential ingredients of words, the letters, must appear in a particular order before we can make sense out of them. The particular order of words or letters (left to right in English, top to bottom in some Asian languages) is not important. The important thing is that we have to assemble them in a linear order before we can derive meaning from them.

McLuhan thought that the shift to **linear information processing** altered people's basic thought patterns. Thought became more linear than it had been in the tribal state. This shift brought about an emphasis on deductive logic and on making sure that every thought connected well to the one that had come before. Messages that reflected the less linear pattern of the tribal age seemed increasingly strange and incoherent. Over time, they diminished in value.

Moving On to the Current Electronic Age

According to McLuhan, the great technology of print completely transformed human culture. Then, in the late 1800s, Marconi's invention of the wireless telegraph gave rise to a new age in human history. The age of electronic communication had arrived. Just as print transformed the old tribal age, so electronic media would transform the great culture of print. McLuhan pointed out that the transition from the print age to the **electronic age** would be similar to the earlier shift away from the tribal state. Both changes would occur over several hundreds of years. According to McLuhan, then, you and I are living at a most unprecedented time in human history. We are living on the cusp of two great communication technologies—print and electronics. If McLuhan is right, then a very provocative thesis presents itself for our consideration. McLuhan asks us to consider the possibility that much of the social upheaval and change that have occurred over the last 50 years are directly due to the shift toward electronic media.

It was in talking about the various consequences of the move to electronic media that McLuhan came into his own as a media guru. He enjoyed the attention he received from TV talk shows and movie celebrities (he made a brief appearance in Woody Allen's 1977 film *Annie Hall*). All of the media attention, combined with the obscurity of some of his ideas, caused him to lose favor in the eyes of the academic world. Still, McLuhan had some interesting things to say about what was happening to our culture with the steady rise of electronic communication forms.

First, McLuhan believed that, in the electronic age, human culture was returning to a form of communication that was much more similar to that of the tribal age. He often talked about the **global village** produced by electronic media—a reference to the power of instantaneous communication to unify the world into a massive, modern-day, tribal community. Almost everyone who was alive at the time remembers exactly where they were on November 22, 1963. On this date, John Kennedy died at the hand of an assassin. McLuhan often explained that the media coverage that followed an event of this magnitude allowed people to experience "one big group emotion." Since 1963, we have often seen the power of the electronic media to unite large portions of the world by drawing their collective attention to the same event. Think about the space shuttle *Challenger* exploding in midair, the first night of fighting in Operation Desert Storm, the Berlin Wall tumbling to the ground, the death of Princess Diana, the O. J. Simpson car chase on the Los Angeles freeways, the tragic shootings at Columbine High School, or the twin towers of the World Trade Center tumbling to the ground. On occasions like these, it is not hard to appreciate what McLuhan meant when he said that electronic media bring about the experience of the global village.

Because television was the dominant medium of the electronic age, McLuhan often used it to illustrate his basic points. Unlike the linear processing of print, television encourages a kind of information processing similar to the acoustical principle of the tribe. Processing a TV message is much more like the all-at-once processing of the ear than the linear processing of the eye reading a printed page. McLuhan was fond of pointing out that most people were in error in regarding television as a visual medium. On the contrary, he argued, television is fundamentally an acoustic medium. To make this point clear, he invited people to try a simple experiment. First, turn the sound down on the TV set for one minute during your favorite program. Now, for another minute, adjust the TV so that you can hear the sound but you can't see any picture. Which condition was more frustrating? Which condition gave you less information? McLuhan believed that people who tried this little exercise would invariably report more frustration in the condition where the picture was visible but the sound was inaudible. So, even though we think of television as a visual medium, McLuhan argued that it was primarily a medium of sound.

Second, McLuhan argued that the electronic communication forms were in direct opposition to the great technology of print. Linear thinking, deductive logic, and the private, information-packed experience of reading would gradually give way to the new electronic experience of radio and television. At the same time, the familiar way of thinking would gradually give way to a mode of thinking that was less linear, less logical, more spontaneous, and more like the thinking of our tribal ancestors. As far as McLuhan could tell, there was no way to stop these changes from occurring. The power of instantaneous electronic information would overwhelm the great culture of print in a matter of time. Although McLuhan claimed that he was almost always against the changes that he saw the electronic media instigating, he remained determined to understand exactly what was happening to us.

In his determination to communicate what he thought, McLuhan often relied on pithy sayings. His most famous of these, **"The medium is the message,"** was really an attempt to summarize his view of human history just outlined. A closer look at this saying will reveal a key principle of McLuhan's analysis of the media age.

THE MEDIUM IS THE MESSAGE

Part of McLuhan's popular appeal was his habit of coining slogans and phrases that he eventually referred to as "McLuhanisms." It was this habit that often got him into trouble with scholars, who typically wanted more depth and more explication of ideas than a simple slogan could provide. Nevertheless, McLuhan seemed to sense that these slogans were important tools of communication, and he churned them out with some regularity. As noted, perhaps his best known saying was "The medium is the message." McLuhan seemed to realize that one of the advantages of a slogan like this one is that it could mean different things to different people at different times. He took full advantage of this feature and provided a number of different twists on the meaning of the phrase. It is no wonder that scholars often disagree strongly about exactly what McLuhan meant when he uttered these words. Some scholars have given up trying to understand what he meant and tend to dismiss all of McLuhan's ideas as little more than creations of an intellectual charlatan.

But if we understand how McLuhan viewed human history, it is possible to get some insight from the idea that the medium is the message. The first thing to understand in considering this phrase is that it plays off the common notion that people change as a result of processing persuasive messages. When we think of television affecting a person's behavior, we usually think in terms of a particular program or particular message that provoked the change. Such thinking has good support from research studies. There are hundreds of research studies that lend credence to the fact that human behavior changes from processing messages. Almost every chapter in this book revolves around the idea that some particular type of media message has a specific effect on human attitudes, feelings, or actions.

McLuhan realized that most people tend to think of the messages in a given medium of communication as the agents of change. He didn't deny that messages have impact, but he wanted to get across what he believed was a much loftier and more far reaching proposition. In claiming that the medium is the message, McLuhan was saying that what really changed people the most was not the message in any given medium of communication, but the medium itself. Hence, the medium *is* the message.

McLuhan believed that most people would find his concept to be a little strange and difficult to think about. His reason for this belief may seem stranger than the belief itself. McLuhan thought that all media were extensions of people: The wheel is an extension of the foot. The book is an extension of the eye. The electronic circuit is an extension of the central nervous system. McLuhan believed that these various extensions of ourselves intensified the particular organ or sense that found itself extended. In response to this intensification, he argued that the affected sense or organ would act to protect itself and engage in a numbing process that he equated with Freud's concept of repression. The result of this process in the case of electronic media would be to make people quite unaware of the media's effects. If we are unaware of the media's impact on our culture, the slogan declaring that the medium is the message is likely to sound a little strange.

But look back at McLuhan's view of human history. He claimed that the invention of print brought about cataclysmic change in human culture and that the invention of electronic media started a major revolution that we have yet to complete. McLuhan saw the important changes in human life arising from the changes in the dominant communication medium at given points in human history. This view stands in sharp contrast to the one that asserts that change arises from messages within a given medium. As he once said, "Societies have always been shaped more by the nature of the media with which people communicate than by the content of the communication."[2] This is probably the best way to understand the well-known slogan "The medium is the message."

THE EFFECTS OF ELECTRONIC
MEDIA ON HUMAN BEINGS

McLuhan liked to emphasize that the dominant medium of communication changed human behavior more than the individual messages that the medium contained. He played with his own slogan a bit and changed it to **"The medium is the *massage.*"** By this play on words, he meant to underscore the fact that communication media are not neutral. They affect people. He once commented that media "rough people up" and act "chiropractically." Comments like these prompted some to charge that McLuhan's mind could only think in metaphors—that he would make a metaphor even when there wasn't need for one. But despite this criticism, McLuhan actually had quite a bit to say about the specific ways that electronic media were changing us. That is one reason that this chapter is included in this text.

The remaining portion of the chapter presents some of McLuhan's thoughts on the effects of electronic media. Keep in mind that he couldn't really prove that any of these effects were actually taking place. He did try, however, to point out the things that were consistent with his claims. And although many scholars scowled at McLuhan's inability to offer hard evidence for the effects he talked about, there was always that nagging doubt that maybe, just maybe, he was onto something. As author Tom Wolfe put it in one article, "Suppose he is what he sounds like, the most important thinker since Newton, Darwin, Freud, Einstein and Pavlov? What if he is right?"[3] Because little hard evidence one way or the other presents itself, most scientists throw up their hands when it comes to a serious consideration of McLuhan's ideas. They hark back to the notion of falsifiability of theory (see chapter 2) and point out that since the ideas can't be falsified, their validity cannot be established. In the next section, I present McLuhan's ideas on several topics that he talked about frequently. To what extent do you find McLuhan's thinking about the media effects outlined here to have the ring of truth? Can you think of ways that they could be subjected to scientific test?

Education in the Electronic Age

During the 1960s, it became clear that television had completely changed the typical household in the United States. Almost every home had a TV set, and viewing time was increasing daily. Interestingly, something else was also starting to happen at around this same time. The scores that students earned on standardized educational tests started to drop slightly. That decline has remained almost steady ever since. Since the 1960s, scores on the verbal portion of the SAT have dropped 50 to 60 points. Educators often bemoan the fact that many of today's college students demonstrate reading and writing skills that are far below the levels of their predecessors.[4] The crucial question that demands an answer is "Why?" Without a carefully controlled study (which is practically impossible in this case), a definitive answer seems to be beyond our grasp. Many things have changed in society since the dawn of TV. There are more single-parent homes, there is more drug abuse, political instability has increased, and the quality of schools in the inner cities has declined. Any one of these things might be responsible in part for a decline in standardized test scores. But according to McLuhan, none of these things is the real cause. According to him, declines in test scores were very predictable in the age of television. He argued that this has to do with the fact that the traditional educational system thrives on the great print technology. Since television took over as the dominant medium of communication, the print-based educational system is a system under siege. By the time today's children arrive in the classroom, they have spent thousands of hours processing electronic information in a nonlinear, acoustic fashion. When they encounter the print-based educational system of the typical classroom, there is a huge incompatibility. Print-based education finds it difficult to win out over the instantaneous acoustic form of television.

McLuhan had a very interesting way of articulating one of the dilemmas of traditional, print-based education in the electronic age. Prior to the mid-1900s, he argued, a person knew that when he or she entered the classroom, the information level inside that room was always going to be *higher* than the information level outside the room. Think about that for a minute. Before electronic media, people simply couldn't find out about the workings of government or foreign affairs or almost anything else of importance, unless they went to school and spent time *reading*. Books were literally the only window on the world. But today, this is no longer true. In fact, McLuhan said that when today's children enter the classroom, they soon realize that, because of electronic media, the information level outside the room is *higher* than the information level inside. In a sense, McLuhan said, today's children know that going to school is an interruption of their education.

McLuhan was very fond of pointing out all of the various signs of the failing educational system. Elementary school teachers who had taught for 20 years before the rise of television frequently reported that the children raised on a steady diet of TV were harder to teach. They were more impatient, less well behaved, and more eager for entertainment than for learning through books. McLuhan argued that we should come to expect such reports. It made perfect sense to him that the rise of electronic media would throw the old print-based educational system into crisis.

McLuhan once noted that we are "playing the old story backwards." In ancient Greece, he pointed out, a well-educated person was someone who had memorized the great epic poems like Homer and could sing them to his harp. This style of learning was consistent with the old acoustic form of the tribal age. The rise of literacy completely wiped out this definition of an educated person. As McLuhan put it, literacy wiped out Homer. And, he argued, if literacy could wipe out Homer, then rock 'n' roll music could wipe out literacy. He believed rock 'n' roll was a new acoustic form of education that threatened the entire print establishment. He predicted that rock music would thrive, while the traditional educational establishment would falter and grope for a way to survive. McLuhan empathized with frustrated parents, raised in the old print culture, who thought that something profoundly disturbing was taking place when rock music captured the imagination of their children. But these parents probably took little comfort in McLuhan's explanation of what was happening. He made one famous remark that combined his belief about rock 'n' roll with his notion that the electronic media ushered in a communication environment similar to that of the tribal age. Parents of the Western world, McLuhan said, were in the process of watching their children become "third world" kids.

If he were alive today, McLuhan would not be surprised to learn that many people describe our educational system as being in disarray—while, simultaneously, the music industry is thriving. I remember thinking about McLuhan's analysis as I watched the first feature-length film on an Omnimax projection system as it enjoyed its second holdover for a longer run at Chicago's Museum of Science and Industry. The Omnimax system uses more than 70 speakers for the sound track and projects the film's images onto a domelike screen. The entire projection system, complete with sound equipment, costs around $2 million. McLuhan would probably smile confidently upon learning that the film that people were flocking to see at $15 per person was a documentary about the infamous rock group the Rolling Stones.

McLuhan believed that education would be successful in the electronic age only to the extent that it adapted to the new electronic forms. This process of adaptation would not be easy, because the ways of print die slowly. As in almost every other area of human life, McLuhan predicted turmoil and struggle as the two great communication technologies clashed in the 20th century. Although he believed that successful adaptation was possible, he wasn't sure how it would emerge—or if it would emerge at all.

War in the Electronic Age: Not So "Hot"

For most of the latter part of the 1960s, Americans witnessed a real war on television for the first time in history. World War II, in contrast to the Vietnam War, was a radio war. Yes, there were newsreels that people could see in local movie theaters before the weekly feature film began. But these didn't have the same impact on our emotions as watching and hearing our favorite news anchor (in most cases, Walter Cronkite of CBS) narrating the details of the latest battle each night. And the war went on and on . . . and on . . . and on. Each Thursday evening in the New York area, one of the local news stations would play the Vietnam "honor roll," consisting of a list of all of the soldiers from the New York/New Jersey area whom officials had pronounced dead as a result of the Vietnam conflict during the week. The list of white names on a blue background scrolled slowly up the TV screens of hundreds of thousands of viewers. On some evenings, the list would continue scrolling for many minutes before all the names had been displayed. On a daily basis, as well, news reporters from the battlefields of Vietnam sent back film footage of live conflict, filled with images that were often deeply disturbing.

As Americans experienced this steady diet of images of war, they grew increasingly uncomfortable. More and more people came to believe that the United States had involved itself in a conflict that was hopeless. The war became a political hot potato. In 1968, President Lyndon Johnson refused to run for a second term, and many speculated that he would not have won, anyway, because of his unpopular Vietnam policy. Richard Nixon won the White House by promising an honorable end to the war in Vietnam.

Why was the Vietnam War so unpopular? Marshall McLuhan thought he knew the answer to that question. He argued that people experiencing the war through television found the brutal images to be extremely unpleasant and ultimately unbearable. Television, McLuhan argued, was a cool medium. **Cool media** were those that allowed high levels of participation and involvement. **Hot media** were those that had higher information definition and, consequently, did not involve the recipient of the message as intensely. Newspapers and radio were relatively hot media. Film was also a hot medium. According to McLuhan, hot media could tolerate higher levels of violence because people could not become actively involved in the processing of their messages. Newspapers and film thrive on violence, but television must be more careful in its portrayal of violent events because it is so involving.

If the distinction between "hot" and "cool" media seems a little vague to you, you are not alone. McLuhan never really explained the difference between hot and cool media in a way that made it easy to grasp. On some occasions, he would simply say, "Cool is involving—hot is not." At other times, he would launch into a much more technical explanation. For example, he argued that the reason television was highly involving was that there was never really a complete picture on the screen at any given instant. This is because the TV picture consists of hundreds of lines that the screen fills in over fractions of a second. At any given instant, the screen contains only a partial picture. Consequently, McLuhan argued that the viewer had to work to fill in or complete the screen's image. This process of filling in the picture with one's mind was highly involving and helped to make television a very intense experience. Film, in contrast, consists of individual frames. Each frame is a total picture when it flashes by the projection bulb and appears on the movie screen. It does not require the viewer to fill in anything. Thus, the level of participation in processing film images is much lower than for television. Film is a hot medium relative to TV.

It is difficult to appreciate how this technical difference between the television image and the film image could have such a huge impact on the psychological experience that viewers have with TV and film. McLuhan's critics questioned him about this: "What happens when you take films and put them on television? Is the result a hot medium or a cool one?" McLuhan might answer, perhaps in frustration, that the result was lukewarm. These sorts of answers were not very satisfying.

McLuhan's distinction between hot and cool media may confuse as much as it enlightens. But it is difficult to argue with McLuhan's general thesis that Americans found a television war to be most unpleasant. Consider the nature of war on television since Vietnam. The crisis in Kuwait was over in a matter of weeks. The recent war in Iraq dominated the 2004 presidential campaign. In both of these cases, the nature of the news coverage was very controversial. During the Kuwait crisis, the government argued that strict control of the press was necessary in order to protect strategy and tactics. But critics argued that these controls went too far and were unnecessary. In any case, there were few TV shots of real human suffering. Some observers compared the typical news footage to a video game. We saw exploding buildings—but little more. More of the same type of coverage followed when NATO bombed Serbia over the crisis in Kosovo. McLuhan would probably say that the government learned to adjust to the electronic age. They learned their lesson from Vietnam: War does not play well on TV. When it does occur, someone must take steps to sanitize the images and get it over with quickly. One reason that George W. Bush's handling of the Iraq war is not earning him very high ratings in the current polls may have to do with the fact that Americans have seen much more gruesome war footage on TV news reports than they did during the Kuwait conflict. Although Bush defeated John Kerry to win a second term as president, many voters were conflicted about the war in Iraq. A good student of McLuhan would probably warn Bush that the steady stream of TV war images and reports of casualties is political wildfire that could threaten to shape his second presidential term in extremely unfavorable ways.

Politics in the Electronic Age:
Was Bill Clinton "Cooler" Than George Bush?

In the 1960s, when McLuhan was at his peak of media popularity, he offered his own political analysis of the presidential campaigns. John Kennedy, McLuhan explained, was the first television president. In an insightful interview that McLuhan granted to *Playboy* magazine (the entire interview is available at the second Web link listed at the end of this chapter), he remarked:

> TV is an inherently cool medium, and Kennedy had a compatible coolness and indifference to power.... Any political candidate who doesn't have such cool, low-definition qualities, which allow the viewer to fill in the gaps with his own personal identification, simply electrocutes himself on television—as Richard Nixon did in his disastrous debates with Kennedy in the 1960 campaign. Nixon was essentially hot; he presented a high-definition, sharply defined image and action on the TV screen that contributed to his reputation as a phony. (p. 61)[5]

If McLuhan had been observing the 1992 political campaign, he would undoubtedly have seen Bill Clinton as the cooler of the two presidential candidates. Clinton was eager to stand up and step forward during one of the presidential debates and talk more conversationally to the live audience. He communicated more relaxation, casualness, and "coolness" than George H. W. Bush. McLuhan, who was a fierce critic of the standard debating format, would have viewed the more spirited and spontaneous exchanges that marked the 1992 debates as more consistent with the "coolness" of the television medium. He argued that the usual debating format had the candidates standing behind elaborate podiums in some of the "hottest" stuff that television was capable of producing. This style of debating was, in McLuhan's view, totally incompatible with the cool medium of television.

Did McLuhan's Perspective Predict
a Winner Between John Kerry and George W. Bush?

One way to put McLuhan's observations to the test is to try to apply them to current political campaigns. From what you've just read about McLuhan's views on TV wars and hot and cool candidates, who do you think McLuhan would have predicted to win the 2004 presidential race—John Kerry or George W. Bush. Why? Although we can't know for certain what McLuhan would have said, it certainly appeared as if Kerry was the "cooler" of the two candidates. During the second of the three presidential debates, Bush particularly looked like the "hotter" candidate. Some commentators remarked that he seemed angry during the entire debate. McLuhan would probably also have noted that with each passing day of the campaign, the nightly TV news was showing the deaths of more American soldiers in Iraq. If war on TV does not play well, then this should have hurt the fortunes of the presidential incumbent. Although George Bush won the election, my understanding of McLuhan's analysis would have led to the opposite prediction.

Many political scientists would probably consider it naïve to predict the outcome of a complicated presidential election by appealing to one or two fuzzy concepts in McLuhan's theory. The fact that Bush defeated Kerry may indicate that perhaps the political scientists are right. The fact that McLuhan

---

STUDY BOX 12-1   McLuhan's Failed Experiment: The Wonders (?) of Prohtex

If you are on the fence about how to evaluate the ideas of Marshall McLuhan, perhaps this little tidbit will push you over. One of the themes in the "theory" of Marshall McLuhan is that when the print age supplanted the tribal age, the sensory balance of communication was disrupted. According to McLuhan, tribal communication involved all the senses—including the olfactory. The sense of smell was an important and valued commodity in the tribal state. If, as McLuhan argued, the electronic age was a return to the acoustic communication environment of the tribal era, then it was also a return to an environment where more of the senses would once again become involved in communication. Consequently, McLuhan thought that the electronic age would be an age in which the sense of smell would become increasingly important.

McLuhan was a person who was not afraid to invest in his own theoretical ideas. According to Gary Wolf, who wrote in *Wired* magazine, McLuhan announced a new product in 1971. In collaboration with his nephew, Ross Hall, who was a chemist, McLuhan actually patented a unique chemical solution that was designed to be applied to people's underpants. That's right, there was no misprint in that last sentence. It was designed to be applied to people's underpants. It gets even better. The secret formula, registered under the trademark Prohtex, worked marvels. It removed the smell of urine from one's underpants while leaving the more interesting body aromas associated with perspiration. McLuhan was convinced that natural body aroma was an important part of communication in the tribal state. According to Wolf, McLuhan really believed that "when electronic technology turned the world into a global village, tribal odors would make a comeback too." Needless to say, Prohtex didn't make McLuhan rich. Perhaps it was ahead of its time. Maybe the coming revolution that will usher us into the electronic age will pave the way for this odd formula to become an everyday best seller. Then again, maybe not.

SOURCE: Wolf, G. (1996). The wisdom of Saint Marshall, the Holy Fool [Online]. Available at: www. wired.com/wired/archive//4.01/saint. marshal.html?person=marshall_mcluhan&topic_set=wiredpeople

---

comes across as a startling prophet on some issues and yet seems hopelessly naïve on other issues makes it difficult for many people to arrive at a final conclusion about the merit of McLuhan's ideas. You will definitely want to read the material in Study Box 12-1 before you make your final decision about how to evaluate McLuhan's ultimate contribution.

Drugs in the Electronic Age

When George H. W. Bush became president in 1989, he launched a war on drugs. Four years later, although his administration would claim some success, the drug problem that plagued the United States was worse than ever before.[6] McLuhan would not be at all surprised. In the same *Playboy* interview, he commented on the drug problem:

The upsurge in drug taking is intimately related to the impact of the electric media. Look at the metaphor for getting high: turning on. One turns on his consciousness through drugs just as he opens up all his senses to a total depth involvement by turning on the TV dial. Drug taking is stimulated by today's pervasive environment of instant information, with its feedback mechanism of the inner trip. The inner trip is not the sole prerogative of the LSD traveler; it's the universal experience of TV watchers. . . . The attraction to hallucinogenic drugs is a means of achieving empathy with our penetrating electric environment, an environment that in itself is a drugless inner trip. (p. 68)[7]

McLuhan would probably be very sympathetic to what some scholars have called "television addiction." Although the evidence for a true physical addiction to TV is relatively scant, some believe that there are those individuals who have a literal addiction to the tube. In support of their claim, they point to people who seem to suffer the familiar symptoms of withdrawal—anxiety, physical nervousness, and depression—when deprived of TV viewing.[8]

MCLUHAN'S INFLUENCE

Because McLuhan's ideas seem to defy direct empirical testing, his theory has been of little value from a scientific perspective. But scientists often give high marks to a theory that instigates new discussion and controversy—even though the theory itself may not enjoy much direct support. If we use this standard to evaluate McLuhan's contribution, perhaps there is some shred of scientific value.

McLuhan started writing about the media more than 30 years ago. Communication scholars still use his ideas and extend them to new areas. McLuhan's basic perspective of **"technological determinism"** (the medium, not the message, determines changes in human behavior) is particularly evident in two books that have received wide acclaim. In his book *Amusing Ourselves to Death: Public Discourse in the Age of Show Business,* Neil Postman argues that television has trivialized public discourse. He states:

There is no more disturbing consequence of the electronic and graphic revolution than this: that the world as given to us through television seems natural, not bizarre. For the loss of the sense of the strange is a sign of adjustment, and the extent to which we have adjusted is a measure of the extent to which we have been changed. (p. 80)[9]

Another scholar, Joshua Meyrowitz, has written a very provocative book, *No Sense of Place: The Impact of Electronic Media on Social Behavior.* The following excerpt from the book's introduction sounds like McLuhan himself:

[T]his book suggests that the widespread use of electronic media has played an important part in many recent social developments, including the social explosions of the 1960s, the many "integration" movements (blacks, women, elderly, children, disabled, etc.), the rise of malpractice suits, the development of "halfway" houses for prisoners and the mentally ill, the decline of the nuclear family. . . . The theory suggests that a broad, seemingly chaotic spectrum of social change may be, in part, an orderly and comprehensible adjustment in behavior patterns to match the new social situations created by electronic media. (p. 9)[10]

To be sure, both Postman and Meyrowitz go well beyond McLuhan's notions in advancing their own thoughts on electronic media. But McLuhan's influence on these widely read scholars and others writing about media impact is quite evident and openly acknowledged. There is no escaping the fact that McLuhan's basic ideas about media impact are at least worthy of some attention.

SOME FINAL REFLECTIONS

You should recognize McLuhan's perspective on media effects as qualitatively different from the ones represented in the other chapters in this book. In the case of Marshall McLuhan, there is very little, if any, scientific evidence to support his ideas. And yet, no book on the effects of mass media is able to ignore McLuhan. The media effects that he talked about were not trivial ones. If his assertions are right, the effects documented in the preceding chapters should take a second seat to the kind of sweeping cultural effects that he claimed the electronic media initiated. If you are like most people, you found some of McLuhan's thinking to be provocative and full of insight. But you may have reacted with skepticism to other parts of his analysis. In the end, media effects scholars don't really know what to do with McLuhan, because his ideas fall short of the testability criterion that scientists embrace. Nevertheless, we must credit McLuhan with stimulating the entire scholarly community to think about the power of the electronic media. If he was right, we may only be at the dawn of the full realization of the electronic age.

SUMMARY

Some media effects scholars may question the extent to which a chapter on Marshall McLuhan belongs in a book of this type. Three arguments for including such a chapter were presented. McLuhan saw the field of communication historically. He described at least three major eras in communication history: the tribal age, the print age, and the electronic age. His observations about the fundamental nature of communication in each era formed the core of his "theory." He achieved fame in applying his insights to all sorts of modern-day phenomena, including drugs, education, politics, and war. Many of his ideas were difficult to grasp, and he disliked scholarly criticism. His perspective is nearly impossible to test scientifically. Although this fact did not ultimately endear him to the scholarly community, it did permit him to roam freely with his speculations. No one could really prove him wrong. In the final analysis, McLuhan's perspective on the impact of the electronic media is worth thinking about—even while recognizing that gathering empirical evidence in favor of it seems unlikely.

KEY TERMS AND CONCEPTS

Prober versus proofs 226

Eras of communication 227

Tribal state 227

Sensory balance 228

Print age 228

Linear information processing versus all-at-onceness 229

Electronic age 229

Global village 230

"The medium is the message" 230

"The medium is the massage" 232

Hot vs. cool media 235

"Technological determinism" 239

To learn more about the topics in this chapter, enter the Key Terms and Concepts found in this chapter as subject and keyword searches on your InfoTrac® College Edition.

NOTES

1. Pember, D. R. (1992). *Mass media in America.* New York: Macmillan.

2. Playboy interview: Marshall McLuhan. (1969, March). *Playboy,* 53–54, 56, 59–62, 64–66, 68, 70, 72, 74, 158.

3. Public Broadcasting Corporation [Video]. Marshall McLuhan: The man and his message.

4. Shanker, A. (1992, January 6). The higher education crisis. *New Republic, 200,* 2.

5. Playboy interview: Marshall McLuhan.

6. McKernan, V. (1992, September 21). The real war on drugs. *Newsweek, 120,* 14.

7. Playboy interview: Marshall McLuhan.

8. Smith, R. (1986). Television addiction. In J. Bryant & D. Zillmann (Eds.), *Perspectives on media effects* (pp. 109–128). Hillsdale, NJ: Erlbaum.

9. Postman, N. (1985). *Amusing ourselves to death: Public discourse in the age of show business.* New York: Penguin.

10. Meyrowitz, J. (1985). *No sense of place: The impact of electronic media on social behavior.* New York: Oxford University Press.

IMPORTANT SOURCES ON
MARSHALL MCLUHAN

Canadian Broadcasting Corporation. (1984). McLuhan: The man and his message [Video].

Innis, H. A. (1972). *Empire and Communication,* rev. ed. Toronto: University of Toronto Press.

McLuhan, M. (1951). *The mechanical bride: Folklore of industrial man.* New York: Vanguard Press.

McLuhan, M. (1962). *The Gutenberg galaxy: The making of typographic man.* Toronto: University of Toronto Press.

McLuhan, M. (1964). *Understanding media: The extensions of man.* New York: McGraw-Hill.

Ong, W. J. (1982). *Orality and literacy: The technologizing of the word.* New York: Methuen.

Playboy interview: Marshall McLuhan. (1969, March). *Playboy,* 53–54, 56, 59–62, 64–66, 68, 70, 72, 74, 158.

Appendix

■

Theories and Theoretical Concepts Discussed in the Text (by Chapter)

Addiction to Media (4)

Agenda-Setting Theory (9)

Ceiling Effect (3)

Copycat Phenomenon (5)

Cultivation Theory (8)

Desensitization (5)

Developmental Theory (7)

Displacement Hypothesis (4, 11)

Dual-Coding Theory (9)

Elaboration Likelihood Model (8)

Excitation Transfer Theory (6, 7)

Face-ism (10)

Facilitation Effect (5)

Forbidden Fruit Effect (1)

Framing (9)

Gender-Role Socialization (7)

Illusion of Personal Invulnerability (8)

Illusory Placebo Effect (8)

Limited Effects Model (3)

Magic Bullet or Hypodermic Needle Model (3)

Mainstreaming (8)

Mix of Attributes Approach (11)

Mood-Management Theory (2, 7)

Parasocial Relationships (4)

Perpetual Linkage (11)

Priming (5, 10)

Protection Motivation Theory (8)

Psychological Reactance Theory (1)

Resonance (8)

Safety Valve Theory (6)

Selective Exposure (3, 9)

Social Comparison (10)

Social Construction of Reality (10)

Social Desirability (4)

Social Learning Theory (3, 5)

Spiral of Silence (9)

Stereotypes (10)

Subliminal Persuasion (8)

Symbolic Catharsis Theory (5)

Technological Determinism (12)

Third–Person Effect (8)

Threshold Effect (4)

Trigger Hypothesis (6)

Uses and Gratifications Perspective (4)

Voter Volatility (3)

Werther Effect (9)

Name Index

Subject Index